Radical Christianity:
A Reading of Recovery

Christopher Rowland

Wipf & Stock
P U B L I S H E R S
Eugene, Oregon

First published in the United Kingdom by Polity Press, Dales Brewery, Gwydir Street, Cambridge CB1 2LJ, UK, in association with Basil Blackwell Ltd., 108 Cowley Road, Oxford OX4 1JF, UK, and in the United States by Orbis Books, Maryknoll, New York, 10545

Wipf and Stock Publishers
199 W 8th Ave, Suite 3
Eugene, OR 97401

Radical Christianity
A Reading of Recovery
By Rowland, Christopher
Copyright©1988 by Rowland, Christopher
ISBN: 1-59752-011-X
Publication date 12/9/2004
Previously published by Polity Press, 1988

Contents

Acknowledgements

Many people have helped, whether directly or indirectly, with the writing of this book. Nicholas Lash, Ed Sanders, W. D. Davies, Morna Hooker, Robert Morgan, Andrew Chester and Mark Corner have discussed various ideas from time to time and provided encouragement and guidance. Before his death Gordon Rupp introduced me to contemporary Muenzer studies. I treasure a conversation with him about Thomas Muenzer at the end of the 1984–5 Miners' Strike in Britain. John Vincent of the Urban Theology Unit has shared the experience of his years of participation and reflection in inner-city Sheffield. Alan Kreider of the London Mennonite Centre discussed the anabaptist tradition with me. I only wish that I had been able to take more account of it in this book.

It has been an enormous privilege to share more closely in the work of Christian Aid and Traidcraft over the last few years. Many friends, particularly Wendy Tyndale, Michael Bailey, Alonso Roberts and others in the Latin America and Caribbean group, have offered advice and enabled me to understand something of what is going on in contemporary Latin America. The present Director of Christian Aid, Michael Taylor, has offered support and friendship in his own inimitable way, and the previous Director, Charles Elliott, gave me practical support when I was making my first tentative enquiries about a visit to Brazil. The friendship and optimism of Richard Adams, the Managing Director of Traidcraft, have been a constant source of encouragement.

Various friends and colleagues read and commented on earlier drafts of this book, including Walter Brueggemann, Jane Tillier, David Sanders, Linda Woodhead, Wendy Tyndale, John Pulford, Robert Mitchell, Lawrence Moore, Nick O'Sullivan and Eamon Duffy. They have helped me enormously, but, of course, I am entirely responsible for any shortcomings which remain. Grants from the British Academy, the Faculty of

Divinity of the University of Cambridge and Jesus College have enabled me to spend time in Brazil and Central America and to gain insights and learn much which would not have been possible otherwise. John Thompson of Polity Press encouraged me to write the book. His support and advice have been invaluable as is that of other members of the Polity team. Finally, my children, Christopher, Rebekah, Benedict and Thomas have put up with periods when I have been away from home or writing this book. I hope that at some point they can glimpse something of that vision of hope in this particular communion of saints which made me want to write it.

I have made many friends on two visits to Latin America, but it is to my friends in São Paulo, Brazil, that I owe a special debt. Sumio Takatsu, Gilberto Gorgulho, Ana Flora Anderson, Jaci Maraschin and Vando Valentini offered me hospitality and opened my eyes to theological horizons which I am only just beginning to explore. Over the last five years I have shared much of this book in various forms with Phil and Vicki West and my wife, Catherine. They have read the manuscript and given me invaluable advice on style and content as well as offering support when it was most needed. I dedicate this book to them and to all my friends in São Paulo.

The quotation from Leonardo Boff, *Way of the Cross – Way of Justice* (Orbis Books, 1980) is used by permission.

The Scripture quotations contained in the text are from the Revised Standard Version Bible, copyright 1946, 1952, 1971 by the Division of Christian Education of the National Council of Churches of Christ in the USA and are used by permission.

For convenience I have continued the convention of the RSV of referring to God with masculine pronoun and adjective.

To Catherine, Phil and Vicki and all my friends in São Paulo

History is usually told by the victors.
It is they who preserve the written documents,
erect monuments,
and have epics sung about themselves
in order to immortalise their deeds.
Who will tell the history of the vanquished, the losers?

All these people fell.
They are Jesus falling again and again
in the course of history's Way of the Cross.
Jesus is already risen from the dead, already in the glory of the Father.
But his resurrection is not complete
because his passion still goes on
in the passion of his brothers and sisters.

It is to such people that God promised the Kingdom.
And it is all the more theirs
in so far as they do not succumb to feelings of impotence,
in so far as they work to anticipate it by enacting profound changes
that create the real conditions for justice, peace and reconciliation.

All memory of suffering awakens dangerous visions,
visions that are dangerous for those who try to control the
present or the future.
They are visions of the kingdom of justice,
which enable the suffering people to shake off their bonds
and to keep moving along the road to liberation.

From Leonardo Boff *Way of the Cross - Way of Justice*

Introduction

This book seeks to look at parts of Christianity's foundation documents in the New Testament and to relate them to themes of hope, protest and social change in later Christian tradition. It also marks the start of a personal pilgrimage to recover those strands of the fabric of tradition which have been woven into the texture and whose effect has had to yield to the dominant strands. That journey into forgotten paths of the Christian story has begun to help my understanding of contemporary Christian discipleship. So much more remains to be done, but it is my hope that this initial essay will turn out to be accessible to as wide a circle of readers as possible.

Perhaps the time has come to put together the fragments of evidence at our disposal which relate to the radical movements on the fringes of Christianity. They have often been despised and excluded from the mainstream of the Christian tradition, but their ideas have continued to re-emerge, provoked by the licence given to them in the canon of Scripture. The canon of Scripture itself manifests the uneasy compromise between consolidation and innovation which has been so characteristic of all religions. It is a heterogeneous collection of documents. The reasons for the inclusion of many of them are now largely hidden from us.[1] But we may be right to suppose that they reflect the struggles between proponents of competing ideas and interests. The inclusion of so much challenging and subversive material alongside the socially conservative is a testimony to the former's deep-rootedness in the tradition; it was easier to tame rather than to remove. Its opponents tamed its power by subsuming it into their own ideology so that its impact could be lessened. But the very act of appropriating and neutralizing opposition ideas and making them part of the dominant ideology had the effect of preserving them. As a result they provided a potent resource for agents of change in subsequent generations of Christian history.

The details of the stories of many of the saints have been submerged for ever beneath an ocean of contrary opinion. It is important to piece together the story of the opponents of the dominant religious ideologies from the hints and fragments available to us. The task of recovery is an arduous one but is long overdue; we have for too long accepted the story offered by the powerful. I have not sought to offer an argument for my preferred reading of the tradition, though my personal preference is evident in the choice and treatment of material. There is need to embark on the process of what I have called 'a reading of recovery', in order to allow those faint voices of protest on the very margins of the tradition to be heard more clearly. The powerful voices of theological orthodoxy must be mute for a while; they need to listen to the wisdom and insight offered by the still small voice of protest. In any case, the powerful have their own protagonists. It is not my intention to add to that list in what I write. Both Thomas Muenzer and Gerrard Winstanley have been either discredited or forgotten, and yet the power and perceptiveness of their writing need to be heard by Christians as well as by the long line of Marxist historians who in various ways have claimed them as their own.

Writing a history of radical social movements within Christian history would require a more wide-ranging enterprise than is possible within this particular project. The scope of the book is of necessity limited. I recognize that Jesus of Nazareth, Paul, Thomas Muenzer and Gerrard Winstanley did not stand alone in their generations in espousing such views nor were they without successors or predecessors. There are omissions and large gaps in the story I have to tell (particularly with regard to the medieval period), partly because of the fragmentary nature of the story, but also because the choice of material reflects my interests and concerns. My scholarly expertise is in the area of Christian origins which helps to explain the balance of the book. The New Testament material forms the heart of the book, and the references to later movements indicate ways in which the threads of the story can be taken up in later periods. No attempt has been made to offer complete accounts of those later movements, a task which has been carried out very adequately by others. Needless to say, I am indebted to the studies of others to illuminate areas where I can make no special claims at competence. Those debts are acknowledged in the notes where further reading is suggested.

I have learnt much from the study of religion in the human sciences and, like many others, welcome their fruitful convergence with biblical study in recent years. I have received much stimulus from my reading of the encounter between Marxism and religion, the variegated character of which has been well set out recently by David McLellan.[2] This has contributed to my understanding of the phenomenon of Christianity and sent me back to look again at the tradition from different perspectives. While I am indebted to study of the sociology of knowledge, it is primarily from the impulses of the contemporary study of the biblical tradition and the consideration of its competing social and political options that is the starting-point for this particular reading of the Christian tradition. It is in the light of this background that I am using the term 'radical'. Radicalism may involve tearing things up by the roots but within Christian history this is done from the perspective of a commitment to the roots of the religion, the story of Jesus of Nazareth and his proclamation of the reign of God which confronts us in the pages of the gospels. The fact is that the shape of the canon of Scripture offers an invitation to the continuous critique of every project and institution, whether temporal or spiritual, in the light of the reign of peace and justice to come. Scripture has provoked the continuous stream of appeals to the inadequacies of the present, leading to the undermining of the foundations of structures painfully built. That process seems to be at the heart of the Christian religion.[3] That is not to deny that some semblance of institutionalization is inevitable but along with it there must exist that prophetic protest which points out its imperfections and demands at the very least that the costs of those compromises should be as small as possible.

Students of movements of protest and hope are indebted to investigations of the character of the millenarian spirit. Among the most important studies of millenarianism are the books of Karl Mannheim and Norman Cohn.[4] It is Mannheim's theoretical study and his outline of what he terms 'the chiliastic mentality' that offers a paradigm which is particularly applicable to many of the texts and movements we shall be examining. In this type of outlook there is the conviction that the present moment is one of critical significance within the whole gamut of salvation history, in which action is necessary, as it is no ordinary moment but one pregnant with opportunity for fulfilling the destiny of humankind. Thus the future hope is not merely a regulative ideal which acts as a stimulus to action and a norm by which one can judge the present state of affairs.[5] Mannheim suggests that the present offers the possibility of realizing the millennium . . . 'for the real chiliast, the present becomes the breach through which what was previously inward bursts out suddenly, takes hold of the outer world and transforms it'. The absolute perfection of the millennium ceases to be a matter of speculation and becomes a pressing necessity for active implementation. The reason is that the *Kairos*, or Propitious Moment, has arrived. As a result the chiliastic mentality 'has no sense for the process of becoming; it was sensitive only to the abrupt moment, the present pregnant with meaning.' For those gripped by this conviction the divine breaks into human history and is active through those who respond to the call to inaugurate the millennium. In this the chiliastic mentality contrasts with that strategy which sees the enlightened elite as a 'leaven in the lump of society'.[6]

With the conviction that the age of perfection can become a reality here and now there is an inevitable distancing from the present age of imperfection. As Mannheim puts it, the 'chiliastic mentality severs all relationships with those phases of historical existence which are in daily process of becoming in our midst. It tends at every moment to turn into hostility towards the world, its culture, and all its works and earthly achievements'. But such attitudes do not last and lead to mutation and the diminution of the original millenarian impetus : 'it became watered down into mere enthusiasm, and the ecstatic element came to life once more, though in a gently soothing form, only in the Pietistic experience of awakening'.

Those who are convinced that the *Kairos* has arrived respond in various ways. Violence is one possibility, in which the elect take up the sword inspired by the divine impulse in a Holy war. But the tradition of peaceful direct non-violent action is another alternative. There is an opportunity to compare these two strategies in the lives of Thomas Muenzer and Gerrard Winstanley, and this contrast illuminates contemporary discussion about the role of violence in the pursuit of the millennial dream which is still a live option in our day.

The New Testament continues to be the battleground for competing interests. That is reflected in the markedly different political options of contemporary Christians as it has been throughout the history of Christianity. That point is well brought out in a recent study of contemporary usage of the eschatological tradition of the Bible in the USA. The threat of nuclear annihilation and environmental pollution have been responsible for a more pessimistic attitude in the contemporary world. It is a mark of our generation that the startling imagery of the apocalyptic tradition and the hope for a better world have become potent modes of discourse in a way which would seem unthinkable to the optimistic minds of even two decades ago. The use of this imagery is to be found right across the political spectrum. On the one hand Daniel Berrigan finds inspiration in the eschatological material of the book of Revelation for his anti-nuclear activism. But at the other end of the religious and political spectrum the book of Revelation more often serves as a dream of miraculous rescue and as a licence for escape from political struggle.[7] The interpretation of Revelation and other pieces of eschatological imagery in the New Testament by born-again Christians absolves them from any concern to do anything about militarism or unjust social arrangements. This contemporary usage indicates the ways in which a common stock of ideas is used to legitimate very different interests, a point well made by Stuart Hall:

> Ideology is not autonomous of the socio-economic and political contexts in which it operates. Ideologies do express and advance certain interests; they are used to legitimate particular structures of power, to defend a particular order of society (or to oppose it); they do become linked with certain groups and classes and, as such, either help to preserve their position of privilege and domination or are used by others to contest that position. In this sense, most

conflicts, whether they arise from economic exploitation, political oppression or social inequality, will also be articulated in the domain of ideology because it is the domain in which, as Marx said, 'men (and women) become conscious of their contradictions and fight them out'.[8]

One area above all other has compelled a reassessment of the form of the Christian religion: the recognition of the importance of eschatology.[9] There are complex reasons for the rediscovery in the second half of the nineteenth century of eschatological beliefs as a significant aspect of earliest Christianity. The exploration of Abyssinia, for example, led to the discovery of Jewish apocalyptic works like 1 Enoch, which for centuries had been part of the Old Testament canon of the Ethiopic church. Awareness of these Jewish texts gradually infiltrated the world of New Testament scholarship.[10] Another concern was one which is endemic in the Christian tradition: it seemed to open a door to the Jesus of history and to offer a very different understanding of reality to that which the church had developed around the central figure of the Christian religion. Such ideas made their most dramatic impact on the study of the New Testament in the work of Albert Schweitzer.[11]

Schweitzer reviewed the various attempts over the previous hundred years to penetrate behind the pages of the New Testament to the historical Jesus. He proposed that Jesus' mission could only be understood if one took seriously those eschatological convictions found in Jewish apocalypses like 1 Enoch. Jesus, argued Schweitzer, was convinced that the reign of God was so near that when he sent out his disciples on a mission through the towns and villages of Galilee they would not return before the heavenly Son of Man came in glory to establish the Kingdom. Matthew 10.23 ('you will not have gone through all the towns of Israel, before the Son of man comes') provides Schweitzer with a central piece of evidence of Jesus' expectation of the imminent end of the old order. When this did not take place, Jesus resolved to go up to Jerusalem and by his death seek to bring about the Kingdom by taking upon himself the messianic tribulations which had to precede the Kingdom of God.

If Schweitzer's thesis is correct, the early church had to deal with an initial and dramatically disappointed hope.[12] Schweitzer argues, for example, that the ideas of the apostle Paul himself were shot through with an eschatological scheme derived from Judaism which had to be revised. Much of what has been written since Schweitzer's work has been an attempt to come to terms with the impact of the eschatological ideas brought to the fore in such a dramatic way by Schweitzer in particular.

The effect of the discovery of eschatology was to force Christians to deal with a strange figure locked into the world of first-century Jewish hopes and to separate Jesus from the concerns of the present world. After all, what had a dreamer about a new age to say about the world where people were anxious about what they had to wear, to eat and to drink? Thus, when Schweitzer spoke of Jesus *eschatological* expectation, he was in no doubt that the kingdom of God which Jesus expected was otherworldly and would be brought in by God alone without any human agency. Many have followed him in assuming that the eschatological character of the gospel necessarily means that the early Christians denied both a historical fulfilment of their hopes and the need for human agency in their fulfilment. Humankind, according to this view of the messianic age, was made up of merely passive spectators of a vast divine drama with the cosmos as its stage. So, reserve is expressed towards a close alignment with historical projects which takes sides in contemporary political struggles. This prevalent reading retains a clear contrast between history and eschatology, the latter being conceived as something totally *beyond* history. This has had unfortunate consequences for the use of the New Testament in Christian social ethics. By refusing to look for the reign of God in human history supporters of such ideas have, often unwittingly, helped to bolster consensus or even a conservative attitude towards the status quo in society, academy and church. That legacy can be challenged in one important respect: early Christian and Jewish writings offer a this-worldly materialistic hope which did not depend on a cataclysmic irruption from the world beyond and the destruction of the present world for the manifestation of the divine righteousness.[13] When we recognize that the teaching in the New Testament, particularly that attributed to Jesus, consists of the ideals applicable to God's reign *on earth*, the New Testament writings can be seen as the struggles of those who looked forward to a new age recognizing the obligation to live in the present *as if* they were living in the age to come.

Radical movements in Christianity have always gone back to the foundation documents to find support for their ideals and distinctive ways of looking at the world. The synoptic gospels with their portrait of Jesus have offered a catalyst for men and women in later generations to respond to the challenge presented to those who would follow Jesus. Prominent themes from the New Testament find echoes from time to time in unexpected parts of the Christian tradition. The Marxist philosopher, Ernst Bloch, indicated the power of the utopian inheritance and its contribution to Marxism as well as the Judaeo-Christian tradition.[14]

His views are somewhat tangential to the mainstream Marxist tradition and have been received with considerable scepticism by other Marxists. But what is most important from the point of view of Christianity is his role as promoter of the eschatological traditions which mainstream Christianity has preferred to forget. Thus one of his early books was on Thomas

Muenzer as theologian of revolution. His promotion of millenarianism and the this-worldly eschatology of Judaism and Christianity stands in stark contrast to the way in which theologians have tended to accept the orthodox eschatology which has concentrated on life after death or life in another world. He has been keen to point out the ways in which basic patterns of hope were submerged by less subversive images.

One example of Bloch's approach to the Christian tradition must suffice. In it he contrasts Jesus, the Son of Man coming on the clouds of heaven to establish justice for the poor, with the Lord Christ, enthroned in heaven in a glorious state similar to the imperial oppressors of the poor. He contrasts the expectation of the Son of Man as liberator and vindicator who would come to transform the lot of the lowly with the figure of the heavenly lord (*Kyrios*), buttress of church and authorities. He shows how the former expectation has moved to the margins of the Christian tradition, ostracized by the exponents of the dominant ideology. Gradually, this Son of Man belief has been displaced by the divine *Kyrios*, a title 'which', as he puts it, 'admirably suited the purposes of those who would reduce the Christian community to a sort of military service of their cultic hero'[15]:

> the Son of Man passed over to the poor. . . . It passed to the heretical brethren . . . to Thomas Muenzer with his Allstedt sermon on the vision of the Son of Man in Daniel and on Jesus the true corner-stone, whom the builders rejected. . . . The other future, the dawning of the 'better age', belonged to the early community and to its Son of Man. This future has, to put it mildly, been a constant stone of contradiction to Christianity.

For Bloch utopia is located in the present as well as the future. It is not yet, in the sense that it has never come to fruition and as such functions as a norm to show up the inadequacy of the reality of the present. The utopian is not something far off in the future but is at the heart of human experience; it is already at hand in an anticipatory and fragmentary way. These fragments are themselves an encouragement to human action in the present. Utopia is not fully possible within the limitations of the present order of things, so Bloch looks for its realisation beyond the confines of the present world. But he denies that utopianism is merely a retreat into a fantasy world and maintains it has the effect of laying bare what is utopian in human experience and broadening horizons so that the hope for a better world may inform and change the present.[16]

Examples of the quest for the original vision and the accompanying protest at the ordering of society are touched on in the chapter on the early church. The view that the age of Jesus and the apostles was a golden age which could be repeated if only there were radical reform and renewal is a recurrent theme. The early Christian belief that the messianic age was already in some sense present meant that many believed that Christianity ought to offer an alternative pattern of living which continues to challenge all projects for ordering society. Such an idea is deeply rooted in the mind of the Church and has continued to disturb the complacency and acquiescence.

The Apocalypse in particular has gone on being a potent resource for the religious imagination. Its apocalyptic spirit offers a tool for those who are discontented with the reality which confronts them. Those who wish to pierce behind the bland appearance to demonstrate the reality of injustice find their inspiration in the apocalyptic tradition of which the Apocalypse is the best example. Of course, it also offers a hope for the future of the world which shows up the inadequacy of the present and stimulates those who perceive injustice to costly action in favour of change.

My earlier studies of the antecedents to the book of Revelation in the ancient Jewish apocalypses and of the eschatological hope within the New Testament have stimulated my interest in millenarian movements and utopian ideas in later Christian history. The light shed on my reading of those ancient texts by the later manifestations of the apocalyptic tradition has been a prime reason for wanting to write this book. I believe that there is great benefit in comparing later movements of radical social zeal with similar trends within earliest Christianity. Such comparisons have always been one of the tools of the historian of religion.[17] Although doubts have been expressed about the value of comparing movements which are not contemporaneous, similarity of concern and outlook can often be as revealing as the comparison of texts from groups which were contemporary but did not have so much in common. This has always been a problem for the study of early Christianity. A natural area for comparison is of course the matrix from which Christianity originated, Judaism. But a major difficulty with this comparison is the fact that the Christian texts are unique in one important sense: they purport to offer the ideas of those who believed that the messiah, the agent of liberation and the fulfiller of the promise of righteousness and peace on earth, *had already come*.[18] In contrast, the extant Jewish material still looks forward to the fulfilment of that promise at some indefinite point in the future. For non-messianic Jews, meanwhile, there were other pressing concerns. For the Christians, however, things were different: *if* the messiah had come, what did that mean for the present, the past and the future, not least in dealings with those who shared the same Scriptures (the Old Testament) but rejected the distinctive interpretation of those texts being offered by the Christians? Such differences of emphasis indicate why it is not always going to be as helpful to compare parallels from Jewish (and for that matter, Greek) literature contemporary with the New Testament and expect to find similar concerns. The messianic emphasis in the New

Testament did set up a range of issues which it would not have been necessary to consider unless one believed that the messiah had come. That is why it is useful to look at parallel movements which, allowing for the change of circumstances of their day, do indicate a preoccupation with the belief that a new era in the divine purposes is about to break in and radical social change is once again on the agenda.

But my concern in this book is not merely antiquarian: hence there is a final chapter on the most influential and challenging theological movement in our contemporary world, the theology of liberation. That development in parts of Latin America is indicative of a widespread rediscovery of radical political commitment as part of the Christian gospel. Less influential and politically powerful it may be than the resurgence of fundamentalist religion allied to conservative politics; but its roots are deep and its effects on the shape of the church to come incalculable. I have embarked upon this study because I have learnt much from experiences of those who are committed to the poor and to the liberation of the oppressed in the Third World. The Theology of Liberation claims to be an authentic reading of the tradition, four square within the catholic theology. Proponents of its novelty do well to recognize this claim and its continuation of the thread of hope and radical change in it which has run throughout the fabric of Christian theology.

It is a mark of the success of the conservatives within the church down the centuries that they have been able to construct an ideology which makes a challenge to the status quo appear to be a departure from orthodoxy. But the Christian tradition is itself diverse, and my hope is that a glimpse of some of those texts and movements which bear witness to a very different attitude may reveal the fragility of the conservative ideology and the antecedents of contemporary Christian commitment to social change and greater equality. Identifying the memory of those struggles from the mists of the past is an important part of rediscovering our inheritance. One of the most exciting projects going on in post-revolutionary Nicaragua, for example (as it has elsewhere in post-colonial Latin America) is the attempt to rewrite the history of the country and tell it from the point of view of the oppressed rather than the conquerors. That recovery of popular culture has marked various pioneering studies by English historians who have wanted to lay bare some of the popular religious and political movements which feature as a backdrop to the dominant ideologies of the day.[19] The time has come to do that for other parts of the Christian tradition. It is incumbent upon those of us who have the opportunity and the resources to lay bare this tradition to reclaim it as a resource of hope and an inspiration in our present struggles rather than as a support to maintain structures which perpetuate the triumph of the powerful and the subordination of the weak.

One area where this is now being achieved in the First World is in the area it sounds, it is not easy to hear it in that environment in an atmosphere of concord and nostalgia. The ethos masks the challenge of the message.

It is a similar experience when one attends Anglican evensong. For centuries (and still today) half way through the service the words of a young Jewish woman are sung (more often than not by men and boys). She responded to God's call in the following way:

> He has shown strength with his arm, he has scattered the proud in the imagination of their hearts, he has put down the mighty from their thrones, and exalted those of low degree; he has filled the hungry with good things, and the rich he has sent empty away.[1]

It is difficult to *hear* the words of Mary's song, the Magnificat, in the midst of the opulence of the surroundings and the close identification of that institution with the dominant cultural ethos of the powerful. What do the worshippers make of the claim that the God they have come to worship is about to put down the mighty from their seat and exalt the humble and meek? Not least, when barely two pages later in the liturgy of the Church of England they will be asked to pray for the Queen. The notion of hierarchy will be reaffirmed and the worshippers entreat the deity for the monarch's wealth and prosperity. What incongruence that the song of a young woman celebrating the poor and the outcast will be sung, often with macho zeal, by a choir of men when women are frequently excluded from participating in the music and leadership of the worship in that beautiful building!

All this is not to deny the importance of the comfort which religion can and does bring. But we are confronted with a phenomenon where, whatever the ideas it seeks to promote, Christian religion seems to stand for stability rather than change, hierarchy rather than egalitarianism, the rich rather than the poor, men rather than women, and so one could go on. It is easy to lay the blame for this on certain persons and events in the past. A particular favourite is the first Christian emperor, Constantine, who lived at the beginning of the fourth century. He managed to envelop the Christian religion within the fabric of the late Roman Empire without any substantial shift in its power or ideology.[2] Moves towards an accommodation with the powerful had been made long before, however. The preoccupation of theology in the early centuries with the glorified Christ tended to mask the scandal of the circumstances of the life and death of the human Jesus. The embarrassing fact was that Christ had ended up on a Roman gallows on the opposite side from the mighty.

One of the most interesting characteristics of the Christian tradition is that it has not only worked for accommodation with established powers but also has never rested content with that settlement. A compromised church contained within its life traditions which undermined any cosy settlement. Throughout church history alongside the story of institutionalization, compromise and accommodation (what sociologists call the routinization of charisma)[3] there have been movements of protest. These have been marked by nostalgia for a golden age of discipleship (e.g. the life of Jesus and the Apostles) or a conviction that a future reign of God on earth is possible, provided that present arrangements are radically altered. By their actions such Christians have sought either to offer examples of more appropriate patterns for society or to bring about a new order by anticipating, or inaugurating, a new age in God's dealings with humankind. Such actions have taken place on the basis of the belief that a future fulfilment of God's purposes for creation can take place in this world and through human, though divinely inspired, agents. They are convinced that God's demands involve a return to a pristine practice of the religion which is evident for all to see by a proper reading of the Christian tradition.

The contrast between the concerns of the career of Jesus as they are found in the synoptic gospels and what was made of it in Christian theology has been a pressing problem for students of early Christianity. The transition from the concerns of the Magnificat and the Sermon on the Mount to the complexities of early Christian theology are nowhere better exemplified than in the confession of faith at the centre of the main liturgy of Western Christianity, the Nicene Creed. An earlier form of this creed was promulgated in 325 at the Council of Nicaea, presided over by the Emperor Constantine to combat Arianism, a teaching which denied the eternal divinity of Christ.[4] This creed concentrates in the main on the divinity of Christ with only a few sentences devoted to other items of Christian dogma like the future of the world. This concentration is indicative of the priorities of nascent Christianity. The contrast between the priorities of the dignitaries at Nicaea and those of the first followers of Jesus has long been the subject of debate.

The account of the way in which an obscure Galillean prophet who wandered around the countryside, proclaiming the imminence of the reign of God, came to be regarded as the Incarnation of the divine son of God is a long and complicated one. This much is clear: Jesus was not simply a wise man responsible for advice on the ways of the world. There are extravagant claims made throughout the gospels about his role as the prophet of the reign of God and probably also messiah, the agent of a new order. We shall note later in this study those features in the stories of Jesus which place him very firmly in the tradition of millenarian prophets who not only predicted but acted in support of their convictions. What is unusual is that the followers of Jesus continued to believe in the credibility of Jesus' claims. While his activities are similar in many ways to those of his prophetic contemporaries, they differ in that the movement that he initiated survived. The longer it

The story of a Jewish prophet which was not forgotton

Jesus among the prophets

We can easily fail to appreciate the scandal of Jesus' execution for treason by a Roman prefect. In Christian theology the event has become the focus of a cosmic drama of salvation in which this murder has been seen as the clue to the redemption of humanity. We may be in a better position to comprehend the significance of the career of Jesus of Nazareth if we compare the account of the end of his life as described in the Gospel of Mark with short extracts from the writings of the late first-century CE Jewish historian Josephus.[23] He has left us snippets of information about various figures and movements whose leaders claimed to be called by God to be agents of liberation into a new era of prosperity for the people of God. In the light of first-century Jewish history the story of Jesus of Nazareth is just one more account of the tragic failure of the pursuit of the millennium and the dashing of raised hopes. The following pieces help us glimpse how Jesus and his views might be placed within the turbulence of Roman-occupied Judaea.

The first extract describes an incident in the last hours of the siege of Jerusalem in 70 CE, the culmination of a bitter struggle between Jews and Romans which led to the deaths of tens of thousands and the destruction of city and Temple.

> The Romans, thinking it was useless, now that the Temple was on fire, to spare the surrounding buildings, set them all alight. . . . They then proceeded to the one remaining portico of the outer court, where women and children of the population of Jerusalem and a varied throng of people, numbering about six thousand, had taken refuge. . . . Out of all that number, not one person escaped. They were killed because of a false prophet, who had on that very day proclaimed to the people in the city that God commanded them to go up to the court of the Temple, where they would have positive signs of their liberation.

This may be compared with a more familiar description of the last moments of another prophet who was provoked to prove that God could act to deliver him:

> And they began to salute him, 'Hail, King of the Jews'. And they struck his head with a reed, and spat upon him, and they knelt down to do homage to him. . . . And they crucified him, and divided his garments among them, casting lots for them to decide what each should take. And it was the third hour when they crucified him. And the inscription of the charge against him read, 'The King of the Jews'. And with him they crucified two men guilty of insurrection, one on his right and the other on his left. And those who passed by derided him, wagging their heads and saying, 'Aha! You who would

destroy the Temple and build it in three days, save yourself and come down from the cross'. So also the chief priests mocked him to one another with the scribes, saying, 'He saved others; himself he cannot save. Let the messiah, the King of Israel, come down from the cross, that we may see and believe.' Those who were crucified with him also reviled him. . . .

At the ninth hour Jesus cried with a loud voice, 'Eloi, Eloi, lama sabachthani' which means, 'My God, my God, why have you forsaken me?' And some of the bystanders hearing it said, 'Behold, he is calling Elijah'. And one ran, and filling a sponge with vinegar, put it on a reed and gave it to him to drink, saying, 'Wait, let us see whether Elijah will come to take him down'. And Jesus uttered a loud cry and breathed his last. And the veil of the Temple was torn in two from top to bottom. And when the centurion, who stood facing him, saw that he thus breathed his last, he said, 'Truly this man was the Son of God'.

The next two passages give some inkling of movements which looked for God to repeat those great moments of deliverance from Israel's past:

Thus it was that the wretched people were deluded at that time by charlatans and those who claimed to be messengers from God. They did not give heed to, nor believe, the manifest portents that foretold the coming desolation of Jerusalem, but as if completely thunderstruck and bereft of all rational thought they disregarded the plain warnings of God.

. . . impostors and deceivers called upon the mob to follow them into the desert. For they said that they would show them unmistakable marvels and signs that would be wrought in harmony with God's design. Many were, in fact, persuaded and paid the penalty of their folly. . . . At this time there came to Jerusalem from Egypt a man who declared that he was a prophet and advised the masses of the common people to go out with him to the mountain called the Mount of Olives . . . for he asserted that he wished to demonstrate from there that at his command Jerusalem's walls would fall down. . . .

Finally, we have the story of another Jesus whose prophetic protest was also greeted with persecution and derision:

One Jesus, son of Ananias . . . suddenly began to cry, A voice from the east, a voice from the west, a voice from the four winds; a voice against Jerusalem and against the sanctuary. . . . The Magistrates supposing . . . that the man was under some supernatural impulse, brought him before the Roman governor; there, although flayed to the bone with scourges, he neither sued for mercy nor shed a tear but merely introducing the most mournful of variations into his ejaculation, responded to each stroke with 'Woe to Jerusalem'.

This juxtaposition of the account of Jesus' execution and the derision which attended his suffering and failure with the passages from Josephus is a reminder that with the gospel accounts of the Passion of Jesus we are dealing with an event which has its parallels in the stormy world of the final years of the Second Jewish Temple. Jesus was not the only prophet of his generation to meet a violent death for daring to proclaim imminent divine deliverance. The striking similarity between the passage from the Gospel of Mark in the New Testament and the accounts of prophetic promises and failures should not be ignored. We all too often gloss over the taunts that are reported to have been uttered against the executed Jesus. He is derided for claims made against the Temple and for his belief that some kind of deliverance was on the way.

In the first account by Josephus we have a graphic description of what can happen when revolutionary idealism takes over and dictates the course of events. We can detect in his description of the last days in Jerusalem something of the frantic spirit which gripped some of the most hot-headed inhabitants. When suffering for the populace had been enormous and the Romans were about to take over the city, some still clung to the belief that somehow God would vindicate them. They hoped for a miracle. As a result they persisted with the armed struggle, ending their resistance with a last-ditch stand in the Temple in the conviction that divine deliverance would come even at the last; just as it had centuries before, when Moses, Joshua, Gideon and other heroes of Israel's past had experienced great deliverance when all the odds seemed to be stacked against them.

Many may want to make a clear distinction between Jesus and the Jewish rebels against Rome in 70 CE, either to protect Jesus from the charge of subversion of the existing political order or, more disturbing still, from appearing to be yet another prophetic fanatic proved wrong by history. The view that Jesus shared many of the ideals of the millenarian prophets of his day may seem surprising. Can it really be said that Jesus' view was similar to those of the Jewish rebels who fought and died so tragically amidst the ruins of Jerusalem?[24] The answer to that question must be in the affirmative. The hopes of both Jesus on the one hand and the Jewish fighters for freedom from Roman domination on the other were more or less the same. They both expected the coming of God's reign of peace and justice on earth where sorrow and sighing would flee: 'thy kingdom come; *thy will be done on earth as it is in heaven*'.[25]

So what difference, if any, can we detect between Jesus and other prophets of change? One difference lies in the *strategy* that each adopted in response to these convictions. As we have suggested, both expected the manifestation of God's sovereignty in the affairs of men and women in the present age, not in some otherworldly future or solely in the far distant past of Exodus and entry into the Promised Land. The presence of God in human history was to be seen in present actions; God was not far off enthroned above the heavens: 'the kingdom of God is in your midst'.[26]

According to the Gospel of Mark Jesus began his ministry proclaiming the imminence of this event.[27] His work and message attracted much interest and support, particularly in Galilee, but from a very early stage he attracted a great deal of suspicion and hostility, leading eventually to plans to get rid of him. It is instructive in this context to see how Jesus dealt with opposition. Once he became aware of the fact that he was facing opposition, he could have taken one of two courses: either he could confront it by force of arms and bring about God's will by the sword (possibly believing like the rebels in Jerusalem that the angels would come to his aid as they had done for charismatic leaders in the past). Or, alternatively, he could accept the likelihood that the use of armed force would probably lead to defeat and destruction. Given the political constraints upon him, and the fact that the hostility was so great that it would lead to his death in any case, he could accept death for himself as an act of martyrdom on behalf of God's cause. *It is this latter strategy which we seem to find enunciated in the gospels.*

This emphasis on Jesus' tactics seems to have an air of political utilitarianism about it and prompts the question: would Jesus have resorted to an armed struggle if the political situation had been propitious and there had been some likelihood of success? A reading of the gospels which stresses Jesus' sympathy with the Zealot *strategy* seems to be difficult to substantiate without writing off the clear indications in his sayings that he rejected the armed struggle as a means of achieving the kingdom of God. This is most evident in the Sermon on the Mount (viz. Matthew 5.38ff and Luke 6.27ff). The accounts of the journey to Jerusalem as they have come down to us read better as the determined, provocative act of the prophet who seeks to challenge a people to repentance rather than the march of the army of the saints on the city of God.[28]

With such thoughts in mind we can perhaps see the story of Jesus' arrest and trial in a different light. When the crowd in Jerusalem is asked whether it wants Jesus or Barabbas released by Pontius Pilate there appears to be a contrast between the aims of Jesus and a contemporary political revolutionary, a freedom fighter who had committed murder at 'the insurrection'.[29] Jesus, who refused to engage in an armed struggle against Rome, surely seems to stand in the starkest possible contrast to this 'terrorist'? But the matter is not so simply dealt with. We need to remember that there were executed with Jesus two men whom modern translations call 'thieves', though, as the use of the word in the writings of the historian Josephus indicates, it should probably be translated 'guerrillas' or 'terrorists'.[30] A closer reading of the gospel accounts themselves, therefore, indicates that the circumstances surrounding the death of Jesus place that event in the same category as those where prophetic figures who offer liberation for God's people end up at the receiving end of the violent reaction of the security forces, ever vigilant to prevent activities which might destabilize a fragile political equilibrium.

Similarities between Jesus and contemporary messiahs have been countered by arguing that the kingdom of which Jesus spoke was not of this world. But there is little evidence to suggest that Jesus preached an other-worldly kingdom. One contrary indication is from the Gospel of John where Jesus tells Pontius Pilate that his kingdom is not of this world.[31] But his response to Pilate here is not intended as a rejection of the worldly triumph of God in history, so much as a repudiation of the idea that the *true* under-standing of that divine sovereignty can come without reference to God's purposes for humanity; and an emphasis on the fact that the character of that kingdom is grounded in God's character and does not take its inspiration from the rulers of this world order. Jesus does not say 'My kingdom is not *in* this world', but, he says, 'my kingdom is not *of* this world'. That is, this kingdom is only God's to give and its norms are the result of the power and inspiration of God's spirit without which the best designs of men and women must fail. Elsewhere Jesus explicitly tells his disciples that their way of life should be in marked contrast to the way of the powerful.[32]

The other passage which appears to indicate that Jesus was not prepared to disturb the existing order is the discussion about the Tribute Money.[33] The way this passage has been read both by Matthew and by Paul indicates that it *was* taken as an injunction to pay taxes to Caesar and recognize the demands of the state as legitimate. But the fact that it was included as part of the basis for the case against Jesus before the Roman prefect should make us pause before assuming that the meaning of the saying is entirely trans-parent.[34] Three points need to be made.

Firstly, the context of the saying is one where Jesus is being put to the test by his opponents. In such a situation it is unlikely that Jesus would have given an answer that would have implicated himself either with the rejection of Roman power by the Jewish freedom-fighters, the Zealots, or those colla-borators who had come to some accommodation with the occupying power. Elsewhere in the gospel tradition reference is made to his awareness of the traps which were being laid for him.[35]

Secondly, the context of the discussion indicates that Jesus makes his opponents show him a coin. He himself does not appear to possess one. After being presented with a coin bearing the image of the Roman emperor he asks whose image and superscription it is. The reason for this is not immediately obvious. Is it in order to indicate rights and duties to the one whose image is before him? Or does he wish to point out that the possession of the coin by Jews is evidence that the possessors themselves are contaminated by an alien ideology which, in direct contradiction to Jewish law, allowed images of human beings to be engraved on coins?[36] Those who possess such objects of an alien system might expect, therefore, to have to abide by the rules of that system. In the context of Jewish repudiation of idolatry a distancing of oneself from the marks of idolatry would be entirely comprehensible. Jesus' response, therefore, may indicate that participants in the Roman economic system, based as it was on slavery and conquest, were bound to pay the tax. But those who really recognized the supremacy of God over the universe maintained their distance from Rome and its exploitative and idolatrous practices. Jesus himself did not possess a coin, and elsewhere in the gospels he is reported to have questioned the monetary system: the food for the multitude is to be given not bought;[37] the disciples are sent out without money;[38] the widow's small contribution is praised;[39] moneychangers' tables are overturned;[40] whereas, in contrast, the messiah is betrayed for money.[41]

Thirdly, it is most unlikely that Jesus' words involved an acceptance of a separation between the sacred and secular spheres. Although such a separation between the sacred and the secular has become such a typical feature of our Western Christianity, it was certainly not typical of Judaism in Jesus' day. Jews regarded God as the creator of the world. The whole universe was regarded as God's domain, and no earthly ruler had any absolute right of possession or authority. Thus, giving God what was God's due meant offering to the supreme ruler of the whole world all that belonged to God. But why did Jesus not say this? A simple answer is that *the context in which the question was asked demanded circumspection*. Jesus was not here offering a definitive ruling on relations between his followers and the state but a clever, if ambiguous, answer, given in a situation where he had been put in a tight corner by his opponents.[42]

Finally, it should not surprise us that Jesus has so little to say about Rome. According to the Synoptic Gospels Jesus visited Jerusalem during his prophetic career only once. He seems to have spent most of his time in Galilee which was not under Roman jurisdiction but was ruled by Herod Antipas, for whom he appears to have had little regard.[43] So care needs to be taken not to conclude from Jesus' rejection of the armed struggle that he neither posed a political threat nor preached an otherworldly kingdom.[44]

The messianic narrative

The presentation of Jesus' life in the first three gospels furnishes ample evidence that he thought the critical moment in history had come: 'the time (*kairos*)[45] has come to fruition; the reign of God has drawn near; repent and believe in the good news'.[46] Immediately preceding those words in Mark's gospel Jesus comes to be baptised by John. The account of that baptism resembles the prophetic call-visions of the Old Testament and has all the appearance of a prophetic commission.[47] Jesus believed himself inspired by expected to reflect the situation at the beginning, for Jewish thought viewed the future age of perfection as a return to the situation in Paradise. Past and future are thus united and the yearning for the age of bliss incorporates that nostalgia for the lost age of innocence and perfection.

The account of the powerful deeds of Jesus is eventually understood by one of his disciples, Peter, as an indication that Jesus is messiah, the appointed agent of change and the harbinger of God's reign of righteousness and peace. According to Mark, Jesus immediately explains the need for his suffering and death once the disciples begin to commit themselves to his way.[78] Perhaps Peter had expected Jesus to pursue the strategy in which an attempt would be made to provoke the hand of God by armed revolt. If so, he was to be disappointed. After this Jesus begins to speak more about the need to go up to Jerusalem to suffer and die. What led to this decision to go to Jerusalem we have no means of telling. Our gospels all stress that the journey to Jerusalem became central to his role as the agent of the Kingdom of God. This movement to Jerusalem was not part of an attack on the city. Rather, for the prophet of the reign of God it could not be otherwise; for it was impossible for a prophet to perish outside Jerusalem.[79] Prophets, so the ancient traditions had asserted, had always suffered at the hands of their fellows. Elijah and Jeremiah had both paid heavily for their commitment to the ways of God.[80] Jesus was to prove no exception.

The crisis at that fateful Passover when Jesus was executed was not just the consequence of the acts of a ruthless hierarchy.[81] Jesus' determination to go to Jerusalem contributed to the provocation of the crisis in Jerusalem which led to his death. That determination to journey to Jerusalem must be properly understood. The recognition by Jesus of the probability, indeed the necessity, of suffering, is not to be interpreted as a determination to die, as if death were all along the sole purpose of his career. A clear distinction must be made between the prophet who reluctantly accepts suffering as the inevitable consequence of the prophet's challenge and the one who sees his life merely as the prelude to his death as 'the lamb who took away the sins of the world'.[82] Indeed, there are indications that Jesus went out of his way to avoid capture and death, for example by refusing to stay in the city during the last fateful Passover.[83] These are hardly the actions of the passive victim who meekly accepts death as the *raison d'être* of his mission. Jesus probably would have expected an enthusiastic response to his message of eschatological salvation. Some glimpse of that initial enthusiasm can be seen in the words he addressed to the imprisoned John the Baptist when the latter asked about his messianic status. The credentials offered are those of the harbinger of the reign of God: 'Go and tell John what you have seen and heard: the blind receive their sight, the lame walk, lepers are cleansed, and the deaf hear, the dead are raised up, the poor have the good news preached to them. And blessed is he who takes no offence at me'.[84]

The indications are that an initial enthusiastic response was rapidly clouded by opposition from various quarters. This led Jesus to take a more pessimistic view of the immediacy of divine glory on earth and to project the fulfilment of the hope for the kingdom further into the future. The present had ceased to seem to be the time of fulfilment and salvation as the storm clouds gathered over him and over Jerusalem. But still the need to die to bring about the messianic reign is nowhere mentioned. Only at the very end of his life, at the last meal that Jesus shared with his disciples before his death, did he interpret his death as the sealing of that new relationship between God and humanity which his proclamation of the reign of God had already initiated.[85]

That means the death of Jesus should not be seen as a timeless example of patient and passive suffering. Christians readily assent to the view that Jesus passively accepted the suffering that was his lot.[86] He then becomes an example of a meek acceptance of whatever befalls one, a form of Christian resignation to one's fate. He thus offers a model of patient suffering in the face of political authority, so true Christian discipleship does not get entangled with the things of this world but looks forward to a recompense from God in some ethereal realm. But such a view is based on a partial reading of the gospels. It is not so much a question of his meekly accepting whatever his betters decided for the him. *He himself helped provoke the crisis by going up to Jerusalem.*

To journey to Jerusalem, the seat of religious authority and economic power, was the act of a man who was aware of the political implications of his action. Jesus of Nazareth went up to Jerusalem and died as a martyr for the vision of the reign of God, a vision which he sought to implement as well as to proclaim. It was a vision which was ultimately rejected because the hierarchy in Jerusalem, wedded as it was to the Roman imperial system, preferred the compromises of the old order to the uncertainties and changes of the new. As Leonardo Boff has put it:

> Jesus did not go unsuspectingly to his death. He courageously took on that risk; in his final period he hid himself from the Temple police, but he made no concessions to the danger of his situation; he remained radically faithful to his message. . . . He did not avoid his adversaries, . . . but resolutely took the road for Jerusalem (Luke 9.51) for the final confrontation. . . . (Jesus' martyrdom) was the result of the rejection of his message and person by those who refused to be converted to the kingdom of God. If Jesus was to be faithful to himself and to his mission, he had to accept persecution and martyrdom. . . . As St Augustine said, 'It is not the punishment but the cause that makes true martyrs'. The martyr defends not his life, but his cause, . . . and he defends this cause by dying. . . . The resurrection of the martyr Jesus Christ has . . . this theological significance: who loses his life in this way receives it in fullness.[87]

The triumphal entry on Palm Sunday and the action in the Temple[88] are hardly the behaviour of a man who was content meekly to accept the control of the powerful. Once in Jerusalem he renews his challenge and focuses on the Temple, which is the economic, political and religious centre of Judaism.[89] Not only did the enormous demands of sacrifices and offerings make it an important creator of wealth but also it offered the members of the priestly caste a share in that wealth. This was of particular importance to the ruling elite surrounding the High Priest. Their hegemony in Jerusalem depended on the continuation of the central role of the Temple in the life and affections of Jews both in the Holy Land of Israel and in the Diaspora. The maintenance of Temple worship was above all a reason for the hierarchy in Jerusalem to come to some accommodation with the Roman prefect. The career of Jesus of Nazareth took place during a period of *relative* stability dominated by the High Priest Caiaphas and Pontius Pilate and the long reign of Herod Antipas in Jesus' native Galilee.[90] Caiaphas sought to guarantee that freedom to worship in the Temple by maintaining an uneasy relationship with the representative of Roman power. Challenges to the status quo, whether to Rome or the Jewish High Priest, were to be viewed with suspicion and action was to be taken. The remark attributed to Caiaphas and recorded in the Gospel of John about the activity of Jesus needs to be noted in this context. In response to the assertion 'if we let Jesus go on thus, every one will believe in him, and the Romans will come and destroy our holy place and our nation', Caiaphas replies: 'you do not understand that it is expedient for you that one man should die for the people, and that the whole nation should not perish'.[91] Here is expressed the concern of the Jewish authorities about the destabilizing character of Jesus' activity. After all, Jesus had entered Jerusalem in a demonstration of messianic dignity, proclaiming the function of the Temple as a house of prayer rather than a place of sacrifice, and, possibly, predicting its demise. The future of the Temple was a theme to which Jesus is reported to have returned again when he made a series of predictions about its future destruction and the imminent crisis for his (Jewish) society in an increasingly unstable world.[92]

In the light of this Caiaphas reports that the maintenance of equilibrium can only be maintained if Jesus is removed from the scene. It may not have been the original intention of the hierarchy to eliminate Jesus at that particular juncture because of the risk of insurrection. But as the result of the unforeseen defection of Judas[93] the opportunity was offered to arrest Jesus. When he is brought before the authorities, he has his words against the Temple cited against him.

Jesus' refusal to offer resistance to his captors and his silence before Pilate should not be regarded as a sign of lack of social engagement. Rather they were examples of the exploitation of the limited options open to a person in a situation where room for manoeuvre was almost exhausted. His silence was the response of one who knew that there was no possibility of averting his death and an attempt to ensure that whatever power remained in his hands would be used to speak at the moment which suited him. This is demonstrated by the report of the trial before the Sanhedrin in Mark 14.62, when he utters his dramatic statement about the Son of Man in response to the question about his messianic status at a moment of his choice.

That statement contains an allusion to Daniel 7, a chapter which was to provide resources for political theology. In Daniel 7.13 after the judgement against the Beast, the representative of the oppressive Empire, the prophet Daniel sees a human figure who is given divine sovereignty over the nations of the world and who inherits the worldly sovereignty taken away from the succession of world empires. During his interrogation by the High Priest Jesus appears to identify himself with this figure, the representative of the people of God, and thereby implicitly indicates his conviction that he will ultimately obtain the victory when the Beast, the power of the State, is destroyed. Justice will ultimately be demonstrated for the people of God who will reign eternally.[94] Jesus' messianic confession offers further incriminating evidence, adding to his saying about the tribute money to demonstrate to the Roman Prefect that he must be executed.[95] According to the Gospel of Mark, his last words are a cry of dereliction, a desperate contrast with the optimism of the opening words of imminent expectation: 'My God, my God, why have you forsaken me?'[96]

The gospels leave us in little doubt that the story of Jesus did not end there. The one who in his life had always been on the margins of society and had died rejected by the rich and powerful is proclaimed by his followers as vindicated by God. In his resurrection the controversial way of Jesus is vindicated; the judgement of the principalities and powers is reversed. The story of Jesus would probably have been forgotten if it had not been given a new lease of life by the convictions which were current in the earliest Christian communities about the resurrection from the dead.[97] To proclaim that resurrection had already happened in the case of Jesus of Nazareth, as Paul and others insisted, was to assert that the new creation was already in some sense present amidst an age that was passing away.[98] The Christian proclamation that Jesus was raised from the dead did not alter the message proclaimed by Jesus, for the resurrection was itself a sign of the imminent arrival of a new order and was thus of a piece with Jesus' message about the reign of God. It is the continuing story of the movement which Jesus started which finally separates his story from the stories of the millenial prophets recorded by Josephus, whose hopes and those of their followers were shattered by the swords of the Roman legionaries, never to recover.

The paradox of Paul

History has drawn a reverent veil over much of the earliest history of Christianity after the death of Jesus. We have the occasional glimpse in the Acts of Apostles. But it is the career of the persecutor turned disciple, the apostle Paul, which dominates the New Testament story of early Christianity. His influence has been pervasive.[99]

The case for Paul's social conservatism hardly needs to be argued. Most people are familiar with his statements about the role of women and his condescending attitude to marriage. Yet Paul's reputation for conservatism depends to a large extent on writings which are thought to have been written in his name, the deutero-Pauline letters, namely 1 and 2 Timothy, Titus and Ephesians.[100] In their different ways these letters integrate the theological currents of Paulinism with a quietistic attitude to the world order. Nevertheless in the central letters whose authenticity is undisputed today the beginnings of these conservative elements make their appearance. Indeed, it is in the letter to the Romans that we find that passage which has arguably had more influence on Christian attitude to the contemporary social order than any other, namely Romans 13.1ff:

> Let every person be subject to the governing authorities. For there is no authority except from God, and those that exist have been instituted by God. Therefore, he who resists the authorities resists what God has appointed, and those who resist will incur judgement.

This passage which has been the cornerstone of Christian support of the status quo down the centuries must itself be related to its social context. The likelihood is that it was written in the immediate aftermath of the return of the Jews to Rome following their ejection by the Emperor Claudius in c.49 CE. According to the Roman historian Suetonius this was because of unrest 'at the instigation of Chrestus'.[101] We should take full account of the context in which Paul seeks to dampen messianic enthusiasm and to persuade those who would repudiate earthly governance that this could not be so in the present evil age. As such Paul's advice about the state in Romans 13 should not be seen as his last word on the subject. In other circumstances in 1 Thessalonians 5.1ff we find Paul holding up to ridicule the Roman slogan 'peace and security' in the light of his eschatological expectations.[102] Thus it is not impossible that the description of political power as a manifestation of the forces of darkness and oppression such as we find in Revelation might have been to the forefront of Paul's mind in other circumstances.[103]

Nevertheless Paul's social ethics, like his theology, seem to represent at best a sophisticated amplification and at worst a gross distortion of the message of Jesus of Nazareth. The gospel of the imminence of the reign of God on earth has become a myth of salvation in which Christ has become the key figure. Paul is apparently little concerned with the Jesus of history in his letters where the concentration is on the glorified Christ and his presence in the life of the believers. That Paul changed the character of the religion of Jesus has an air of plausibility about it, but like so many oversimplifications manages to ignore a variety of contradictory and confusing elements in the Pauline letters.

It is the letter to the Galatians, probably the earliest extant letter from Paul's pen, which best enables us to catch a glimpse of a rather different view of Paul. This letter was written at the height of Paul's controversy with opponents of his practice of admitting Gentiles into the messianic community without circumcision. Throughout it there breathes the spirit of fiery enthusiasm and uncompromising conviction in the rectitude of his cause. The first major issue is Paul's claim to be an apostle of Jesus Christ. In the first two chapters of the letter Paul sets out the basis of his claim to authority rooted firmly in the conviction of a direct prophetic vocation.[104] Paul strongly rejects the idea that he is merely the intermediary of the mother church in Jerusalem and therefore subordinate to its dictates, even though he is forced to admit that during his career he has spent time in the city and met the senior representatives of the church there. Once the issues of his authority and his claim to be on a par with other apostles are dealt with, Paul turns to the vexed issue of the conditions for admission of Gentiles into the messianic community. It is important to be aware of the precise terms of the problem. Paul's crime in the eyes of his opponents was not that he admitted Gentiles into the commonwealth of Israel.[105] Any Gentile who accepted circumcision and obedience to the Law of Moses could become a member of the people of God. But Paul believed that the messianic age had come and that there was a new dispensation available for a number of Gentiles who could become children of Abraham by means of faith in the messiah. Thus, the issue for Paul was not that he was abrogating the rules of admission which had for centuries applied to those who espoused Judaism (which, of course, applied to all male Jews who were circumcised eight days after birth). Rather he is convinced that the heavenly messiah has called him directly to be the emissary to the Gentiles to summon them to be inheritors of the messianic kingdom on the basis of faith in the messiah alone, thus fulfilling the Jewish eschatological expectation that some Gentiles would share in the privileges of Israel in the Age to Come. Circumcision was no longer necessary as a sign of entry into the messianic people. Whereas Scripture seems to make it clear that admission into Israel normally involves circumcision, it is very vague on the conditions attaching to the admission of that select body of Gentiles who become children of Abraham in the messianic age. Where Paul disagreed with his contemporaries was over this issue. They clearly thought that the regulations governing the admission of proselytes still applied in the messianic age; Paul clearly did not. He argued that faith in the messiah was by itself sufficient to justify those Gentiles' participation in the messianic community.

It is Paul's conviction that God has revealed to him Jesus the messiah and that he (Paul) is God's agent which is at the heart of his approach to the scriptures. The scriptures are now read in the light of the fact that the age of the Spirit has come. Christians in Corinth, for example, are told that passages in the Bible were in reality addressed directly to those fortunate to be alive when the decisive moment in history came about: 'Now these things happened to them as a warning, but they were written down for our instruction, upon whom the end of the ages has come'.[106] The present has become the moment to which all the scriptures have been pointing, though their meaning can only be fully understood with that intuition which flows from acceptance of the messiah. True perception only comes when the veil is removed and the scriptures are seen to be fulfilled in Jesus the messiah.[107] Paul would have echoed the words of Jesus: 'Blessed are the eyes which see what you see! For I tell you that many prophets and kings desired to see what you see, and did not see it, and to hear what you hear and did not hear it'.[108] Those who accept the messiah can understand the true meaning of the scriptures and taste the goodness of God and the powers of the age to come.[109] It is not that the scriptures are redundant but that they have ceased to be the primary source of guidance for the followers of the messiah. The scriptures are a witness to and confirm the promptings of the indwelling Spirit of God. Like Jesus, Paul compares the present with the situation at the beginning of creation. He describes Jesus as the Second Adam[110] who rectified the pervasive transgression of the first Adam and thereby opened the way to the renewal of creation when the sons of God could share in the liberation which God purposed for the cosmos.[111] The Mosaic dispensation is thereby seen as an interim arrangement made obsolete when the messiah comes and the creation begins to return to the perfection which God always intended.

For Paul then the present had become a time of fulfilment: 'Behold, now is the acceptable time: behold, now is the day of salvation'.[112] That being the case new rules applied which would not have been appropriate for the old aeon. How Paul came to this view and how he worked out the justification of the position he adopted we can only guess. But at any rate in Galatians he is quite clear in his own mind that the scriptures themselves vindicate his position, and in both Galatians and Romans 4 he supports his views on the irrelevance of circumcision by reference to Abraham. This resort to the scriptures indicates that Paul is no opponent of the Jewish tradition *rightly understood*. It was not for him a case of abrogating the authority of the Jewish scriptures. What was important was to see those scriptures in the context of the fulfilment of which they themselves had spoken. What Paul offered his readers was the true meaning of those scriptural texts. For those with the inner eye of perception the true meaning of those texts was readily apparent. Or as Paul puts in one of his daring interpretations, the Jew who does not recognize Jesus as the messiah still has his spiritual sight veiled, just as Moses' face was veiled when he descended from the mountain. But when the Jew recognizes the messiah, the veil is removed. Here in 2 Corinthians 3 Jewish exegetical ingenuity is used to vindicate the messianic understanding of scripture as Paul stresses the superiority of his ministry as compared with that of Moses. For Paul the true meaning of the texts and their real significance is best (perhaps only) understood by those 'upon whom the end of the world has come'.[113]

Elsewhere in Galatians the language of freedom is to the fore.[114] Once again Paul resorts to the Abraham narratives to contrast two covenants: one of bondage and one of freedom. For those who are in the messiah there is a new dispensation with new criteria for morality and a radical way of implementing that morality. Thus Paul can speak about the Spirit as the power which enables those who are part of the messianic community to fulfil the requirements of God. Paul is prepared to sketch out what that ethical rectitude might involve only in the vaguest terms (Love, joy, peace etc.).[115] Indeed, when he does speak about what that fellowship with and in the messiah might mean he stresses the equality which is the consequence of such participation:

> For in Christ Jesus you are all sons of God through faith. For as many of you as were baptised into Christ have put on Christ. There is neither Jew nor Greek, there is neither male nor female; for you are all one in Christ Jesus.[116]

What is more, in speaking of this equality within the messianic community Paul uses language which indicates that those in that fellowship are not merely believers in the messiah but are in some sense clothed with the messiah's person: they put on Christ like a garment.[117] They have the Spirit of the messiah dwelling in them.[118] Paul himself when speaking of his own ministry speaks of the messiah dwelling in him. There is thus identification between the apostle and those who respond to his message and the messiah himself, so that the divine is incarnated in the lives of the messiah's followers.[119]

Such ideas have become so much part of Christian rhetoric that their startling quality can easily be missed. If this is what Paul had to offer to his new converts, it would hardly be surprising to find that such ideas provoked a radical response. That this was in fact the case may be gleaned from

1 Corinthians. In a cosmopolitan environment like Corinth it is likely that the beliefs and ideas which Paul communicated initially would have been heard and understood in ways different to what he intended. But the problems which Paul alludes to in his letters to Corinth are not solely the consequence of the distortions of the gospel by the Corinthians, for Paul himself contributed to the issues with which he is forced to deal in 1 Corinthians.[120] Evidence for this can be found in those places where Paul responds to questions from the Corinthians.[121] In the course of doing so he quotes slogans from them which suggest that 'all things are lawful' and that 'an idol is nothing',[122] views which commentators now conjecture have their origin not so much in the Corinthian misunderstanding of the gospel as in Paul's own preaching. So it was the initial impact of Paul's preaching which set in train a series of events and practices which culminated in Paul having to deal with the consequences of his own ideas in this letter. Indeed, it is easy to understand how this might have happened, given the tone of Galatians. Its emphasis on freedom, intuitive understanding of the ways of God, indwelling of the divine in the believer, the importance of direct acquaintance with the Risen Lord, dispensing with circumcision and the offer of the true understanding of the Law might easily have provoked some of the problems in the Corinthian churches. In 1 Corinthians Paul spends a considerable amount of space seeking to regulate the worship of the community and to order the more ecstatic manifestations of the Spirit, partially to avoid giving offence to outsiders.[123] His attitudes to women and marriage[124] seem rather conventional in the context of the ancient world but are quite comprehensible (though not defensible) if he were seeking to retrieve a situation which had emphasized equality of the sexes and the possibility of a common life without marriage. Both these views would not have been inconceivable given the kind of grand statement of principle in Galatians 3.28. Indeed, in 1 Corinthians 12.13 Paul repeats the formula found there but significantly *without* reference to male and female:

> For just as the body is one and has many members, and all the members of the body, though many, are one body – Jews or Greeks, slaves or free – and all were made to drink of one Spirit.

This may reflect the fact that the role of women in the Corinthian church was a burning issue. Despite these more guarded views on social relations Paul maintains the importance of the role of the Spirit as the means of understanding God and his ways: that emphasis on the charismatic community and the intuitive appreciation of the divine will cannot easily be forsaken.

This evidence fits the supposition that some members of the Corinthian church had embraced a realized eschatology: the conviction that the new age has arrived in all its fulness and that the regime appropriate for that new age could be implemented without reserve.[125] Paul emphasizes the fact that final consummation is still to come, so that precipitate implementation of a new regime ignores the reality that the old order is still very much in force.[126] Faced with this situation Paul seeks to persuade the Corinthians to draw back by demanding a greater accommodation with the existing order and mores (so not giving offence).[127] We may imagine that people of Corinth, fired by Paul's initial preaching, found the advice offered in 1 Corinthians to be an example of Paul drawing back from the implications of the gospel. There is evidence that Paul's relations with the Corinthian church were to become even more stormy, involving a confrontation with prominent members and the impassioned outburst of self-justification with which the second letter to the Corinthians ends.[128]

As far as we can ascertain, the authentic Pauline letters do not bear out the view that Paul abandoned the messianic enthusiasm of his initial message, though it would appear from his first letter to the Corinthians that this enthusiasm was tempered by a more circumspect attitude to socially controversial behaviour. Such an attitude is comprehensible given the evidence of antinomian and immoral actions in Corinth. But Paul goes further. He wants to check developments leading to patterns of behaviour which might upset the stability of the hierarchical social structure into which the messianic ideas had penetrated. Equality of honour and respect were encouraged among the new converts, particularly in the meetings of the *ecclesia*; equality of status and the abolition of subordination within the Christian household most emphatically were not.[129] He continued to look forward to the establishment of the reign of God. But that eschatological–millenarian gospel which had provided such a radical instrument for change in Galatians also contained within it the possibilities of a conservative reaction to attempts to implement its demands when these were incongruent with the existing social order. Thus in 1 Corinthians Paul uses the imminence of eschatological fulfilment as a reason for doing nothing radical in the interim to disturb existing social arrangements: the end is coming soon; therefore remain as you are.[130] Elsewhere, in letters like Colossians and Ephesians there is a resort to pagan household codes which encourage sobriety and subordination of wives to husbands and slaves to masters.[131]

Paul kept alive the messianic ideas in a more subtle way which was to have a pervasive impact on the way the Christian religion developed. He identified his own career so closely with the life of the messiah that he could speak, initially of himself, and occasionally of his fellow-Christians, being contemporary embodiments of the messiah. The background for this idea lies within precisely those millenarian ideas which had seemed so radical in Galatians. We noted there the identification of the apostle and the believer with Christ. That identification, with its capacity for encouraging prophetic and charismatic conviction, also provided Paul with the means of internalizing messianism. 'Christ in me' could gradually cease to be a reason for continuing the messianic activity in the world at large and become exclusively a stimulus for the inward transformation appropriate to the new age.

In Romans 7 where Paul speaks about the struggle which takes place in the human person, between the good intended and the evil actually done, there is the suggestion that the tension between the old order and the new in the present, expressed in the longing for the fulfilment of the eschatological hope, has become internalized and individualized. Thus the tension has become *primarily* a matter for the individual overcoming the passions of the flesh dominated by the old order rather than the power of the new breaking down the old order in the world outside the individual. It is the quest for personal perfection in a world where societal change seems to be a forlorn hope, without the dramatic intervention from beyond to break down the principalities and powers which stand in the way of the fulfilment of the divine promises. In 2 Corinthians that identification with the messiah leads to concentration on identification with the suffering of the messiah and an emphasis on personal holiness. The believer and the messianic enclave are temples of the Holy Spirit;[132] the church in Corinth is called the Body of the Messiah, in which the various individual members are seen as limbs of that body.[133] The Holy Spirit in the Old Testament inspired the prophets to speak the word of God to challenge the existing order; Jesus was anointed with the Spirit to preach good news to the poor. In a situation of political impotence living out the messianic presence individually or ecclesially is a practical response to guarantee the ongoing witness of the way of the messiah. It is a product of restriction and, like martyrdom, a means of continuing to live, in order to tell, the messianic story in unpromising circumstances. As such it does not mark a decline from the messianic task, in so far as it never becomes the goal of the messianic ministry, as it often has in Christian history.

Paul thought of the present as a time of fulfilment, a moment when a new order was being manifest and an old was passing away.[134] The reign of God on earth had not yet arrived, however, for the situation was one where the new was overlapping with the old and there was a cosmic struggle between light and dark as the painfully slow birth of the new order moved towards its conclusion. Paul did not abandon the hope for future transformation. Rather that hope gradually ceased to have the importance of the quest for personal holiness and the consequences of internalizing radical transformation in the present. How other early Christians came to terms with the frustration and disappointment of unfulfilled expectation we must deal with in the following section. What is evident in the letters attributed to Paul in the New Testament is the important role he played in taking up the charisma and translating it into another social milieu where the space for change in the existing order was slight. There can be few doubts about Paul's innovation and zeal, or about the faithfulness with which he took up the initial message. Yet his career and writing represent for us an example of that process of accommo-dation with the outside world and the channelling of the charismatic vision into an order which would guarantee preservation (what Max Weber called the routinization of charisma). This was taken further by his successors as the prophetic spirit, which inspired men and women in different ways, became linked firmly with an ordered ministry. For those who did not belong to the emerging clerical elite the mark of the Spirit was received through the rite of baptism. Restrictions were placed on the exercise of any charisma in the ecclesial sphere. The paradox of Paul is that the energetic innovator and founder of the Gentile church should have been the one who above all sowed the seeds of acceptability and passivity. Yet as the history of Christianity has indicated, the moments of reformation have often looked to the radical Paul as a basis for appeals for social change. He thus began the process of the channelling of the prophetic charisma in such a way that it could be a resource for those who were dissatisfied with the impoverished circumstances and longed for revolutionary change.

Coping with the kingdom

The centrality of an imminent expectation of a new age in the early church raises the question: how did those who look for a new age deal with the non-fulfilment of that hope? This issue has been extraordinarily influential within biblical exegesis over the last century or so.[135] The recognition of the centrality of an eschatological expectation within early Christianity led to the view that the non-fulfilment of their hopes must have presented a problem for the second generation of Christians (commonly referred to as the problem of the delay of the Parousia). When confronted by such disappointment, as well as by threats of doctrinal and ethical deviance, the church shelved egalitarianism in its church order. In its place, so it is argued, there emerged a hierarchical structure which guaranteed purity of doctrine and enabled the messianic community to maintain its identity in a world in which the kingdom showed no signs of coming. There are hints that this may have been happening in the aftermath of Paul's death. In the Pastoral Epistles (1 and 2 Timothy and Titus) there is a much greater concern with the preservation of proper teach-ing, and the role of the charisma of the Holy Spirit is tied more closely to the authorized exponents of the tradition through the laying on of hands.[136] Sobriety is encouraged among church officials[137] and the role of women in the *ecclesia* is excluded completely; they are to be saved through child-bearing.[138] The great and the insignificant all have some role to play,[139] but there is little suggestion of any important change in the order of things. Indeed, the devout

Christian should pray for the rulers.[140] There is no complete capitulation to the form of this world; riches are to be spurned, 'for the love of money is the root of all evil',[141] and they are to be generous with their giving.[142]

A change of attitude does seem to have come over second-generation Christianity, though whether the emergence of orthodox Christian doctrine and ethics is to be regarded as a response to the problem caused by the delay of the Parousia is not so clear. The explicit evidence for this delay being a problem within primitive Christianity is not as convincing as is often believed, 2 Peter 3 being in fact a rather exceptional piece of evidence. But while one would want to question the view that the delay of the Parousia *must* have been a problem, it would be wrong to dismiss some of the issues which this particular theory has highlighted. Two issues in particular call for comment.

Firstly, how groups react to disappointment and the mechanisms by which they deal with the contradictions between their hopes and the reality of the world has been the subject of much study (what some social anthropologists describe as 'cognitive dissonance').[143] It is pointed out that the non-fulfilment of hope does not as a rule lead to the abandonment of that hope. Indeed, there is a tendency to indulge in intensive activity as a compensation for the lack of evidence of the new age. It has been suggested that this can be seen in early Christianity in the rise of the missionary enterprises.[144] But, in addition, early Christianity may have dealt with non-fulfilment of its grandiose hopes by intensifying those hopes such as we find, for example, in the vigorous expectation which is to be found in the pages of Matthew's gospel[145] and in the concluding verses of Revelation.[146]

Secondly, Paul's theology and self-understanding cannot be properly understood without reference to his belief in the partial presence and imminent expectation of a new age. His own sense of calling had an important place within the overall scheme of salvation history. Paul's consciousness of his eschatological role can be illuminated by reference to Karl Mannheim's discussion of the utopian or, to use Mannheim's terms, 'chiliastic mentality'.[147] One aspect of this mentality, he argues, is the way in which the present moment becomes the *Kairos*, the moment to take decisive action. The utopian then takes it upon himself:

> to enable the absolute to interfere with the world and condition actual events . . . the present becomes the breach through which what was previously inward bursts out suddenly, takes hold of the outer world and transforms it . . . the chiliast is always on his toes awaiting the propitious moment . . . he is not actually concerned with the millennium to come; what is important for him is that it has happened here and now . . . the chiliastic mentality has no sense for the process of becoming; it was sensitive only to the abrupt moment, the present pregnant with meaning.[148]

Paul's sense of destiny meant that he believed himself called to be an agent in the dawn of the new age, the means by which the Gentiles became fellow-heirs in the commonwealth of Israel. Once Paul died that sense of being part of the 'propitious moment' disappeared. The understanding of present activity as an integral part of the consummation of the divine purposes gradually disappeared also. The future consummation then became an article of faith rather than an activity forming an indispensable part in 'interfering with the world and conditioning actual events'.

Something similar to the situation in the Pauline churches may be found in the appendix (chapter 21) to the Gospel of John. One issue which is touched on in the closing verses of the chapter is the problem posed by the death of the Beloved Disciple. Verse 23 indicates that there was an expectation current among the members of the community that this disciple would not die before the return of Jesus. Now that he has, a question-mark has been placed about the future coming of Jesus; the sense of being part of a 'propitious moment', the 'present pregnant with meaning', has been replaced by bewilderment in the face of the departure of a figure who had hitherto been the key to the ongoing story of the community; the outlook of the community and its view of its future have been deprived of their eschatological significance. The death of the Beloved Disciple seems to have provoked discussion in the Johannine communities about the validity of the expectation of Christ's return. It had been understood that this glorious consummation of the divine purposes would take place during the earthly life of the Beloved Disciple. The writer of John 21 seeks to enable his readers to come to terms with the disappointment they feel and to prepare them for an uncertain future.[149]

Similar themes emerge elsewhere in the Fourth Gospel where the disciples are those to whom Jesus comes. The one who loves Jesus and keeps his commandments will be loved by him and Jesus will manifest himself to that disciple;[150] indeed, divine indwelling will characterize the life of the obedient disciple, for both the Father and the Son come and make their home with that disciple.[151] The dwellings with the Father which Jesus goes to prepare for the disciples can be enjoyed by the one who loves Jesus and is devoted to his words.[152] Likewise the manifestation of the divine glory is reserved not for the world but for the disciple.[153] In the prophecy of Isaiah 'all flesh will see the salvation of our God'[154] and those who pierced the crucified Son of Man will look upon him when he returns in glory.[155] But in the Gospel of John the world cannot see the returning Jesus. Indeed, whereas in Revelation the goal of the new age is heaven on earth for those who bear the name of God on their foreheads,[156] in John seeing Christ's glory is part of the bliss reserved for the disciples in heaven above.[157] The Paraclete comes to the disciples; the world cannot receive him; and it is the Paraclete who enables the disciples to maintain their connection with the basic revelation of God, the Logos who makes the Father known.[158] The Paraclete thus points back to Jesus, the Word made flesh, and is in some sense at least a successor to Jesus, a compensation by his presence for Jesus' absence with the Father. These Johannine passages probably represent an attempt to come to terms with disappointed *Parousia* hopes.

But we should also note that it seems likely that the Johannine writings are products of a group to some extent alienated from contemporary society. Thus the lack of concern for the future of the world is in part due to the concentration on those who are of the light rather than the children of darkness outside the elect group.[159] The sectarian slant of its writing has given a dominant position to the concern for the elect rather than the world. But the world is still an arena of divine activity. The Spirit, as the advocate of the way of Jesus in bearing witness to the divine righteousness and the judgement of the old order, will carry on irrespective of whether or not the followers of Jesus accept it.[160] But the inward-looking character of the writing testifies to a dominant concern with the life of perfection in a group which feels itself increasingly alienated from a world which prefers darkness to light.

Early Christians had ample resources for dealing with the non-fulfilment of their hopes, particularly from within the apocalyptic tradition.[161] The apocalypses show an interest in the world above where God's reign is acknowledged by the heavenly host and where the apocalyptic seer can have access to the mysteries of those purposes of God for the future world.[162] In most apocalypses that experience of a disclosure of the heavenly mysteries is reserved for the apocalyptic seer, but it was perfectly possible to extend that privilege to a wider group. We find this in the writings of the Essenes discovered near the Dead Sea and in the later Jewish-Christian Odes of Solomon, both of which offer the elect group a present participation in the lot of heaven and a foretaste of the glory which is to come.[163]

The close relationship of the community of the elect with Christ in the heavenly places is stressed in the letter to the Ephesians,[164] so that the present life of the church becomes a foretaste of the kingdom of God, just as the Spirit enables the believers to regard the present as a participation 'in the powers of the age to come'.[165]

The privilege granted to the apocalyptic seer of glimpsing the divine glory which is to come can be paralleled also in Paul's understanding of apostleship. We have noted that he thought of himself as an embodiment of the crucified messiah: 'always carrying in the body the death of Jesus'.[166] In the presence of the apostle whether in person, as co-worker or by letter, the presence of Christ was confronting his congregations.[167] Paul is a father of Christ Jesus in the letters to the Corinthians and Paul's person is to be imitated as he is the embodiment of Christ.[168] Like the Risen Christ who stands in the midst of his churches in Revelation 1.13ff the apostle of Christ comes as a threat and a promise: a threat to those who have lost their first love or exclude the messiah and his apostle; a promise of blessing at his coming for those who conquer.

Accommodation with the existing order[169] and a growing concentration on theology and the life of the *ecclesia* was matched by a diminution of interest in the expectation of a coming reign of the messiah on earth. Of course, eschatological ideas persisted within the early church. At the end of the second century the orthodox writer Irenaeus still demonstrated his millenarian convictions, and Hippolytus indicated an interest in the figure of Antichrist and wrote a commentary on the book of Daniel.[170] Such ideas persisted within the church, particularly among groups which were marginalized by the emerging dominant ideology.[171] But the Donatist writer Tyconius paved the way for the interpretation of millenial ideas which was to triumph, thanks to Augustine of Hippo. Augustine seems to have entertained a millenial belief earlier in his life but in *The City of God* defused belief in the material character of the millennium by his allegorical interpretation. For him the future kingdom of God was purely spiritual.[172] Augustine's views were formulated partly in opposition to millenarian understandings and to the identification between kingdom and empire (for example, in the extravagant claims made by Eusebius of Caesarea about the Christian empire).

The process of accommodation could never eliminate the seeds of hope for a better world because the fundamental convictions centred around Jesus' messiahship and resurrection. Both of these were bound to keep alive the seeds of hope, however much they may have been constricted and diminished by the link with the life of the individual Christian and his/her conduct in subsequent teaching. The message of hope for a better world of which the Resurrection was the sign and seal could never be lost. As they became an integral part of the Christian way of viewing the world, they remained as a continuing reproach to the institutions and arrangements that Christians developed for themselves. However much the language of theology may have been constrained by its links with the powers of an age that was passing away, there could be no permanent restraint to prevent those primary convictions and symbols from being once more the resource for those agents of change in another age and other circumstances.

2

Themes of Protest and Prophecy

'It shall not be so among you'

In the discussion of the New Testament I have argued that the hope for a new age was of central importance. The journey of the prophet of the reign of God to Jerusalem provoked a crisis for the hierarchy there, and the eschatological enthusiasm linked with Paul's gospel was tamed as the Christian movement came face to face with the entrenched economic interests of privilege and wealth. The pervasiveness of that hope for a new age set up a contrast between the old order and the new, so that present realities were shown up in stark contrast to the glory which was to come. The millenarian tradition could not easily be shaken off. For one thing it was deeply rooted in the tradition. Jesus had led the life of a wandering preacher with nowhere to lay his head[1] and had told his disciples not to be anxious about wealth, status or basic needs.[2] He had come to proclaim good news to the poor and outcast and had challenged the rich to sell everything and give to the poor.[3] Particularly challenging was the fact that Jesus and the apostolic church claimed to have a foretaste of God's reign in the present age. The primitive church believed that it was inspired with the Spirit of the New Age to continue Jesus' work. The call to imitation in the power of God's spirit bred dissatisfaction with the present and a nostalgia for the time when the powers of darkness were kept at bay. Despite all the difficulties the taste of Paradise here and now seemed not only a possibility but also a pressing demand: 'You must be perfect as your Father in heaven is perfect'.[4] That command itself echoes the demand made upon Israel in the book of Leviticus to reflect the holiness of God.[5] In this chapter we shall explore some of those strands within the Jewish and Christian tradition which sought to revive or keep alive that life of the age to come amidst the ruins of an order which was passing away.

Way of holiness, way of the wilderness

The holy nation

The Judaeo-Christian tradition has always maintained an ambivalent attitude towards surrounding culture. This is evident within the pages of the Old Testament where the people of Israel are encouraged to use their best endeavours to keep their distance from the Canaanite culture and rebuked when they fail. This distinctiveness is grounded in theology. Unlike the nations Jews have no image for their God and must repudiate idolatrous practices as the sign of that special relationship with God. In this section we shall examine some aspects of that quest for distinctiveness and the contribution that it made to the quest for holiness.

Asceticism[6] and renunciation of the pleasures of the world have become part and parcel of the mainstream Christian spirituality. A glance at the origins of Christianity will indicate that a quest for communion with a holy and perfect God was firmly rooted. Perfection might be a present possibility for those who were prepared to make the necessary sacrifice to achieve it in the life of personal holiness and self-denial.

We need to be clear about the character of the debt to its Jewish matrix owed by Christian asceticism. The Jewish Law, the Torah, contains a variety of regulations relating to diet and purity, cultic practice as well as social legislation. Jews were not allowed to eat certain foods,[7] and sexual activity was circumscribed by the practice of ablutions and abstinence. This was an integral part of the Jewish tradition and was intimately linked to the quest for holiness both communal and personal which lies at the heart of Jewish religion: 'You shall be holy even as I am holy,' God commands his people.[8] That quest for holiness gave identity to the election of Israel as a nation. The practice of holiness, or separation from the surrounding cultures, is deeply rooted in the biblical tradition. When Jews found themselves scattered throughout the world without institutions like the Temple to give focus to their everyday social reality, practices like circumcision, sabbath and food and purity laws had a particularly important role in maintaining that distinctive culture in the face of the constant pressures to conform to the prevailing social mores. It was a pressure felt also in Palestine during the first part of the second century BCE. Attempts were made to integrate the Jewish culture into the increasingly dominant Hellenistic culture disseminated as a result of Alexander the Great's conquests. An overt attempt by the Syrian king, Antiochus IV, to impose Hellenistic practices in Jerusalem was met with armed resistance by the Maccabees.[9] It was symptomatic of the deep-seated hostility to other cultures and the concern of Jews to be distinctive, a holy nation.

That quest for holiness manifested itself in various ways. In the pharisaic tradition[10] which was the basis of the later rabbinic Judaism and has been the cornerstone of Jewish practices throughout the Christian era there was a concerted attempt to encourage lay (i.e. non-priestly) folk to practise in their everyday lives that level of ritual purity applicable to priests when ministering in the Temple. The regulations embodied in the *halakah* of the Mishnah[11] indicate the degree of specificity involved in the quest for a precise delineation of the boundary between the realm of the holy and the realm of the profane. The result was a pattern of existence which, once mastered, enabled a significant degree of intercourse with the ritually impure and participation to a significant degree in the life of society at large. It offered a strategy for being in the world but not of it and the continued assurance of moral rectitude that clearly drawn boundaries offer. The parameters were clearly set, however complicated they may be and however demanding upon those who would commit them to memory. Thus the earliest codification of the rabbis' rulings in the Mishnah offered a kind of utopia in which precise regulations, which took full cognisance of human fallibility, challenged as well as guided those who sought to maintain the perfection of holiness.

The priestly hierarchy in Jerusalem seems to have been content to have a *modus vivendi* with the Roman prefect in Jerusalem in order to ensure that the Temple cult was maintained as the foundation of the maintenance of religion. For some Jews, however, this strategy, and that of the rabbis which sought to combine the practice of holiness while living in a society dominated by the ritually impure (Gentiles and non-observant Jews), were unacceptable. For those who found it difficult to countenance the continued existence of persons and institutions which defiled, in particular, the Holy Land of Israel, this solution was nothing less than an accommodation with the profane. Before the First Jewish Revolt in 66 CE there were those patriots who could not tolerate that spirit of accommodation which allowed priest and pharisee to accept, however reluctantly, the presence of Rome in the Holy Land and city, provided that continuation of cultic activity and space for living the life of personal holiness were guaranteed. To purge the land of all defilement was an eschatological goal which some felt had to be taken in hand by the Elect in the present rather than leaving it to some indefinite period in the future. Following the injunctions in the Bible not to allow anything profane to remain[12] they were prepared to engage in a holy war against the forces of darkness which were defiling the land.

The Essenes in the wilderness of Judaea

The most significant solution to the Christian quest for perfection is that offered by the Essenes who established a community in pursuit of a life of holiness and communion with heaven at Qumran in the desert of Judaea and the (probably related) group, the Therapeutae, who lived in Egypt.[13] The Essenes and their practices are mentioned at length by the Jewish historian Josephus,[14] and the outline he gives of their ideas and practice corresponds to a large extent to the community whose writings were found in the vicinity of the Dead Sea in 1947. Among these documents we have a rule of discipline which seeks to regulate the life of a community some of whose members were expected to practise community of goods and a common devotion to the laws of God. It is apparent from the Manual of Discipline (widely known by its acronym 1QS), the main testimony of the regulations of the community, that there was a sophisticated procedure of admission and regulations all designed to maintain a separate identity of a group which was at odds with contemporary Jewish life. The document indicates that they looked back to the inspiration of a founder, whose precise identity is unknown, but who is referred to in several of the Scrolls as the Teacher of Righteousness. His interpretation of Scripture was regarded as authoritative. Indeed, he was credited with knowing more than the prophets of the Bible themselves and expounding what they *really* meant in their enigmatic oracles. He had been persecuted by the priestly authorities in Jerusalem, probably because he observed festivals on days different from the mainstream of Jewish life as a result of the use of a different calendar for the celebration of holy days as compared with the rest of Judaism. Those who joined the community saw themselves as members of a new covenant, and the language which they use of their common life together indicates that they saw it as heaven on earth: they shared the lot of the angels. For them the era of perfection to which prophets looked forward was already present. The members of the community believed that in their common life there was already a taste of the Paradise to Come.[15] The Essenes believed that communal holiness was only possible within an environment of complete separation from a system (particularly the establishment in the Temple) which was entirely corrupt.

The utopian character of the Essenes' vision for society as a whole is well illustrated by a recently published text discovered in the vicinity of Qumran, the Temple Scroll, which offers us a carefully and well-thought out plan in which the utopian and realistic are interwoven. The scheme which it contains is a blueprint for the Temple to be built after the conquest of the land. As such it stands in contrast to both Solomon's Temple and the Second Temple built in the sixth century BCE after the return of the ruling elite from exile in Babylon, an institution which was disparaged from time to time in Jewish sources. The utopianism of this text, however realistically conceived the plan may have been, would remain a blueprint of those who did not have the possibility of implementing their hopes.[16] But the Essenes did not expect to remain aloof from the struggle with the world for ever. One of their documents, the War Scroll (often referred to as 1QM), presents a detailed programme of military preparations to engage in a struggle on behalf of the sons of light against the sons of darkness in which they would be assisted by the angelic hosts in what would turn out to be a cosmic battle. The Dead Sea Scrolls thus indicate the existence of a dissenting group with a very clear consciousness of election and a sense of superiority over the rest of Judaism.

Similar practices are to be found in the first century CE in Egypt, the country which was to be the birthplace of Christian monasticism. The Therapeutae lived in Egypt near Lake Mareotis not far from Alexandria and were roughly contemporary with the Qumran community. The Therapeutae pierced behind the literal meaning of the words of Scripture which were 'symbols of something whose hidden nature is revealed by studying the underlying meaning'.[17] Men and women lived as celibates in a life of prayer and contemplation of the divinity. In the description of their worship the Jewish writer Philo of Alexandria compares their quest for the vision of God with the ecstatic state of some of more frenzied elements of Greek religion.[18]

Such counter-cultural traditions were not peculiar to the Jewish world of Jesus' day, for they have a long history in Judaism, linked with the quest for holiness and religious identity. The prophet Jeremiah in the seventh century BCE commends a group called the Rechabites[19] who refuse to drink wine, live in tents rather than houses and do not till the land. The Old Testament prophets similarly show features of protest and ascetic restraint, just as Jesus of Nazareth's mentor, John the Baptist, appeared on the margins of society in unconventional garb and with a challenging and uncompromising message. All offered to their contemporaries a living demonstration of the alternative which obedience to the righteous God sets before society.

Rigorist and separatist tendencies in the quest for divine holiness gave to these groups as elitist quality which inevitably separated them from the mainstream of Jewish practice. Such elitism is particularly evident in the apocalyptic tradtion where it was an important preparation for receipt of visions of the divine world. It is the cultivation of additional rites as a means of gaining that purchase on communion with the divine that is particularly evident in some of the Jewish apocalypses written at this period. In them we have accounts of preparations which include fasting, prayers, mortification of the flesh and resort to special foods. To those who practised these rites was vouchsafed divine knowledge about God's purposes and answers to some of the pressing questions of the human predicament. An example of such preparation for visionary experience can be found in the book of Daniel[20] where Daniel mourns for three weeks, eats no delicacies, no meat or wine, and does not anoint himself. In Acts[21] Peter's hunger is the prelude to his ecstasy. Here we have examples of those ascetic practices which guarantee that state of readiness for experience of divine revelation. It is obviously necessary for those who embarked on these exercises to go further than what might normally be expected of lesser mortals.

Christian asceticism

Ascetic strands are simply attested in the early days of Christianity. Thus in Revelation virginity is exalted and those men who have never defiled themselves with women are particularly blessed.[22] There is probably a relic here of the rules governing a holy war when those engaged in God's struggle were expected to avoid contact with women.[23] Celibacy was not generally encouraged in Judaism, but according to the gospels Jesus had never married and is reputed to have looked forward to a time when marriage would be abolished,[24] when those who were fortunate to participate would be like angels in heaven. For those who thought the resurrection had already arrived, the possibility of living like angels was not something reserved for the future but was already a present possibility.[25] Marriage and sexual intercourse were part of the aeon which was passing away. Those who belonged to the new order had no need of them. Indeed, according to Matthew 19.12 Jesus seems to recommend castration for the sake of the kingdom of heaven. Many felt compelled to respond to this call, not least the great Christian theologian of the third century, Origen.[26]

Perfectionism and asceticism are evident in the Pauline churches. In 1 Corinthians 7 Paul seems to be dealing with a problem where men and women in Corinth were attempting to practise abstinence. The chapter appears to suggest that men were living with women without sexual intercourse,[27] a practice which was found in later periods when women were cohabiting with Christian men.[28] Paul answers the questions of the Corinthians with regard to sexual ethics and exhibits a grudging acceptance of marriage. He recommends the unmarried state as being one which enabled the disciple to be without any anxieties and be more ready to enter the kingdom which was near.[29] The practice of virginity was a means whereby the flesh could be subdued to the Spirit and the glories of the age to come demonstrated. As Novatian, an official of the church in Rome, put it in the middle of the third century:

> Virginity makes itself equal to the angels: it excels the angels, because it must struggle against the flesh to master a nature which the angels do not possess. What is virginity, if not a magnificent contemplation of the life to come?[30]

In the letter to the Colossians, however, Paul condemns his readers for ascetical practices when seem to be related to quests for angelic visions and communion with the heavenly world.[31] Also the writer of the Pastoral Epistles confronts ascetical practices of a Jewish origin which in his view lead to eccentric behaviour,[32] indicating that such practices were not uncommon in the earliest period of Christianity. On the fringes of what was to become mainstream Christianity ascetical practices were rife. At the end of the first century Elchesai repudiated sexual desire and was said to have indulged in special diets.[33] In the Syriac-speaking church celibacy was urged; and Tatian's writings in the last quarter of the second century manifest the quest for chastity, while his version of the Four Gospels which conflated them into one narrative (the Diatessaron) reflects this heightened awareness of the need for sexual abstinence.[34] In the same region a century or so later the Pseudo-Clementine literature can describe the problems which might confront the male virgin. From the text it would appear that there had been examples of male and female virgins cohabiting, and the writer gives advice on appropriate courses of action for the wandering celibate.[35] While there were those like the Carpocratians who rejected marriage and advocated free love and community of goods, other 'heretics' like Marcion manifested that ascetic tendency we find elsewhere in second-century Christianity.[36]

There is another dimension to asceticism: keeping one's distance from possessions and the things of the world. This is enjoined in sayings attributed to Jesus in the gospels which speak of the need for the apostles to renounce possessions and engage in a wandering, homeless ministry.[37] Recent study has suggested that these sayings may reflect the life-style of significant groups in earliest Palestinian Christianity.[38] Unlike the churches founded by Paul such wandering preachers may have been concentrated in rural areas and have had a loose attachment to local communities which supported them. In a situation where there was a less hierarchical structure of social relations an alternative pattern of living with a loose attachment to convention and property was much more viable. Indeed such figures may have fulfilled a social role which was a permutation of the classical role in Israel of the prophet.[39]

The call of the wilderness

Such movements of thought and practice with the development of elites dedicated to quests for perfection offer us some antecedents for the emergence of Christian monasticism in the third and fourth centuries. In the middle of the third century monastic asceticism made its appearance in the desert of Egypt in the form of Antony's solitary existence.[40] It drew deeply on the ideas inherent in the gospel tradition. The story goes that Antony was challenged by the saying of Jesus in Matthew 19.21 ('If you would be perfect, go sell what you possess and give to the poor, and you will have treasure in heaven'). Responding to this he sold his possessions and placed himself under the care of God 'not being anxious for the morrow'. His example attracted many disciples in the desert. Essentially, the monastic life as laid down by Antony concerned the way to conquer the inner conflict and keep the passions of the flesh under subjection. Antony's contribution was to the hermit, anchorite existence rather than to the development of monasticism as it was later practised.

In only a limited sense could one regard the life of these Egyptian solitaries as a social protest, though their wise and perceptive ideas may have been a poignant challenge to the decadence of the surrounding culture. Particularly, their way of life with its focus on ethical response as a key to discipleship threw into the sharpest possible relief the growing worldliness of the churches and their concentration on dogma (though it should be stressed that Antony's orthodoxy was not in doubt). Nevertheless they were seen as spiritual supermen offering a way of life which it was clearly impossible for all adherents to follow.

Of perhaps greater significance for the history of monasticism is the contribution of Pachomius, a younger contemporary of Antony, who was himself influenced by Antony's ideas and seems to have lived the life of a solitary for a time.[41] He established a settlement north of Thebes and attracted followers. Pachomius laid emphasis on the importance of manual work of various kinds which alternated with periods of prayer and reflection on Scripture. There was a regular pattern of meeting for liturgy with regular teaching from superiors on the spiritual life during the week. There was a common (cenobitic) life which included eating together and discussion of points at issue from the scriptures. The transition to cenobitic monasticism from the life of the solitary was not easy. The fierce independence which the existence of the hermit encouraged made the obedience and communal discipline involved in the common life very difficult. During Pachomius' life a large number of communities were established under his general supervision. As the Pachomian practice spread, it became necessary to formulate a rule which reflected the pragmatic character of its origin arising from the experience of the issues confronting men as they learnt to live together. The rule itself was given supernatural sanction, as it was reputed to have been written on a brass tablet and given to Pachomius by an angel.

This remarkable movement with its roots firmly in Egypt may have been partly a nationalist social protest which attracted those who wished to escape the law as well as those who wished to escape society. It appealed to many erstwhile slaves, and as the economy of the Empire depended on slavery such a drain on manpower was a cause of deep resentment and embarrassment for the ecclesiastical authorities in the metropolitan areas. It was essentially a lay movement (a feature which was jealously guarded from attempts at episcopal control) with a concern to subjugate the passions of the flesh by starting at new life in an environment completely different from that which the initiate had known previously.[42] In an era of growing crisis, both political and spiritual, the monastic way of life offered a glimpse of eternal values amidst the perplexing flux of existence. Heaven on earth was located in the spiritual supermen of the desert.[43] The vision represents part of that nostalgia for the uncomplicated life of the wilderness when the people of God were free from the encumbrances of urban life. Old Testament prophets like Hosea yearned for that time again[44] so that the people could understand God without the fetters and anxiety of the world. The quest for holiness manifested in the ascetic tradition of the church was part of that recurring cycle of the need for renewal and the demand for perfection of heaven on earth so deeply embedded in the tradition.

Pachomius' rule stands at the start of a process which culminates in the rule of Benedict at the end of the fifth century and the spread of cenobitic monasticism throughout Western Christianity. Compared with Pachomius' rule Benedict's is more realistic, and is not geared to the extraordinary spiritual endeavour of the superman of the desert. If the rule is more lax and more realistic, the social control is greater. Stability and obedience of the monk to his superiors are cornerstones of the Benedictine rule. As in the Pachomian communities the importance of manual work is stressed, and the regular liturgical activity is given prominence. Thus it was that the voices in the wilderness grew into an integral part of church and society, prompting their own renewal movements in the later Middle Ages pioneered by people like Bernard of Clairvaux and Francis of Assisi who in their turn sought to recapture the original vision of perfection and to establish heaven on earth in the common life of the spiritual elite. Francis' vision corresponds more closely to the rigour of the desert than the conventual life. His absolute renunciation of possessions and demands for poverty did not sit easily with the need for a community to have material things in its possession to enable its common life and apostolic task to be carried out. Francis' vision brooked no compromise, and its legacy was the fratricidal struggle which ran through the early history of the Franciscan order in the century after his death. Then the quest for poverty was allied to the apocalyptic tradition, a matter to which we shall have to turn in a later chapter. But now we should return to the life of the early church and note the way in which Jesus's recorded challenge about wealth was handled.

Sell all you have and give to the poor

Theology and social ethics

We have noted the ways in which ascetic attitudes and a counter-cultural communal existence took root in the monastic practice of Pachomius and his companions. Such a concern for the common life is, as we have seen, paralleled in the life of the Qumran sect where some members practised the abolition of private property and led a shared life in the promotion of a community. This was for a time also the case in the life of the earliest messianic community in Jerusalem, though there does appear to have been hardship, as little attention seems to have been paid to the construction of a different style of economic management based on the abolition of private property.[45] There is little evidence of such practices in the Pauline churches. While there is certainly an attempt to distinguish the Christians from the prevailing culture, for example by the repudiation of idolatry, the hard sayings of Jesus about the loosening of family ties and the attitude to wealth do not appear to have made such an impact in communities where a rather different social strategy seems to have been pursued.[46] The Pauline letters indicate that within a short time the church in Judaea was undergoing a period of poverty which necessitated financial support from the non-Palestinian churches.[47] Paul was responsible for organizing the collection for the saints in Jerusalem and in several of his letters argues the case for generous support. But elsewhere, as we have noted, there are clear indications in the tradition of Jesus' sayings that not only is the accumulation of wealth wrong but that the rich can expect no reward in the age to come.

The dominant concerns of most of the theologians of the ancient church were with doctrine, and a study of their writings will reveal the extent to which the pursuit of orthodoxy and ecclesiastical order had become the pressing concern of Christianity.[48] The Christian religion had become a movement where the theological development had relegated ethics to a subordinate position. The reasons for this are many and complex, and some have been alluded to already.[49] What does stand out is the stark contrast to the parent religion, Judaism, where discussion of God's person and character took second place to the understanding of what was involved in obedience to the divine will. That is not to suggest that ethical teaching was unimportant. Indeed, we may suppose that it was the patterns of life of Christians both individually and corporately and the powerful examples of commitment even to death which continued to attract adherents rather than the conviction and sophistication of the arguments.[50] But the main Christian writers themselves focused on the theological task of explaining the mysteries of the doctrine of the Trinity and the humanity and divinity of Christ. Certain patterns of behaviour, particularly in matters of sexual morality, were regarded as essential signs of a salvation that had been accepted by the faithful. But if the writers of the ancient church were keen to promote the importance of personal ethical rectitude, where did they stand on more contentious issues like private property and relations with the state? The fact that most Christians were involved to a greater or lesser extent in the social world of their day meant that accommodation was necessary. Clearcut adherence to rigorist principles *at least when it came to attitudes towards society* could not be sustained. Such rigorism seems to have been driven inwards (or outwards into the desert, as we have seen). The quest for Paradise, heaven on earth, was to be sought in the subordination of the flesh by the Spirit. At least where Christians did have control over their own destinies and their immediate circles, whether it be family or church community, the quest for the perfect life of the kingdom of God could be pursued. The coming of the new creation might not be seen in human affairs at large, but it could come about in that person who was 'in Christ'. Certainly the old struggles would continue but discipleship guaranteed that for those who were willing to make the necessary personal sacrifices the glory of heaven could be actualized.

Coming to terms with a hard saying of Jesus

Christians could not easily live with the rigorist social ethics attributed to Jesus in the gospels.[51] When asked by a young man what he should do to inherit eternal life Jesus tells him to obey the commandments and goes on: 'One thing you lack; go, sell what you have and give to the poor, and you will have treasure in heaven; and come, follow me.'[52]

That advice may have been possible for the wandering teachers and ascetics of Syriac Christianity[53] but was totally unmanageable in the stratified and hierarchical societies of the Greek cities. Equality of status and wealth was replaced in this urban environment by the emphasis on equality of honour within the Christian community, a feature which confronts us within the socially conservative Pauline instructions in the New Testament. With regard to issues of wealth a more 'realistic' approach seems to have been taken after the initial flush of egalitarian enthusiasm. At the end of the second century Clement of Alexandria (*c*.150–215) accepts that material goods are God-given but refuses to allow them to be regarded as a right of the possessor. He sees wealth as a means to achieve two goals: self-sufficiency and community. It was thus the obligation of Christians who did possess wealth to increase their almsgiving, so that the needs of a wider group who did not have the means to provide adequately for themselves could be increased. There is no suggestion of any radical critique of private property.[54] Rather it is redistribution from the rich to the poor which characterizes the proper Christian use of wealth. Clement makes use of an argument which has been employed to great effect by Christian apologists of wealth and property: only if a person possesses property and wealth can anything be done to help the poor and hungry.[55] Even so, Clement's teaching sets an ideal which, though it falls short of the strict demand of Jesus, presents a stark contrast to conspicuous consumption by the rich.

In an age when the divisions between rich and poor were even greater, Basil of Caesarea (c.330–379) was much more attuned to the needs of the poor and the powerless and was ready to admit that the reason for grinding poverty was in part at least to be explained by the continuing acquisitiveness of those who already possessed the wealth. He condemned the exploitation which was going on and sought to demonstrate to those who were engaged in such activities the evil of their ways. He argued that private appropriation of the common land was robbery. All persons have an equal right to the land, just as all have an equal right to the air and other aspects of creation. He taught that as God was the provider for all people, the few must cease expropriating more than their fair share, so that all could have enough: 'If each one would take that which is sufficient for one's needs, leaving what is in excess to those in distress, no one would be rich, no one be poor.[56]

The treatment of the subject by John Chrysostom (347–407) and Ambrose of Milan (c.339–397) is characterized by a similar combination of a rejection of an absolute right to property and an appeal to equal access to the benefits of nature. Emphasis is placed on the importance of human need as a factor in determining rights to property. Material goods are ordained for the needs and requirements of *all* the human race. Chrysostom also points to human solidarity as men and women were created in God's image to serve God. Therefore, it was incumbent upon human beings called to a common destiny to enable all to reach that goal. Augustine of Hippo (354–430) too emphasized that goods must be used and not become idols or fetishes. Indeed, it is worthy of note that idolatry, for which many were willing to suffer martyrdom,[57] is compared with property ownership. Hoarding is contrary to the participation in a common destiny and calling. Chrysostom also exposes the way in which the emphasis on acquiring commodities has effects on human relationships. The yearning for private property and acquisitiveness promote oppressive, dehumanizing actions. Both poverty and anxiety about subsistence were the consequence of preoccupation with personal wealth and the perpetuation of that money in a family. As Augustine pointed out, the concern to maintain each individual's right to property was the cause of the fragmentation of humanity. The accumulation of wealth in the hands of the few led to war and continuing oppression in order to maintain the right to what had been gained by those means. All of this was a distortion of human solidarity and the purposes of the Creator.

In the twilight of the Roman Empire in the fourth and fifth centuries there was growing unease about the inequalities between rich and poor. The rise of monasticism allowed the quest for perfection to be hived off to an elite group of Christians without making the rest of the Christian church feel too guilty about its wealth. Indeed, Augustine of Hippo gave practical effect to his concern by founding a number of monastic communities dedicated to the common life. The challenge posed by the sayings of Jesus still had to be met. Matthew's version of Jesus' advice to the rich young ruler had modified the uncompromising 'Sell all you have and give to the poor' by the addition of the clause 'If you would be perfect'.[58] This variation provided the opportunity to see the renunciation of property as a counsel of perfection, suitable for those who sought to emulate Jesus in the desert but not for ordinary Christians. Even so, Christians should not pursue riches without any constraints, for, as we have seen, Clement stressed the need for sufficiency. But definitions of what was sufficient for individual Christians varied. The problem is well posed in the ambiguous character of some words of Gregory Nazianzus: 'Cast away all and possess God alone, for you are the dispenser of riches which do not belong to you. But if you do not wish to give all, give the greater part; and if not even that, then make a pious use of your superfluity'.[59] There is a recognition that riches are not the right of the possessor, but the vagueness of the advice allows the wealthy to escape when it comes to taking practical steps about wealth.

The Christian conscience could be satisfied by placing the emphasis on almsgiving, a feature of much of the patristic literature. But almsgiving is a way of remedying the ills caused by society without making any serious attempt to cure the causes of those ills. As Geoffrey de Ste Croix has put it, 'almsgiving enabled the propertied class not merely to retain their wealth without any feelings of guilt, but even to glory in it, investing it with a moral aura derived from using a small proportion of it (fixed entirely at their own discretion) for ''good works'' that would help to ensure their own salvation'.[60] The encouragement of dependency and self-righteousness on the part of the donor is something which is difficult to square with the tenets of a religion whose major thrust is the growth of all into mature personhood, the measure of the stature of the fulness of the messiah.[61]

De Divitiis: An orthodox ethic from the heretical margins

By far the most radical text dealing with the subject of wealth is the document De Divitiis which was written by Pelagius or one of his disciples in the fifth century.[62] Pelagius was a British theologian who achieved fame as the target of Augustine of Hippo's theological ire for suggesting that Christians by their own efforts could practise good works to achieve salvation. Such a view conflicted with Augustine's emphasis on the fallen nature of humanity and the centrality of divine grace as the sole means to achieve anything in God's sight. Pelagius' suffering at the hands of the theological giant of the early church should not detract from the extraordinary character of this document which offers a potent critique of wealth and property, even if it too stops short of advocating community of goods[63] or suggesting that the actual possession of wealth is wrong (rather, it is something which is likely to lead to sin). Nevertheless there is a frank recognition that wealth is the result of covetousness and theft and is the cause of violence: 'for the sake of wealth the earth is daily stained with innocent blood'.[64] But the author is not content merely to inveigh against the rich, for there is an attempt to analyse the origin of wealth, not merely its possession.[65] Wealth causes difference of status between rich and poor and blinds the rich to their common humanity.[66] Like other writers the author of De Divitiis appeals to the justice of an equal share of nature but presses home the point that no theory of justice can allow one person freedom of abundance and the other the bondage of poverty[67]: 'if God had willed universal inequality, he would have distributed all creation unequally'. Not only does he appeal to nature, for he also notes that both rich and poor share the same rite of baptism within the Church: 'are the rich reborn from one baptism, the poor from another? . . . If God distributes the gifts of flesh and spirit with fully equal affection towards all people, it begins to be clear that inequality of wealth is not to be blamed upon the graciousness of God but upon the iniquity of humanity'.[68] The author criticizes those who use fanciful scriptural interpretation to allow them to avoid the plain meaning of the text and dismisses those who look to the examples of wealthy men from the Old Testament in preference to the example of Christ.[69] So there is a pungent comment on the double standards applied by those who want to avoid the implication of the scriptural text:

> now we must discover the reason why those who are accustomed to expound nearly all the Old Testament allegorically and mystically and interpret the sayings or actions in the New Testament literally and as historical incidents . . . yet in the single instance of riches either forget their custom or change it and reverse the process . . . in this matter they try to justify their own manner of life rather than the forceful words of Scripture and by every ingenious device and false interpretation of the law to defend what they live . . . they wish the commandments to harmonise with their lives and not the reverse.[70]

Those attempts made to 'explain away' the meaning of Jesus' saying 'It is easier for a camel to pass through the eye of a needle than for a rich person to enter the kingdom of heaven' are subjected to ridicule.[71] There is an uncompromising condemnation of all the rich on the basis of the woe pronounced by Jesus in Luke 6.24.[72] Repentance comes about only if the rich man makes a careful disposal of all his wealth, leaving himself only the bare necessities of life or nothing at all. Only then will he be able to strive to enter where the rich man cannot. The writer rejects the notion that it is more important to have one's life straightened before giving away one's wealth: 'an argument invented to justify sin as well as wealth.'[73] There is a rejection of rights of inheritance, and those who possess as the result of inheritance are urged to 'act that you may keep it as an eternal inheritance . . . to transfer it from earth to heaven', as the accumulation of wealth is lost at death.[74] Such an action will be of benefit to the following generation in whose name the wealth is accumulated.

A remarkable link is made between wealth and political power. The rich are the ones who seek to sit on the tribunals, such as the one before which Christ stood when he was on trial. This provokes a devastating critique of the consequences of such political involvement:

> With that proud ambitious spirit that covets all earthly glory for itself, the rich commonly seek worldly power, and sit themselves upon that tribunal before which Christ stood and was heard. . . . See the slave seated where the Master stood, judging where the Master was judged. . . . You sit upon the tribunal. . . . Under your eyes the bodies of men like you in nature are beaten. . . . To watch is horrible enough; what am I to say when you give the order?
>
> Any Christian feels such disquiet. . . . You who plead you were a servant of the law . . . were a little earlier claiming to live according to the law of Christ. What is the explanation of this great difference between men who are described by the same word, Christianity, and are bound by the same sacrament of the same religion? . . . It is worth enquiring closely into the reasons which produce such wide differences between people of the same religion. . . . It is the rich, dripping with excessive wealth, whom the will to cruelty leads into acts of such savage wickedness.[75]

In the post-Constantinian age when Christians were involved in secular magistracies such a distancing of the followers of Jesus from the running of society would have seemed as strange as it does in our own day. It is a clarion-call to Christians to look closely at their profession of faith and to note the discrepancy between their beliefs and their practice. The recognition that division in society is caused by private property is clearly grasped, and the remedy is quite clear[76]: 'they do not understand that the reason why the poor exist is that the rich own too much. Abolish the rich and you will have no more poor. If no one has more than he needs, then every one will have as much as he needs. For it is the rich few who are the cause of the many poor.'

This is a long, and sometimes verbose, tract, but any deficiencies in its analysis are amply compensated by its single-minded concern with its subject. As John Morris has commented, 'the crisp argumentation that wealth and property had arisen in the past through "oppression"; that the existence of the rich, the fact that society is divided into such "general" (classes), is the cause of poverty, cruelty, and violence; and that society should be wholly reshaped, now and in this present substance by abolishing the rich and redistributing their property to the poor – is by any textbook definition socialism.'[77]

It may be an unusual document among the corpus of patristic literature. But what it does show is that the concern for social justice and equality as general principles was alive and well even if little is suggested about how such a restructuring of society might take place. The uncomfortable fact that Jesus of Nazareth had said some harsh things about the wealthy was a subject which Christian theologians were compelled to handle, though the ingenuity of exegesis enabled its force to be lessened. The *De Divitiis* is evidence that the subversive challenge of the foundation documents of the Christian church were to haunt the ecclesial organization, particularly at those times when its place in the social fabric seemed most snug and secure. It took the writing of a heretical school to remind mainstream Christianity of the sharpness of Jesus' challenge about wealth and property.

Rekindling the embers of the prophetic spirit

The claim to inspiration by the Spirit of God is a central theme of the New Testament. In the final discourses before his death in the Gospel of John, Jesus promises to send the Spirit who will act as an Advocate (Paraclete in Greek), to remind the disciples of Jesus' words and to guide them into all truth. The presence of the indwelling spirit in the earliest Christian communities was regarded as a return of the spirit of prophecy affirming the continuity with the absent Jesus in his words and work. Access to the spirit was open to all, whether women or men. In his programmatic speech on the Day of Pentecost Peter alludes to the prophecy of Joel: 'your sons and your daughters will prophesy'.[78] It was a mark of the reign of God already at work. It will come as no surprise, therefore, to find that the quest for a revival of that prophetic inspiration came from a generation of Christians who had not known the initial enthusiasm of the church. It is to an examination of one such movement in the early church that we now turn.

Montanism: inspiration from the promised Paraclete

The second century[79] saw a bewildering variety of claims to direct access to the testimony of the first followers of Jesus in apocryphal documents and also of claims to direct communications from the world above. Nowhere did these claims present such a potent threat at the end of the second century as in the rise of a movement in Phrygia under the leadership of Montanus and two female companions, Priscilla and Maximilla.[80] We cannot be sure when the movement started. The usual date given is 172 (alternatively 156-7). What distinguished the movement from other claims to esoteric revelation was that its doctrine was remarkably free of the extraordinary complexities and distortions which so characterize the gnostic cosmological systems which were current in the middle of that century; it is much more akin to the apocalyptic religion which we shall be examining in the next chapter. It claimed to have the inspiration of the Spirit (or Paraclete as the Montanists chose to call the Spirit, after the usage found in the Gospel of John 14-16). The Montanists believed that the prophetic spirit now spoke through them as a guide for conduct. They claimed access to the Paraclete whom Jesus had promised as the divine inspiration which would 'guide them into all truth'.[81]

Three things particularly annoyed the opponents of this new movement: (i) its claim that inspiration of the Spirit came through an ecstatic state in which the human became a passive channel for the divine oracles; (ii) the important position it gave to women; and (iii) its millenial beliefs. Montanus spoke of God inspiring the prophet in the following terms: 'man is like a lyre, and I strike him like a plectrum'.[82] There is no suggestion here (to quote Paul's words) that the prophetic spirits are subordinate to the prophets. Rather the Spirit descends on whomsoever the Spirit chooses, man or woman, lay or ordained.[83]

The important role given to women and the millenialism of the movement are well exemplified in this quotation from a later writer:

> In Pepuza she (one of the Montanist female prophets) was asleep and Christ came to her and and slept with her . . . she said: 'transformed in the likeness of a woman, in a bright robe, Christ came to me and put wisdom into me, and revealed to me that this place was holy, and that here Jerusalem came down from heaven.'[84]

Here the hope of Revelation 21 is picked up and an insignificant location in Phrygia chosen as the site of the descent of the heavenly Jerusalem.[85] Of course, by itself such a millenial belief would not have been particularly unusual at this period. Mainstream writers like Irenaeus and Justin still looked forward to a fulfilment of the divine promises in this world.[86]

Prophecy: giving space to women in a church ruled by men

What is much more remarkable is the role given to women in the Montanist movement and the emphasis on the importance of spiritual inspiration, the fulfilment of the promise of Jesus about the coming of the Paraclete. Attempts have been made to explain this ecstatic religion as the result of the impact of indigenous Phrygian religion on Christianity in the area, but that can hardly be an adequate explanation of the phenomenon.[87] It is at least as likely that Montanism represents a protest against greater ecclesiastical organization by those who clung to ancient and more flexible practices. The relationship between the divine charisma and the ecclesiastical organization had become more clear partly as the result of the need to draw boundaries against claims to inspiration and doctrine which did not conform with emerging orthodoxy. In a situation of tighter control and a narrower view of divine vocation the Montanist movement appeared to open the floodgates to spiritual anarchy just at the time when the storm caused by gnosticism seemed to have passed. Its appeal to the past was appropriate in an area which seems to have kept alive the prophetic and ascetical spirit as the book of Revelation shows.[88] Its nostalgia for the pristine freshness of the Spirit which inspired the apostles would have contrasted with the routine character of contemporary Christianity.

One feature of this movement in particular calls for attention. The reaction to Montanism indicates the way in which the church had narrowed the options open to women. Origen in the first half of the third century had stated that women should be excluded from the prophetic office,[89] despite Peter's words on the Day of Pentecost. The reasons for the squeezing out of women from the forefront of ministry are various. But one potent force is indicated in a late second-century liturgy, the *Apostolic Tradition* attributed to Hippolytus,[90] which spoke of Christian bishops in language derived from the Old Testament image of the High Priest. This effectively excluded women from that high office, for, according to the biblical rules for priesthood, only men qualified for the office. When that priestly vocation had attracted to itself the prophetic spirit in the rite of laying on of hands, or ordination, there was little room left for women in the higher echelons of the church's ministry. As women were ritually unclean because of menstruation,[91] there seemed to be every reason for excluding them from the holy offices, a situation compounded by the growing accommodation of Christian practice to the prevailing culture.

The part which women played in Montanist origins raised the spectre of a role for women in an organization increasingly dominated by men. In the book of Revelation a prophetess in the city of Thyatira had been castigated as a Jezebel for her teaching, not at this stage because she was a woman, for it appears that it was the character of her teaching which was at issue.[92] But the problem with prophecy is that it is far less predictable in its manifestation and its effects. The rebirth of prophecy in Montanism enabled that ever-diminishing space for women in the church to be opened up once more. After all had not the apostle Paul specifically allowed women in Corinth to pray and prophesy even when normally they might expect to be silent in church?[93]

In the history of religion prophetic religion has enabled women to express themselves and thus give rein to that intuitive element which the cold rationality of male-dominated institutions has so readily suppressed. Various texts indicate that attempts were made to enable women to have more than a passive role within the life of the church. Virginity and their role as widows and as passive recipients of the ministrations of the male clerical elite were rapidly becoming the norm. The involvement of women in ascetic practices and celibacy was itself a protest against the current expectations about the woman's domestic function and against the concept of woman as a sexual object and mother of children. The adoption of celibacy offered the woman control of her life apart from the dominance exercised by husband, brother or father. In the Acts of Paul and Thecla[94] Thecla's conversion by Paul's preaching and her adoption of a celibate life brought her into conflict with the patriarchal values of contemporary society. Her example was appealed to as a precedent for a woman to teach and baptize.[95] In the case of the martyrs Perpetua and Felicity at the beginning of the third century, martyrdom could lead to a position of enormous influence over ecclesiastical affairs in the short time available before death.[96] The promise of the martyr's crown was sufficient to guarantee a hearing, for the voice of a martyr was that of one who was about to wash her robes and make them white in the blood of the Lamb. Renunciation and death then offered only a drastic and very limited opportunity for women to speak with authority, so it is easy to see why Montanist prophecy was greeted with enthusiasm as it seemed to offer hope of greater opportunity for participation.

Evidence about women's involvement in the corporate life of the people of God from all periods of church history is difficult to come by, and the history of Montanism is indication enough of the way in which traces were erased from the tradition or distorted by the prevailing ideology. As with all movements and ideas which mainstream Christianity preferred not to recognize, the role of women, in whatever form, both within established patterns and more particularly outside mainstream Christianity, has to be reconstructed with patience and imagination from the distortions of ideology and the occasional glimpses vouchsafed to us.[97] Montanism is one attempt to cling to an ever-decreasing role for women which was foundering in the face of a culture where men and the quest for predictability were to have the final say.

This process impoverished religion, not only because women were relegated to the role of consumers of a religion concocted by men but also because the incorporation and subordination of the prophetic in the role of the priest meant that the powerful cutting edge of radical criticism was blunted: 'without vision the people perish.'[98] The presence of the book of Revelation in the canon of the New Testament is a potent reminder of that prophetic responsibility, to an explanation of the character of which we must now turn.

3

The Apocalypse

Hope, Resistance and the Revelation of Reality

The Apocalypse: voice from the margins of the canon?

Throughout the history of the church the book of Revelation has posed problems of interpretation and doctrine for Christian thinkers. Its association with fringe movements from Cerinthus and the Montanists to the enthusiastic followers of Joachim of Fiore and the Reformation radicals has added to the suspicion which Christians have felt towards this work.[1] Its peripheral place in the New Testament canon accurately reflects its influence in Christian theology. Eschatology is a matter to which one turns (if at all) only after other doctrinal issues have been fully explored. A glance at the readings prescribed for the Sunday Eucharist in the Church of England shows that the compilers of the readings do not consider the bulk of Revelation an appropriate resource for the edification of contemporary Christians in England. Even when the text does seem to have something challenging and apposite to say (as it surely does on the matter of the State in chapters 13 and 17), the less opaque (and less disturbing) thirteenth chapter of Romans is served up for the edification of believers. That contemporary point is merely an indication of the acute problem posed by the Apocalypse for mainstream conformist Christianity. In the Lutheran tradition the reputation of the book of Revelation is of being 'weakly Christianised Judaism';[2] this is a view shared by many. Its violence stands in stark contrast to the oft-repeated assertions that adherents of the Christian religion should espouse reconciliation and non-violence, rhetoric which has been subjected to critical scrutiny in recent years.[3] Much of this has been the result of an 'internalizing' reading of Revelation in which the struggle represented in its imagery is related not to the historical plane but to the soul of each Christian on its pilgrimage through this vale of tears to the City of God.

But the cataclysmic horizon of late twentieth-century life with the threat of disaster on a cosmic scale has meant that the images of Revelation have had a new appeal, often to those on opposite ends of the political spectrum. The members of New Right groups in the USA have resorted to the apocalyptic symbolism of Revelation as a resource to confirm their convictions that disaster is coming to the world order. Revelation can encourage a fatalistic attitude to the nuclear holocaust and an acceptance of the need to use it to keep at bay the hordes of darkness. In such a scenario there is little doubt on the part of the interpreters that the hosts of darkness are to be identified with the forces of world communism, while the elect can easily be seen to be the evangelical Christians and the President of the 'free' world whose resoluteness alone can expose the ways of darkness in the face of the insidious activities of the communist Beast. The fact that Revelation explicitly criticizes the kind of complacent assumption of rectitude and moral decency in the letter to the Laodicaean church[4] seems to make no impact on those who have already assumed that the new age is based on evangelical fundamentalism and a particular version of the American dream. One reason is that concern for the future of the cosmos and God's purposes for it have been deprived of their power by the assurance offered to born-again Christians that before the Great Tribulation comes they will be whisked off to be with the Lord in Paradise. Their only responsibility is to make sure their spiritual state is maintained so that their position with the saints away from a world of sin is not affected.

At the other end of the social spectrum peasants in Latin America find in the stark dualism of the book and the conflict between good and evil a graphic portrayal of their own struggles, as they seek to subsist amidst the violence and destruction of counter-insurgency campaigns in El Salvador, Contra-terrorist raids in Nicaragua or the powerful forces of the owners of large estates who seek to drive peasants off their land[5] in the remote areas of Brazil. What is more, the challenge of imminent disaster to an unrepentant world has begun to find a response in a Western world which has come to despair of the platitudinous certainties of its culture based as it is on exploitation of land and people. The Apocalypse has become a means of unmasking reality and exposing the iniquities which lurk behind the bland utterances of the powerful and the evil structures which undergird a facade of humanity in a sick society.

The centrality of eschatology in the New Testament

While the book of Revelation may be a product of the Jewish Christian culture of Asia Minor,[6] there is much in it which suggests that it also reflects the beliefs of the mainstream early Christian tradition. The central theme of its presentation of the eschatological drama is the conviction that the death of Christ (who is symbolized by a Lamb) and his exalation to the throne of

God is the decisive moment of change in the relationships between heaven and earth and the old age and the new.[7] This was the view of Paul in particular, as is evident in the way in which he talks of the resurrection of Jesus and the indwelling Spirit of God as 'the firstfruits' of the new age.[8]

But what of the other features of Revelation? Are the belief in the millennium (a reign of the messiah on earth), the destruction of the hostile powers and the stark dualism typical of other early Christian texts? The answer to that question is in the affirmative. The presentation of the main features of early Christian hopes for the future is no easy task.[9] For one thing nowhere do we have a systematic presentation of these beliefs. Rather we have various hints in contexts which usually deal with some other subject.

Of the centrality of the belief in Christ's imminent coming in glory there can be no doubt. Most New Testament documents focus on this hope, sometimes without much discussion of the consequences of this belief for the rest of the cosmos. In one of the most extensive passages dealing with the final change from the old order to the new we find material concerning the reign of Christ, but nothing is said about the lot of the saints in the new age, save that at the last trump the dead will be raised and the righteous will be changed into bodies of glory and will share the messiah's kingdom.[10] In 1 Corinthians 15.24ff the subjection of the principalities and powers (and in that Paul includes human as well as angelic potentates) to Christ is a feature of the eschatological process. Nothing is said explicitly here about Rome, but we cannot think that Paul supposes that the status quo will remain permanently. Rather he believes that God has allowed the powers on earth and in heaven free rein for a certain period.[11] Ultimately, however, the powers are called to account, punished and made subject[12] to the authority of God's messiah and in some cases destroyed.[13]

The gospels indicate that a form of the millenial belief was accepted by the early church. In the Beatitudes we find that a promise is made to the meek that 'they will inherit the earth'.[14] It is difficult, however, without excessive spiritualization to suppose that the filling of the hungry and the inheritance of the earth refer to events in a world very different from the present when a new order would bring about a reversal of values.[15] When one adds to these sayings the vow which Jesus is reported to have made at the Last Supper not to taste of the fruit of the vine until he drinks it anew in the kingdom[16] it appears that he was thought to have looked forward to a day when a new order under God would be established on earth: a time when many would come from the east and the west to sit down at table with the patriarchs in the kingdom of God.[17] It is special pleading to attempt to spiritualize all Jesus' hopes. Without resorting to a blind literalism this symbolism should not be evacuated of its evocative force in conjuring up in the minds of hearers and readers the hope for a new and better order in the near future.

Similarly in the Pauline corpus the classic statement of Paul's eschatological belief in Romans 8 includes a statement that the whole creation is moving towards the birth of a new age[18]:

> I consider that the sufferings of this present time are not worth comparing with the glory that is to be revealed to us. For the creation waits with eager longing for the revealing of the sons of God; for the creation was subjected to futility, not of its own will but by the will of him who subjected it in hope; because the creation will be set free from its bondage to decay and obtain the glorious liberty of the children of God. We know that the whole creation has been groaning and travailing until now; and not only the creation but we also ourselves, who have the firstfruits of the Spirit, groan inwardly as we wait for our adoption as sons, the redemption of our bodies.

This is a process centred on the present world order, not in some other realm. The majority of early Christians expected a reign of God on earth in the future when the elect would reign with the Messiah Jesus. Thus while there are certainly no signs in either gospels or epistles that a specific period of a thousand years was countenanced (such a belief was by no means common in Judaism in any case),[19] belief in the reign of God on earth is an idea which is central to the foundation documents of the Christian church and is demonstrated by its persistence well into the second century.[20]

The conquest of the powers

The hostility towards the Roman state and the rejection of its claims and power in Revelation contrast with the blander attitudes expressed elsewhere.[21] Nevertheless the conviction that all that was opposed to God would ultimately be uprooted and destroyed, so graphically portrayed in Revelation 17–20, is at least implicity stated elsewhere in the New Testament.[22] For example, in 2 Thessalonians 2.3f we find Paul using the imagery of apocalyptic literature to speak of the ultimate expression of hostility to God which would be overcome by Christ at his coming. Similarly the traditional features of Jewish eschatology, the messianic woes and other cosmic catastrophes, are set out in Mark 13. Nothing is said in this chapter or its parallels about the overcoming of the forces of darkness and their destruction. Indeed, as it stands Mark 13 seems to be a torso of the traditional eschatological pattern. It mentions the messianic woes and the attendant features which would indicate the coming climax, for example the setting up of the abomination of desolation and the political and social crisis facing those in Judaea, but after the coming of the Son of Man and his angels to save the elect nothing is said about the fate of the rest of creation.[23] As it stands, the chapter leaves the contemporary reader with the impression that the redemption of the elect is from a world fast sinking to destruction (hence

the doctrine of rapture which forms part of the stock of current fundamentalist eschatology today). One can only assume that one reason for this
truncated eschatological passage has much to do with the preoccupation of
the author with the immediate concerns of the elect, their need to persevere
in the midst of tribulation and the hope of their ultimate vindication. Possibly
Mark 9.1 with its promise of visible signs of God's reign for the followers of
Jesus is evidence of Jesus' complete presentation. Also, implicit within the
message of Jesus on the reign of God is the belief that the powers of darkness
(i.e. everything opposed to God) would be overthrown.[24] In so far as the
might of Rome stood in the way of the reign of peace and justice, the
co-existence of Roman sovereignty with the dominion of God would have
been impossible. Jewish hopes for the future, on which the New Testament
ideas are based, made no provision for any such co-existence of the reign of
God with the reign of the kings of the earth.

The pervasiveness of apocalyptic

Even if parallels can be found to the various items of eschatological belief in
Revelation this work at first sight seems to stand out from the rest of the New
Testament because of its style of writing. It is the only full-length apocalypse
in the New Testament. The absence of the apocalyptic genre from the New
Testament does not mean that the apocalyptic religion finds its only example
in Revelation. The features which we have categorised as typical of the
apocalyptic are in no small part derived from the distinctive experience and
claims the work makes.[25] John of Patmos tells his readers that what he saw
and heard came while he was in the Spirit,[26] in all probability a reference to a
visionary trance. What follows has many of the characteristics of a dream or
vision. The beasts and the angels are the product of the visionary imagination taking up scriptural passages which were widely used as a basis for
visions, particularly Isaiah 6.1ff and Ezekiel 1. In the context of such visions
it is only to be expected that their contents may drift towards the bizarre and
exotic. Other early Christian writers probably shared this outlook. There is
abundant evidence that the claims to visions and revelations were indeed a
prominent feature of primitive Christianity. The belief that the spirit of
prophecy had returned to the Christian community meant that they thought
the voice of God was to be heard directly through the mouth of prophets or
by the intuitive apprehensions of the believers themselves.[27] Paul speaks of
the importance of glossolalia and prophecy.[28] In the story of the growth of
the church in Acts the writer tells of the visions which mark decisive turns
in the story: the change in the life of Saul the persecutor of the church;[29]
the strange experience of Peter at Joppa which led to the conversion of the
Gentile centurion Cornelius.[30] Also, as we have seen, according to the

synoptic gospels the decisive moment in Jesus' ministry was marked by a vision in which he saw the spirit descending upon him like a dove.[31] Such passages are not common, but they do come at crucial moments in the narratives, so that it would be a mistake to regard their scarcity as evidence of their insignificance. The private nature of such experiences make it likely that many more remained uncommunicated and, therefore, unrecorded, in the tradition. We can see from 2 Corinthians 12.2ff that it was only under severe provocation that Paul resorted to disclosing an experience which he would have preferred to have kept confidential. Such isolated outcrops are an indication of the importance of the claim to knowledge of divine mysteries which Paul refers to occasionally in his letters.[32]

Early Christianity emerged in a world where contact with the divine by dreams, visions, divination, magic, supernatural enlightenment and other related forms of insight in the quest for knowledge was common.[33] To abstract the early Christian movement from such a quest and from the aspirations to radical change which are frequently embodied in the collections of such knowledge would be to ignore the reasons for its attractiveness within the ancient world. Claims by Christians to be indwelt by the divine Spirit and as a result to know the very mysteries of the divine purposes validated the understanding of the world necessitated by the apparent absence of the fulfilment of the divine will in human affairs. Visions of the divine purposes were an essential component which enabled the continued adherence to religious traditions by those who found little in human affairs to indicate their veracity. Early Christianity offered access to divine power and insight by confession of Jesus' messiahship and acceptance of the rite of baptism. When such convictions about communion with the divine world are linked to the initial assertions about the imminence of a new world order and a pattern of common life where fellowship and mutual support were to the fore it becomes entirely comprehensible why primitive Christianity should offer such an attractive social system for many in the ancient world.

Thus the hints from the rest of the New Testament suggest that the book of Revelation may not be such an idiosyncratic member of the canon. However much its theology may strike a discordant note with the tender spirits of our age we must reckon with the likelihood that both its apocalyptic and its millenarian outlook were vitally important for most early Christian writers. It is a measure of the success of the opponents of millenarianism in Christian theology that suspicion of the book has been endemic in Christian history. To pretend that the centrality of visions and revelations in Revelation is an aberration which perverts the truth of the gospel of Jesus and Paul is to misunderstand the significance which the apocalyptic outlook had for these two figures as well.

Apocalyptic: unmasking reality

Since the end of the last century, commentators on early Christian doctrine have had to reckon with the possibility of the pervasive influence on early Christianity of Jewish beliefs concerning the hope for the future derived from the apocalypses.[34] Few today would deny that the hope for a glorious new age in which sorrow and sighing would flee away, loosely referred to as eschatology, has a significant part to play either explicitly or implicitly in the presentation of the early Christian message. While admitting that the word 'eschatology' itself has been, and continues to be, a source of confusion, the relationship between apocalyptic and eschatology is frequently left unexplained. Many use the word 'apocalyptic' to describe the beliefs concerning the arrival of a new age and see apocalyptic merely as a form of eschatology. This is an area of confusion where some clarification is needed both with regard to the antecedents of the apocalyptic movement and the best way of characterizing it.

In all recent discussions of apocalyptic, a clear distinction is made between apocalyptic (or apocalypticism) and the apocalypse. The latter is a particular literary type found in the literature of ancient Judaism, which is characterized by its claims to offer visions or other disclosures of divine mysteries concerning a variety of subjects. The apocalypse, of which the books of Daniel and Revelation are the two canonical examples, is to be distinguished from apocalyptic, usually viewed as a cluster of mainly eschatological ideas which impinged generally on the theology of Judaism. The distinction between the apocalypse and apocalyptic ideas is an important one. But what is the cluster of ideas, usually labelled apocalyptic? The following summary may help to indicate one pole of the contemporary discussion[35]:

> We may designate apocalyptic as a special expression of the Jewish eschatology which existed alongside the national eschatology represented by the rabbis. It is linked with the latter by many ideas, but is differentiated from it by a quite different understanding of God, the world, and man.

According to such an interpretation characteristic features of apocalyptic include the following:

1 a contrast between the present age, which is perishable and temporary, and a new age, which is still to come, and which is imperishable and external;
2 a belief that the new age is of a transcendent kind, which breaks in from beyond through divine intervention and without human activity;
3 a wider concern than merely the destiny of Israel;

4 an interest in the totality of world history;
5 the belief that God has foreordained everything and that the history of the world has been divided into epochs; and finally;
6 an imminent expectation that the present unsatisfactory state of affairs will only be short-lived.

I would like to draw attention to two features of this treatment of apocalyptic. Firstly, its belief that the future hope is of a particular kind; secondly, its view that there is sufficient cohesion in the ideas contained in the different apocalypses to distil from them an outline of the essential features of apocalyptic; and thirdly, that transcendent eschatology, the hope for a new order *beyond* this world, is the key to our understanding of the thought-world of apocalyptic.

According to this view of apocalyptic there existed in Judaism two types of future hope: a this-worldly, national eschatology found principally in the rabbinic texts (produced by Jewish teachers in the centuries following the fall of Jerusalem in the year 70), and an other-worldly eschatology found principally in the apocalypses. The evidence from the apocalypses themselves, however, indicates that such a dichotomy cannot be easily substantiated. Apart from a handful of passages *the doctrine of the future hope as it is found in the apocalypses seems to be remarkably consistent with the expectation found in other Jewish sources. If* the point of departure for our understanding of the pattern of thought which we call apocalyptic is the apocalypses, and *all* the apocalypses, not just Daniel and Revelation, then we shall have to admit that the description of apocalyptic outlined above is inadequate.

Apocalyptic: higher wisdom through Revelation

The belief that eschatology provides the key for understanding the essence of apocalyptic is now seen to be inadequate. We can, however, understand the disparate elements of the book of Revelation if we see the underlying theme to be one which derives from its initial statement 'The Revelation of Jesus Christ' (Revelation 1:1) rather than from the eschatological message running through much of the rest of the book. Revelation is not merely an eschatological tract satisfying the curiosity of those who wanted to know what would happen in the future. Though it contains much teaching about 'what must happen after this', its purpose is to reveal something hidden which will enable the readers to view their present situation from a completely different perspective. When seen in this light, the significance of many of the visions in the Apocalypse falls into place: the Letters to the Churches offer an assessment of their churches' worth from a divine perspective: the vision of the divine throne room in Revelation 4 enables the churches to recognize the dominion of their God; in Revelation 5, the death and exaltation of Christ is shown to mark the inauguration of the new age; and in chapters 13 and 17 the true identity of the Roman emperors and the City of Rome is divulged. Revelation is a text which seeks to summon to repentance and to give reassurance by showing – by means of direct revelation from God – that there is another dimension to material existence, which could be, and was being, ignored by the churches of Asia Minor.

If we think of apocalyptic as 'higher wisdom through revelation',[36] the claim of the apocalypses to reveal mysteries about the future, the movements of the stars, the heavenly dwelling of God, angelology, the course of human history and the mystery of the human plight can *all* be seen to fall within the category of the mysteries which can only be solved by revelation. Such a quest makes sense of the apocalypses, *including* the book of Revelation. Indeed, the impact of the message of the latter depends very much on its claim to be a direct revelation of how things *actually are*, rather than the mere opinion of the wise teacher. Apocalyptic thus offers its readers an answer to that heart-felt plea from the prophet in Isaiah 64.1: 'O that thou wouldst rend the heavens and come down . . . to make thy name known to thy adversaries'. Many felt that this echoed the question of oppressed Jews of a previous generation: 'where are thy zeal and thy might? The yearning of thy heart and compassion are withheld from me'. The apocalypse offered a basis for hope in a world where God seemed to be restrained, by unmasking the reality of what the past, the present and the future of human history were actually about.

There is a kind of historical determinism undergirding this view of human history. The apocalyptic unveiling reveals that the future triumph of the divine righteousness is assured. But the apocalypses do not portray *individual* human destiny as preordained. That is open; and one of the functions of an apocalypse is to provoke a response of identification with the divine purposes by the individual or community in view of the inevitable outcome of the triumph of God. Several apocalypses do portray the present as the decisive moment in human history when the flowering of the historical development has reached the time for harvest. What stands out in all of the apocalypses is the need for the fulfilment of the totality of God's purposes in history before the new age can finally come. Consequently, it is futile to take any short-cuts to bring that about before the decisive moment in the history of salvation arrives.

Apocalyptic visions offer a hope of a better world which shows up the inadequacy of the present. As such they played an important part in creating a critical outlook on the world order and promoting a distance from the fabric of society as presently constituted. This alternative perspective on the world is the vehicle for reality to be unmasked. The injustice in the world and the temporary nature of the present order is demonstrated as a spur to action in pursuit of the goal of the reign of God.

Understanding the Apocalypse

The word apocalypse today is generally synonymous with catastrophe and disaster: *Apocalypse Now* sought to capture in horrific and lurid detail the horror of war. The images of Revelation are what make the book both compelling and frightening; but they seem to be most pertinent to the break-up of society and the world order which comes in war. But if we confine our understanding of the Apocalypse simply to the horrors brought by the Four Horsemen and the torment of the Lake of Fire we shall miss much of significance in this remarkable book. As we have just noted, apocalypse concerns the unmasking of the reality lying beneath the surface of the society and personal attitudes. The New Testament Apocalypse sets out to reveal things *as they really are* both in the life of the Christian communities and in the world at large. In so doing it gives little comfort to the complacent church or the powerful world. For the powerful and the complacent it has a message of judgement and doom, whereas for the powerless and oppressed it offers hope and vindication. The characterization of contemporary society in the apocalyptic symbolism of beast and harlot[37] is a vigorous unmasking and denunciation of the ideology of the powerful, by which they seek to legitimize their position by persecution and economic exploitation; it is an ancient Christian form of the critique of ideology. The critique of the present is effected by the use of a contrast between the glories of the future and the inadequacies of the present. The process of unmasking involves an attempt to delineate the true character of contemporary society and the superhuman forces at work in the opposition to God's righteousness in the world. The enormous power of those forces which undergird the oppression and lack of righteousness of the world order are shown to be unstable and destined to defeat. In contrast the apparent fragility of the witness of those who follow the way of Jesus is promised ultimate vindication.

The structure of the Apocalypse

To assist with the exposition of themes from the Apocalypse, a survey of the book and its imagery is here outlined:

1.1-8 Introduction
1.9-end Call Vision
2-3 Letters to the Seven Churches

4   The vision of heaven: a door is opened for the seer to witness the contrast between the acknowledgement of God's sovereignty in the world above and an unresponsive humanity below.

5   The Lamb is shown to be worthy to open the seals and thus to initiate the process of divine judgement and the reconciliation of God and humanity which reaches its climax in 21–2.

6, 8–9, and 16   The sequence of seals, trumpets and bowls which periodize the eschatological process which must precede the establishment of the divine reign on earth.

7   First interruption in the sequence of seals, trumpets and bowls. The opening of the seals in 6ff is here interrupted with a description of the sealing of the elect and the promise of ultimate vindication for those who are faithful in the period of divine judgement.

10–15   Second interruption in the sequence: the eschatological witness of the Church

    10–11   the prophetic task of the Church

    12   Divine protection for the people of God and the acknowledgement of ultimate victory but with the imminent threat from the Devil.

    13   the earthly embodiment of the Devil in the state revealed and the consequences for those who refuse to compromise (i.e. having the mark of the Beast)

    14   the Elect are those who are marked with the mark of the Lamb; they will be the ones to achieve ultimate vindication: the contrast with the fate of those who have the mark of the Beast.

    15   Song of victory over the enemies of God

17–19.10   Babylon's identity and character revealed and her judgement described.

19.11–end   the victory of the Son of Man over the enemies of God.

20. 1–10   the messianic reign on Earth with the restraining of evil

20.11ff   the Last Judgement

21–22.5   New Creation, New Jerusalem

22.6–end   Final admonitions

    The first three chapters of the book describe the call of John the seer who is imprisoned on the isle of Patmos,[38] followed by a series of letters to the angels of the seven churches in Asia Minor in which the Heavenly Christ offers reproof and encouragement in varying degrees, fostering a steadfast witness and the arousal of the complacent from attitudes of compromise. The apocalypse proper begins in chapter 4 where John sees God enthroned in heaven surrounded by the heavenly host who laud him as creator and redeemer. That scene is transformed in the very next chapter which describes the coming of a Lamb to God to receive a sealed scroll which symbolizes the historical process leading up to the establishment of divine justice on earth. The Lamb has earned the right to open the scroll and start this process leading to the climax of human history. The book of Revelation is interested in human history as the arena where the divine promises will be fulfilled. There is an unequivocal link between God and the historical process; in continuity with the Jewish tradition there is no suggestion that the world is out of God's control. Rather, unseen to human eye, but laid bare by the apocalyptic seer, the action of God is shown to be behind the dissolution of the stability of the cosmos and society. The dramatic picture of the coming of the Lamb (a symbol of the executed and martyred Jesus) to the throne of God in chapter 5 expresses the conviction that already God's purposes for humanity are in the process of being fulfilled.

Life in the last days

The sequences of seals, trumpets and bowls outlines the predetermined evolution of the divine purposes in history as the structures of the world give way to the messianic age (the millennium). That process which is symbolized by the repeated sequence of sevens is long and drawn out; there is no rapid transfer of the world to the sovereignty of God. The millennium only comes at the end of the predetermined process of divine judgement. There can be no short-cuts to the millennium; the period of tribulation and suffering must be accepted with fortitude and patience, the latter being a favourite word in the book of Revelation. Judgement is necessary because there is no sign of repentance. Human reaction to the horrors of the surrounding world is not to repent but to curse God.[39] God's righteousness reveals itself in judgement against humanity because of the alienation of human society from the way of God. The maintenance of that structural injustice which is unresponsive to the need for change in line with God's will results in ultimate destruction.

The reasons for the shortcomings of the state are laid bare also. The Beast is the incarnation of the powers of the Devil and attracts universal admiration for acts which *appear* to be beneficial.[40] The pressure is to conform and be marked with the mark of the Beast.[41] Those who refuse to do so are offered reassurance that being marked with the Lamb is a sign of righteousness even if it means social ostracism.[42] In the present age those marked with the Beast apparently have freedom to go about their business, whereas those who refuse to be so marked and side with God and the Lamb are persecuted and their deaths are greeted with glee by the inhabitants of the earth.[43] In reality it is those who maintain their integrity, even at the price of their lives, who will be vindicated, whereas those who have the mark of the Beast 'drink the wine of God's wrath'.[44] Those who persevere are shown that the might of state power is itself extraordinarily fragile, and its affluence, so attractive and alluring, is destined for destruction at the hands of that power which has maintained it.[45]

The prophetic witness of protest

The apocalypse contrasts with the utopian tract offering its readers a blueprint of some future, ideal society. As an evocation of a future age of glory it challenges the present order and enables those who accept its message to have their own consciousness infused with its critical spirit and an optimistic attitude towards the future. But Revelation is not a detailed blueprint of an ideal society to be contemplated at leisure or one which engages the reader only temporarily. Hope inspires action, readiness to suffer, and an awareness of the urgent need of repentance in the face of catastrophe. It seeks to persuade its readers that the present moment is a time of critical importance. The outline of future history is offered as the basis for a change of heart to engage the whole of life in its drama which will have drastic consequences for the one who reads it. Acceptance or rejection of its message is nothing less than the difference between alignment with the reign of God which is to come and sharing the fate of the Beast in the Lake of Fire.

That demand is evident in the letters to the churches which introduce the vision of hope and in the concluding admonitions which stress the authority of the text and the imminence of the fulfilment of its message.[46] The readers of the Apocalypse are not allowed to dream about millenial bliss without being brought face to face with the obstacles which stand in the way of its fulfilment and the costly part to be played by them in that process: they have to wash their robes and make them white in the blood of the Lamb, and avoid being marked with the mark of the Beast.[47] The strictures against those who recommend eating food sacrificed to idols indicate the need to create some distance between the conduct of Christians and the typical behaviour of society.[48] The references to idolatry and immorality in these passages are to be understood as in the tradition of the Jewish concern for holiness, that distinctive pattern of life over against the nations: 'it shall not be so with you'.[49] There is a challenge to the assumption that the disciple will be able to take part without too much comfort in the social intercourse of the contemporary world. As Klaus Wengst has put it:

> According to John the decisive question with which he sees the Christians of his time confronted is not 'How can I survive this situation with the least possible harm? . . . Rather, the question of the possibility of his own survival is completely put in the shade by the one question which is important to him: In this situation, how can I bear witness to the rule of Christ, his claim to the whole world? . . . He calls for an exodus . . . as joining in, life along the usual

lines, necessarily means complicity with Rome. The consequence is social separation. . . . By refusing to 'join in', by contradicting and resisting, they dispute that the world belongs to those who claim to rule over it. . . . 'Here is a call for endurance of the saints, those who keep the commandments of God and the faith of Jesus' (14.12). This sentence can be regarded as a summary of all that John wants to say. This endurance puts Christian life into the role of the outsider.[50]

The role of the follower of the messiah is not quiet resignation. Revelation 6.9–11 suggest that martyrdom actually contributes to the coming of the Kingdom. There has to be a quota of martyrs who must share the testimony of Jesus and take their stand against a rebellious world before the vindication can finally come. According to chapters 10–11 the seer is involved in the unfolding eschatological drama of the apocalypse when he is instructed to eat the scroll and commanded to prophesy. This is a direct call to participate actively as a prophet rather than to be merely a passive spectator. Revelation is insistent that the role of the martyr or witness is of central importance. Jesus of Nazareth is the faithful prophetic witness, and his followers have to continue his testimony.[51] That will involve suffering in the great tribulation, but those who join the messianic throng are those 'who have washed their robes and made them white in the blood of the Lamb'. In chapter 11 the church is offered a paradigm of the true prophetic witness as it sets out to fulfil its vocation to prophesy before the world, utilizing the figures of Moses and Elijah. That prophetic witness takes place in a setting opposed to God and ends in martyrdom and death: 'the martyr defends not his life but his cause'.[52]

This is similar to the main thrust of the message of the eschatological discourse in the synoptic gospels[53] which must not be separated from the narrative of Jesus' proclamation and inauguration of the reign of God. It is that context which is necessary to prevent the discourse about the future becoming the focus of the narrative. Discipleship involves sharing the way of the cross of the Son of Man as he goes up to Jerusalem. What is offered the disciple is the sharing of the cup of suffering of the Son of Man rather than the promise of sitting at his right hand or his left when he reigns on earth.[54] This request is not repudiated but, as the eschatological discourse makes plain, there can be no escape from the painful reality of the present witness with its need to endure the tribulations which precede the vindication. That is the challenge which faces those who wish to live out the messianic narrative in their own lives; no short cuts to the messianic reign are to be found here. Similarly, in Revelation the promise of a part in the New Jerusalem is linked with present behaviour.[55]

Overcoming the contradictions of the present in the New Creation

In reading the unfolding eschatological panorama of Revelation it is not often realized what a significant piece of theology is to be found in this work.[56] First and foremost, Revelation offers canonical justification for the cosmic and historical context of divine activity. That view, so deeply imbedded in the Jewish scriptures, was subordinated in mainstream Christian doctrine to the concern for the individual soul, a process already evident in the New Testament. The struggle between darkness and light in human affairs was neglected in favour of that conflict in the human heart. The book of Revelation has provided encouragement for all those who look for the fulfilment of God's righteousness in human history.

There is similarity of language between the description of the New Age in Revelation 21 and the prologue of the Fourth Gospel.[57] In Revelation 21.3 the tabernacling of God with humankind is fulfilled in the new creation. It is an eschatological hope which awaits the completion of that process of judgement on the unrighteous institutions which barred the way to God's reign. In contrast John 1.14 speaks of the tabernacling of the Divine Word in history as an event not in the future but in the past, in the person of Jesus of Nazareth: 'the Word became flesh and tabernacled among us and we beheld his glory, the glory as of an only son from his father'.[58] While in Revelation 21 the dwelling of God with humanity takes place in a world made holy and acceptable for this, in John the Incarnation takes place in an environment where the 'world knew him not'.[59]

The contrast between the vision of the new Jerusalem in Revelation 21 and the initial vision of the heavenly court in chapter 4 also should be noted. In Revelation 4 the seer is granted a glimpse into the environs of God. Here God the Creator and Liberator is acknowledged, and, as we notice from the following chapter, it is from the God of the universe that the historical process begins which leads to the establishment of a new aeon. In the chapters following 4 and 5 we find the picture of a world afflicted but unrepentant; indeed, manifesting precisely the kind of misguided devotion to evil which has to be rooted out before God's kingdom can finally come. In Revelation 4ff God is still in heaven, and it is there that the heavenly host sing his praise and magnify his name.

HEAVEN: God surrounded by those who do God's will ⌐

EARTH: Humankind unwilling to do God's will   Heaven on earth in
                                                   new creation
                                                   (Revelation 21–2)

This contrast between heaven and earth disappears in the new creation. Now the tabernacle of God is with men and women, and they shall be his people. God's dwelling is not to be found above the cherubim in heaven; for his throne is set right in the midst of the New Jerusalem where the living waters stream from the throne of God and his servants marked with the mark of God will see God face to face.[60] Here we have an example of theological immanentism which is predicted for the New Age. It is only then that there will be the conditions for God and humanity to dwell in that harmony which was impossible while there was rejection of the divine righteousness in human affairs. Heaven on earth is what the new age is all about. God is no longer transcendent but immediate – part and parcel of that world of perfection and evident in it. Indeed, those who are his will be his children and carry his name on their heads: they will be identified with the character of God and enjoy his presence unmediated.[61]

As we have seen, early Christian writers were convinced that this divine immanence was not reserved solely for the New Age. The glory which the apocalyptic seer enjoyed in his revelation was a matter of living experience here and now for those who confessed Jesus as messiah and participated in the eschatological spirit. Already those who possessed the spirit of God were sons of God;[62] already those in Christ were a new creation[63] and a Temple of divine spirit.[64] That hope for the final resolution of the contrast between heaven and earth was already perceived by those who had eyes to see and know it. Already the people of the messiah were being 'taught by the Spirit . . . what God has prepared for those who love him, God has revealed to us through the Spirit'.[65]

The Apocalypse can remind readers of early Christian literature of the hope for a reign of God on earth, when injustice and oppression will be swept away and the structures of an evil society replaced. This is an important component of the Christian gospel. One can imagine how easy it would have been for the early Christians to have capitulated to their feelings of political powerlessness by concentrating on individual holiness only. But even Paul finds it necessary to speak of a process of salvation which is firmly rooted in the process of liberation for the whole of creation.[66] The Apocalypse does not easily allow a retreat into the conventicle as the main arena of divine activity, for it persuades the saints to prophesy before the world about the righteousness of God and the dreadful consequences of ignoring its implementation. In the midst of the old order the presence of God is to be found in the prophetic witness of protest, the unmasking of injustice and the pointing forward to the messianic age. The visions of a world above where perfection reigns are symptomatic of the fractured existence of injustice and an expression of longing for resolution and an end to alienation.

The legacy of the Apocalypse

The book of Revelation stands firmly in the prophetic tradition, and its appeal to the spirit of prophecy made it a resource for subsequent generations of Christian prophets. We have seen how the Montanists appealed to aspects of its message at the end of the second century. Its close association with them may have contributed to the suspicions which attached to it, leading some figures in the early church to question whether it should be in the canon of scripture at all.[67] Its millenarian outlook was not a problem until towards the end of the second century, when such ideas were regarded with increasing contempt.[68] When in the fifth century Augustine offered an interpretation of the prediction of the millennium which effectively undermined the expectation of the age of divine righteousness on earth, a pattern of interpreting eschatological material which had already been set in train was firmly established and millenarianism pushed to the sidelines. Augustine's repudiation of millenarian ideas and his identification of the millennium with the era of the church can be seen in the following quotation from *The City of God* Book xx 7ff:

> It is therefore of this kingdom at war, in which conflict still rages with the enemy, that the Apocalypse is speaking in the passage we are considering [i.e. Revelation 20.1ff]. . . . And so the passage is concerned with the first resurrection which is now in being . . . then he gives a summary of what the church does during those thousand years, or what is done in it, when he says, 'I saw thrones, and those who sat on them, and judgement was given'. This must not be supposed to refer to the last judgement. The thrones are to be interpreted as the seats of the authorities by whom the Church is now governed, and those sitting on them as the authorities themselves.

This work was composed to refute the suggestion that the fall of Rome and the imminent threat to civilization was the vengeance of the gods of Rome for the capitulation of Rome to the Christian religion. By describing humanity as consisting of two societies of human beings, one of which is predestined to reign with God from all eternity, the other doomed to undergo eternal punishment with the Devil (Book xv.1), and seeing the former as pilgrims to a celestial city, radically different from the present world, Augustine set the agenda for an understanding of the relationship of God's salvation to human history. How that Augustinian position was challenged and the millenarian strand given new life at a crucial point in the twelfth century will be the subject of brief discussion in the next section.

Joachim of Fiore

It is difficult to explain why Joachim of Fiore, an obscure Cistercian abbot in
Southern Italy, should have turned to the book of Revelation and stressed
the idea of imminent fulfilment of God's purposes *within* human history.
One explanation may be that such ideas proved attractive in an era of rapid
social change.

From the tenth century onward in Central Europe there emerged a relative political stability which facilitated the growth of economic activity and
an increase in population. One consequence of this was an increase in a
rural proletariat – people who had no smallholdings and who flowed into
the growing commercial centres to become part of an ever-increasing urban
poor.[69] It was in such a situation that Joachim wrote his fascinating and
complicated exegesis of Revelation and expounded his convictions about the
imminence of the fulfilment of God's purposes in history.[70] When the
promise of perfection related not to some world beyond this but to the world
of poverty and inequality, the fantasies began to have a potent air of reality
and encouraged expectation of social change. Joachim of Fiore was born
*c.*1135 in Calabria. He was a member of a well-connected family at the
Sicilian Court. He turned his back on the career that had been mapped out
for him and became first a hermit, an itinerant preacher, and then a Benedictine monk at the monastery of Croazzo. He became abbot and in due
course went off with a few followers to set up another community at San
Giovanni da Fiore.

During his life he was much sought after because of his apocalyptic
insight. His was a pessimistic message about imminent troubles coming
upon the world. Indeed, Joachim thought that Saladin's conquest of Jerusalem in 1187 was a sign that the church's tribulation, symbolized in the attack
of the dragon in Revelation 12, was reaching its climax, with the imminent
appearance of Antichrist in human history; his days were a time of unique
crisis. Antichrist (who, Joachim believed, had already been born) would be
a false teacher from Western Christianity who would ally himself with the
Islamic infidels. Hope was to centre on a righteous remnant offering a
renewed commitment to a superior form of religious life. Joachim looked for
the most perfect form of monastic life, and it it this which is still to come as
the climax of the third age. While there has been debate over the relationship
between this ideal community and the present institutions of the church, it
would appear that Joachim did have some actual communal existence in
mind rather than some inner disposition which did not shatter contemporary institutional arrangements. His own Fiorensian community which was
given official recognition at the Fourth Lateran Council in 1215 might have
been expected to have been the embodiment of this ideal; but there seems

little evidence that he ever thought of it in these terms. In his expectation and quest for the perfect religious life Joachim reflects the restless spirit of the age which sought a return to the primitive apostolic life of a lost golden age. There would be 'a coming monastic utopia', a holy pope[71] who would preach in the age of Antichrist and two new religious orders would arise to confront the Antichrist, to lead the church into the final age of the Spirit, an order of preachers and an order of ascetics.

Joachim's importance for Christian theology was that he affirmed that the pattern of history was incomplete and that process of completion was imminent *within* human history, not in some eternal realm. He took the Augustinian concept of the pattern of seven ages derived from the seven days of creation. But whereas for Augustine the seventh and final age, of rest and blessing, lay beyond history, for Joachim the eschatological sabbath coincided with the third age imminent in his day. There is a clear contrast between the way in which the millenial traditions had been used and interpreted by Augustine and the legacy of interpretations which stem from Joachim. As we have seen, Augustine in *The City of God* Book xx had set in train a pattern of interpretation which viewed the conflict between God and Satan as one which took place now within the individual soul rather than some eschatological conflict in the world which would herald a new era. Thus preoccupation with a future earthly millennium was thereby excluded, and that hope of an alternative paradigm for the world order on which millenial dreams depend was subtly undermined. However orthodox Joachim might have thought himself and his opinions, such a view of history was, in Marjorie Reeves' words, 'concealed dynamite'[72] which enabled the challenge to the status quo that a millenial view encourages.

Joachim offered a history of salvation divided into three major periods corresponding to the three members of the divine Trinity. The close link between the divine Trinity and the process of human history is a distinctive feature of his thought; the real meaning of the flux of history could not be understood without recourse to the mystery of the Trinity. The first period began with Adam and lasted to Christ (in a similar vein the apostle Paul has carved up human history into dispensations in Galatians 3 and Romans 5). It was linked with God the Father and was the era of the order of the married. The second lasts until the present (i.e. the time of Joachim, the moment of salvation). It is linked with God the Son and is the time of the order of clerics. The third, the time of the monastic order, is linked with God the Holy Spirit. It began with Benedict and will bear fruit in the last times. What is most significant about this view of history is the progressive character of the saving work of Christ, for it maintains that the purposes of God still have to be fulfilled in the era of the Spirit, when humanity would manifest a moral perfection under the guidance of the Spirit. While Joachim apparently did not expect the New Testament to be superseded, he does seem to have expected the final era of the Spirit to have been superior to all that had gone before. The significant point about Joachim's exegesis, however, it that this exegetical enterprise was employed to elucidate the whole history of the human race rather than individual Christian piety.

In the complexities of Joachim's thought we have an exegetical kaleido-scope in which the quest for inner meaning reached extravagant proportions. Some of the complexity of his periodization of history can be glimpsed in the following quotation[73]:

> The first of the three *status* of which we speak was in the time of the Law when the people of God served like a little child for a time under the elements of the world. They were not able to attain the freedom of the Spirit. . . . The second status was under the gospel and remains until the present with freedom in comparison to the past but not with freedom in comparison to the future. . . . Therefore the third status will come toward the end of the world, no longer under the veil of the letter, but in the full freedom of the Spirit when, after the destruction and cancellation of the false gospel of the son of perdition and his prophets, those who will teach many about justice will be like the splendour of the firmament and like stars for ever. The first status which flourished under the Law and circumcision was begun with Adam. The second which flourished under the gospel was begun by Uzziah. The third, insofar as we can understand from the number of generations, was begun at the time of St. Benedict. Its surpassing excellence is to be awaited near the End, from the time Elijah will be revealed and the unbelieving Jewish people will be converted to the Lord. In that status the Holy Spirit will seem to call out in the Scripture with his own voice,. . . . The letter of the prior testament seems by a certain property of likeness to pertain to the Father. The letter of the New Testament pertains to the Son. So the spiritual understanding that proceeds from both pertains to the Holy Spirit. Similarly, the order of the married which flourished in the first time seems to pertain to the Father by a property of likeness, the order of preachers in the second time to the Son, and so the order of monks to whom the last great times are given pertains to the Holy Spirit. According to this, the first status is ascribed to the Father, the second to the Son, the third to the Holy Spirit.

Apart from the obvious interest in the book of Revelation evident in his complicated exegesis of that book, there are clear features of the apocalyptic outlook evident in Joachim's writings. He emphasized that he was above all an interpreter of Scripture:

> God who once gave the spirit of prophecy to the prophets has given me the spirit of understanding to grasp with great clarity in his spirit all the mysteries of sacred scripture.[74]

This claim to be an interpreter resembles the authority given to the teacher of Righteousness in the Dead Sea Scrolls to whom God has made know the real meaning of the mysteries divulged to the prophets,[75] though the interpretation offered by Joachim does not amount to an exclusive claim to have the true interpretation. He also received visionary insight which he believed enable him to make sense of Scripture and doctrine: 'a revelation of the fullness of the Apocalypse and of the complete agreement of the Old and New Testaments perceived with clear understanding by the mind's eye'.[76] This is evident also in his account of the illumination he received about the mystery of the Trinity when he saw a ten-stringed psaltery which enabled him to resolve his doubts about the doctrine. The experience of illumination was not something which was peculiar to Joachim alone, but a foretaste of that spiritual insight which was to be the prerogative of all flesh in the New Age.

The Legacy of Joachim: the Franciscans and holy poverty

Within a decade of Joachim's death his prophecy of two new orders seemed close to fulfilment in the rise of two new mendicant orders, the Franciscans and the Dominicans. A sense of destiny is evident in the opening words of a joint encyclical issued by the generals of the Franciscan and Dominican order in 1255: 'nivissime diebus istis in fine saeculorum ('in these latest days at the end of the ages'), indicating an important role for the mendicant friars in the last days.[77] It was the Franciscans in particular who found in Joachim's prophecies warrant for their role as the key to the struggle against the forces of Antichrist which would lead the world into the glories of the final monastic utopia. As we have noted, Joachim had predicted a pivotal role for orders of 'spiritual men' in the imminent crisis. Accordingly, those who would be perfect could not afford any kind of compromise on the perfection necessary as they had a divinely appointed role in the crisis of history.

Later the Franciscans engaged in a bitter struggle over the correct interpretation of Francis' rule of poverty, and in this the influence of the Joachite ideas played a significant role as they continued to provide the motor of the quest for perfection.[78] The utopian practice of the Franciscan order had became a bone of contention already during the life of Francis of Assisi. Francis had insisted in 1226 towards the end of his life that no modifications should be made to his own practice of poverty. But as is so often the case the wishes of the founder of a radical movement were interpreted rather more flexibly. Within five years a papal bull had declared Francis' testament null and void and the process of accommodating the rule to the demands of a growing international monastic order had begun. The complete renunciation of private property by the order seemed to some an impossible ideal, and there arose a struggle between the Franciscan Spirituals, who wished to preserve the initial practice of Francis, and those who wanted to come to some kind of accommodation with surrounding culture. A prolonged struggle ensued, resulting in the final triumph of the compromisers and the condemnation of the Franciscan Spirituals, the heirs of the literal interpretation of Francis' ideals.

Franciscans learnt from Joachim the expectation of an imminent end to the present age but also considered that within the church there was to be a struggle between good and evil, with the collapse of the present church (some believed it would happen in 1260) and its replacement by the monastic utopia predicted by Joachim. To the rigorist Franciscan Spirituals the advent of Francis represented a turning point in salvation history. By identifying Francis with the angel of the sixth seal of Revelation 7.2 they indicated that in Francis was revealed the character of the final order which opened the door of spiritual understanding. The advent of Francis was regarded as being a third testament, and the Franciscan Spirituals had a role in bringing about the eschatological reformation. In the debates which ensued among the Franciscans the Joachite influence prevailed even among those who could not accept the conviction of the Spirituals that they already enjoyed that perfection of the new age. Like the apostle Paul when dealing with the eschatological enthusiasm of the Corinthian Christians, Bonaventure, the leader of the Franciscans at the end of the thirteenth century, accepted some of the planks of Joachite exegesis but his leadership was marked by the attempt to square the circle of absolute poverty and the need to possess and use things in the world. For Bonaventure poverty was not the highest ideal that it was for the rigorists. While Bonaventure managed to maintain an uneasy balance between the two factions, after his death the profound split in the Franciscan order was to manifest itself.

There were inevitably tensions with the ecclesiastical authorites as the Franciscan rigorists extended their criticisms to the lack of evangelical poverty in the ecclesiastical hierarchy. So much so that the opposition of the church could in some cases be sufficient indication to the persecuted minority that it must be not the true church but Antichrist itself. Other enthusiasts like Fra Dolcino (d. 1307) were inspired by Joachim and believed that the eschatological agents to bring about the true apostolic life were to be human figures. In Dolcino's view the Roman Church was no longer the church of God but of Babylon and the pope would be replaced with a pope appointed by God. He advocated anti-clericalism and a form of spiritual anarchism and antinomianism. Eventually Dolcino gathered his followers together on a mountain near Novara to await the fulfilment of eschatological events (reminiscent of the accounts of the eschatological prophets of the first century

CE contemporary with Jesus of Nazareth and much later the defeat of Muenzer and the peasants outside Frankenhausen). Traces of this kind of Joachite-inspired millenarianism persisted for decades. Eventually, in 1317 Pope John XXII, whom many Franciscan Spirituals regarded as the Christian Antichrist prophesied by Joachim, condemned the Spirituals in the Bull *Sancta Romana et Universalis Ecclesia*. In 1322–3 John condemned the view that Christ and the apostles had owned nothing. The outcome of this was the continued adherence of groups to the original vision and a continuing struggle within both church and order. The wheel had come full circle; radical renewal had been tamed.

As in first-century Palestine where the message of the prophets of the millennium was greeted by an increasing number of landless peasants and labourers, promises of deliverance in this period fell on receptive ears also. Here again was the quest to recapture the original vision within the church, not least in the growth in new religious orders. Radical Christianity finds no more ready exponents and sympathizers than those who were heirs to Joachim's vision. The turbulence of the late medieval ages and the contribution of the millenarian spirit is an essential ingredient of the story of radical Christianity. Its importance does not reside merely in the feelings of dissatisfaction with church and society which are manifest but is also found in the legacy of such ideas to the Reformation period. In the years after Joachim's death there was a proliferation of Joachite literature, in which pseudonymous writings were attributed to the abbot of Fiore and became very influential in subsequent centuries when the significance of the obscurities of his exegesis was explored and applied to contemporary events. Protest movements like the Hussites were probably influenced by Joachite literature,[79] and there is a direct link between Joachim and the radical movements of the late medieval and Reformation period. The commentary on Jeremiah was used and admired by Thomas Muenzer, for example,[80] and possibly also by Winstanley.[81] It is to these examples of radical discipleship that we must now turn.

4

Muenzer and Winstanley

Two Models of Radical Discipleship

The legacy of Joachim of Fiore ensured that a historical approach to eschatology was kept firmly on the agenda. At the Reformation that legacy was appropriated once more in outbursts of revolutionary millenarian enthusiasm. It is not my concern to trace all the meanderings of the path of visions and social change so much as to offer a glimpse of the impact of such ideas at certain selected points in history. In this chapter I want to outline the life and thought of two radicals of the early modern period who shared many ideas but whose understanding of the application of these ideas in an environment of rapid social change led to contrasting patterns of radical discipleship.

Thomas Muenzer: a new Daniel at the head of the army

On 13 July 1524, less than a year before his death outside Frankenhausen in the Peasants Revolt, Thomas Muenzer preached one of the most remarkable sermons of the Reformation period.[1] It was preached before Duke John, his family and town officials in Allstedt. It was Muenzer's opportunity to put his case for the radical reformation before those who had the military power to effect change in society by force. What is more, it enabled him to speak directly to a supporter of Luther and in the presence of the Duke who had himself come under more radical influence.[2]

Muenzer is one of the most misunderstood figures in early modern history. He is often seen as nothing more than a rabble-rouser and dangerous fanatic whose espousal of the holy war against his enemies drew upon himself a justifiable retribution. Muenzer's views are frightening in their insistence on human agency in the exercise of the divine wrath. But Muenzer's pitiless attitude should be seen in its historical context. It is as well to remember that

Martin Luther, the hero of the Protestant Reformation in Germany, had nothing but contempt for the 'marauding peasants' and encouraged the authorities to engage in their suppression, just as he manifested a crude anti-semitism which shocks us greatly.[3] This has to be said, as from the moment of his death opponents set about vilifying Muenzer and even those whose ideas might be considered similar to his have distanced themselves from the stormy career of the young Reformation radical. But the story of the dispute over Muenzer has not stopped with his notoriety among his immediate contemporaries. In current Reformation studies Muenzer's role in the Peasants Revolt has been the subject of considerable dispute between church historians and Marxist historians.[4] Most problematic is his role in the early bourgeois revolution, a particular concern of Marxist historiography. One of the problems with Muenzer studies has been the difficulty of steering a middle course which recognizes the specific socio-economic realities which undergird and condition the theological ferment at the beginning of the six-teenth century without necessarily wanting to deprive those ideas of their power and determinative significance in provoking actions in the social sphere. Any study of Muenzer's writing leaves the impression of the breadth of his biblical knowledge and the sophistication and power of his exposition. No doubt Muenzer would not have been aware of the larger social process of which he was a part (though he clearly believed he was living in a critical moment of history). We would deprive his ideas of their power for social revolt if we saw them merely as the expression of protest of a segment of society. But Christian assessments of Muenzer have also found it difficult to explain the relationship between Muenzer's mystical pietism and political activism. We have to appreciate the subtle relationship between the triumph in the inner battle of overcoming what is opposed to God and the parallel, but distinct, obligation to change the world according to God's purposes. Only if we do so can we grasp how Muenzer saw the ultimate triumph of God's sovereignty in the world as so closely linked to undergoing inner suffering.[5]

Zwickau, Bohemia and the Prague Manifesto

Muenzer was born in Stolberg in what is now the German Democratic Republic round about 1491. He seems to have had an academic education, with periods spent at the universities of Leipzig and Frankfurt an der Oder. At some point he was ordained priest and he became provost of a nunnery in 1516. His early career gives no indication of the fiery radicalism to come, though his contact with various nunneries may partly explain the profound influence of the German mystical tradition, particularly Tauler.[6]

His first contact with Zwickau (the centre of his initial outburst of radical activity) came in April 1520 when he was appointed to a supply preachership there at the Church of our Lady. There were already social tensions in Zwickau, and Muenzer's anti-clerical sermons contributed to the growing unrest in the city. Muenzer became associated with the revolutionary and radical elements in the city among whom were the so-called Zwickau prophets who proclaimed that the last days were at hand and that a holy war against the godless fought by the Elect was due to start.[7] In his St Stephen's Day sermon of 1521 Muenzer embarked on a clerical diatribe which provoked the congregation to attack a priest who was sitting in the church. Finally, in April 1521 after a further disturbance, Muenzer was ejected from Zwickau, thus beginning an itinerant life which was to last for the next four years.

From Zwickau Muenzer made his way to Bohemia where he probably linked up with Lutheran sympathizers in Prague. Bohemia had been a centre of social unrest and political subversion based on religious radicalism.[8] The legacy of Huss and the English theologian John Wycliffe was still felt there, and movements inspired by Joachite eschatology as well Wycliffe's ideas were widespread and had caused uprisings decades before.[9] In Prague Muenzer issued his Prague Manifesto which has come down to us in various recensions.

A basic theme of this Manifesto is the need for inner knowledge of God and divine sonship, and the close identification of the true believer with God himself, knowledge of which is said to be self-authenticating and does not depend on the book faith of intellectual assent. There is emphasis on the need for the period of trial which leads to true faith ('Therefore I will suffer those things which Jeremiah had to suffer'), and a sharp attack on preachers and teachers in the church for their unwillingness to teach 'the true order of God, which he has set in all his creatures'. The problem, in Muenzer's eyes, is the lack of any experience on the part of preachers of the words 'heard from the mouth of God'. It is assurance of that Spirit within which is the mark of the elect:

> St Paul writes to the Corinthians that the hearts of men are the paper and parchment on which God writes with his finger the irrevocable Will and Eternal Wisdom, and this writing any man can understand if his understanding has been opened . . . and God has done this from the very beginning in his elect, in order that they may not be uncertain, but have an invisible witness from the Holy Ghost.

The problem, in Muenzer's eyes, is that book religion is the scourge of true Christianity. Most Christians do not appreciate the importance of immediate apprehension of the divine will. Muenzer points to the prophets' conviction that they were mouthpieces of God, a method of God's communication which

is still active: 'that is why all the prophets have used this manner of speaking –
"Thus saith the Lord", they do not say, "Thus did the Lord say", as though
it were all over, but they say *now in the present time*'. He touches on a theme
which was to be repeated later in the Sermon before the Princes, namely that
the church has lost the innocence of the apostolic age. The true church is one
'which shall rather be the Elect friends of the Word of God, who learn to
prophesy as Paul teaches that they may truly know, how friendly and how
heartily God loves to talk with all his elect'. He indicates a role for himself as
one who comes in the Spirit of Elijah, the prophet who comes before the
'great and terrible day of the Lord'.[10] The present is a time for decision, for
'if you will not do this God will let you be beaten by the Turk in the coming
year'. In the longer, German, version of the Prague Manifesto he defined
his own role as the wielder of the eschatological scythe: 'the harvest time is
here, and this is why God himself has put it out to harvesting. I have made
my sickle sharp, for my thoughts are firmly centred in the truth, and my lips,
hands, skin, body, life itself curse the unbeliever'.[11]

Allstedt and the Sermon before the Princes

Muenzer's appeal to the Christians of Prague was a failure. He was expelled
from the city, and entered a period of hardship both spiritual and economic
in which he interpreted his sufferings as an identification with the sufferings
of Christ. This fallow period came to an end in 1523 when he was appointed
preacher at the parish church of St John in the town of Allstedt close to the
mining areas of Mansfeld. At this time he finally broke with Luther and
embarked on that career of idiosyncratic innovation, fiery radicalism and
fanaticism which was to culminate in his condemnation by his former mentor
and his execution after the failure of the Peasants Revolt in Thueringia.
Meanwhile his career in Allstedt was marked by an extraordinary mixture
of radical preaching and invective and a creative development of eccelesias-
tical life which itself flew in the face of the clamp-down on liturgical experiment at the time. His liturgical experiments attracted large numbers of
people to Allstedt.[12] Muenzer consolidated his support by forming leagues
of the elect,[13] a kind of new covenant, which included local peasants from the
surrounding area. It would appear the he hoped to turn Allstedt into an
alternative centre of Reformation to Wittenberg where Luther was based.

Allstedt's relative remoteness from centres of authority meant that local
officials preferred to take no action rather than risk an uprising which they
did not have the resources to contain. Muenzer's reputation attracted the
hostility of Count Ernest of Mansfeld and the suspicious interest of Duke
John, brother of the Elector of Saxony, Frederick the Wise. The upshot was
that John and Frederick resolved to hear Muenzer preach in Allstedt. This

evoked from Muenzer the famous Sermon before the princes in July 1524 to which we have already alluded. In it he sought to persuade the princes that they should take up the sword on behalf of the Elect and wipe the godless from the face of the earth.

The challenge in the spirit of Daniel

Muenzer takes as his text for the Sermon before the Princes a passage from the prophet Daniel in which the Jewish seer interprets a dream of the Babylonian king Nebuchadnezzar, which the wise men of the court were not able to interpret.[14] The dream is of a statue made of various substances which is hit by a stone made without human hands and shattered, after which the stone becomes a great mountain filling the whole earth.[15] Christ is the rock made without human hands, insignificant in human eyes and trampled underfoot by an ignorant humanity. The interpretation offered by Daniel is the destruction of four world empires (symbolized by the different substances of which the statue is made) to be replaced by the kingdom of God which will never be destroyed.[16] For his interpretation of the dream Nebuchadnezzar gave Daniel great power and acknowledged that Daniel's God was 'God of gods and Lord of kings, and a revealer of mysteries',[17] an indication of the appropriate response of wise rulers to the inspired prophetic word.

Then Muenzer proceeds to interpret the various parts of the vision of the statue. Christ is the stone which is about to shatter the final empire, a fact which is appreciated better by 'the poor laity and the peasants'. In the face of this destruction the princes are exhorted to side with Christ the Stone whose empire will replace the kingdoms of the present rulers. What is needed now is for the princes to recognize the incompetence of the clerics, just as Nebuchadnezzar rejected the wise men of his court. In their place he urges them: 'A new Daniel must arise and interpret for you your vision and he . . . must go in front of the army. He must reconcile the anger of the princes and the enraged people'. Christ the Stone is about to shatter the schemes of the Lutheran clergy.[18] The princes should heed Christ's words 'I am not come to send peace but a sword' and eliminate the wicked, thus showing themselves to be ministers of God as Paul commanded[19]: 'if you want to be true governors, you must begin government at the roots, and as Christ commanded, drive his enemies from the elect. For you are the means to this end'. In a daring exegesis of Romans 13 he points out that Paul's reference to rulers 'not bearing the sword in vain, for they are the servants of God to execute wrath on the wrongdoer' should be interpreted as an obligation to root out the wicked who are opposed to the ways of the New Daniel.

So Muenzer does not allow the rulers to use the argument that judgement must remain in God's hands and reminds them of their obligation to wield the sword as executors of the divine wrath. He exposes the ideological camouflage of those who seek to appeal to the gentleness of Christ to suit their own ends. Instead he asserts the continuity between the Old and the New Testaments[20]: Christ fulfils the Law and the Prophets. This justifies use of the Old Testament, so that he enjoins the repudiation of idolatry by a programme of iconoclasm. There can be no quiet waiting upon God to destroy the works of the Antichrist, for it is human agents acting under the power of God who will effect the divine purposes. If the rulers refuse to do so, the sword will be taken away from those who 'confess him all right with words and deny him with the deed'. They will be replaced by the 'angels, who sharpen their sickles for this purpose'; they 'are the serious servants of God who execute the wrath of the divine wisdom'. Those who repent will be spared but those who refuse to co-operate in the task of returning the church to its original state cannot be spared: 'the weeds must be plucked out of the vineyard of God in the time of harvest'.

Muenzer stresses the importance of a diligent reading of Scripture. This leads him to a realization of the Church's error in forsaking the way of Christ and the apostles. The church, he says, has lost its pristine glory, and by reference to the early Christian writer Hegesippus, Muenzer points out that the 'church did not remain a virgin any longer than up to the time of the death of the disciples of the apostles'. In order better to understand what prevents devotion to Christ the Stone it is necessary to be attentive to revelation from God, particularly so in a 'dangerous age' such as the one his hearers were living in. The clergy teach ordinary people that 'God no longer reveals his divine mysteries to his beloved friends by means of valid visions or his audible Word'. Muenzer lists examples of visions from Scripture, and insists that opponents of visions are in fact opponents of the Holy Spirit, poured out in the Last Days. That Spirit is revealing to the elect 'a decisive, inevitable, imminent reformation with great anguish'. Muenzer contrasts the way in which the people of God rejected the words of the prophet Jeremiah with the ready acceptance of Daniel's interpretation by the pagan king Nebuchadnezzar.

Muenzer admits that there have been false prophets and deceivers. But he rebukes those who deny the possibility of continuing revelation as faithless men. Those who have fellowship with heaven are in a position to interpret. It is the 'learned divines who are the soothsayers who publicly repudiate the revelation of God and thus attack the Holy Spirit'; they suppose that what is contrary to their understanding must be of the Devil. Martin Luther, 'Brother Fattened Swine and Brother Soft Life' rejects such claims to visions. The proof of the rectitude of the revelation will be evident to the spiritual person.

Muenzer maintains that to gain 'the self-disclosure of God a person must be separated from all diversion and have a heart resolute for truth and must through the exercise of such truth distinguish the undeceptive vision from the false one'. That means abandoning all consolation of the flesh and attending to 'the field of the Word of God which remains full of thistles and thorns and of big bushes, all of which must be got out of the way for this work of God'. Spiritual turmoil and suffering are a mark of the divine approbation. It is in such circumstances that God vouchsafes visions and dreams to beloved friends. Then will such a person receive the vision in the present; only then is it to be tested in the light of Scripture: first experience, then Scripture. Knowledge of the Scripture, therefore, is inadequate without the enlightenment which comes from the Spirit. Scripture is a witness to the faith of the writers, and it is the appropriation of that inner illumination which prompted the writing which is at the heart of true discipleship.

Whether Muenzer at this point had any realistic conviction that the princes could be won over to his side is not clear. Even at the very point of his departure from Allstedt he wrote to Elector Frederick the Wise in measured tones hoping that he might be able to continue his work. But events were to close the door on any accommodation between Luther and the princes. Firstly, refugees who were followers of Muenzer arrived in Allstedt from Sangerhausen. The continued pursuit of these men by Duke George of Saxony provoked Muenzer into an outraged response, asserting that the authority of the princes over the common people was at an end. In the interestingly titled 'The explicit unmasking of the false belief of the faithless world' Muenzer rejects a role for the princes and considers them merely a prop for the status quo: 'the great do all in their power to keep the common people from perceiving the truth'. Shortly afterwards, in an attack on Luther he accuses him of being a stooge of the powerful and responsible for offering an ideology which supports private property. Muenzer points to the way that the mighty lay claim to the whole of creation as their property (which he deems robbery) while forbidding the poor to do the same by resort to the commandment: 'Thou shalt not steal'. The only way for ordinary people, Muenzer believed, was to take up the struggle for the overthrow of the ungodly. Not surprisingly, at about this time Luther wrote his letter to the princes of Saxony in which he warned them of the dire effects of Muenzer's activities. Muenzer now rejected any godly role for the authorities as they held nothing of the Christian faith; their rule was at an end and would shortly be handed over to the common people. Muenzer was eventually deserted by former supporters and his stay in Allstedt came to an end when he escaped in August 1524.

The last battle

Muenzer finally ended up in Muehlhausen, a town south-west of Allstedt. Here Heinrich Pfeiffer had been active in preaching, and there was already a political struggle against the establishment. In May 1523 the power of the local dignitaries had been challenged and reforms instituted. Anticlericalism and iconoclasm were thus already part of the fabric of existence when Muenzer arrived on the scene. Pfeiffer and Muenzer soon began to work together and drew up articles of reform. While there was support in the town, they did not receive the backing of the rural peasants and both Pfeiffer and Muenzer were eventually expelled in November 1524. Muenzer went to Nueremburg, and it is from this period that we have his most bitter piece of invective against Luther, in which Luther is roundly condemned for supporting social injustice by his theological opinions and lending support to the oppression carried out by the godless princes. After further wanderings Muenzer returned to Muehlhausen in March 1525 whither Pfeiffer had returned. The revolutionary party was now dominant, and Muenzer was appointed as parish priest of the Church of Our Lady.

It was then that the full effects of the Peasants War began to affect Thueringia. There had for some time been various regional grievances, but underlying it all was a common burden of oppression and discontent in a world of rapid social and ideological change. The peasants ransacked religious houses and terrorized local gentry. There was little concerted action by the landlords, and the peasant revolt was hardly well organized, though Muenzer did send an appeal to his old friends in Allstedt. A large contingent of peasants assembled at Frankenhausen some miles from Muehlhausen. Muenzer led a contingent there, leaving Pfeiffer behind. There was little support from the miners of the Mansfeld region. Six thousand poorly equipped peasants occupied a hill overlooking Frankenhausen. In their midst was a banner proclaiming 'the Word of God endureth for ever'. Duke George arrived and issued an ultimatum that Muenzer should be handed over with a vague promise of an amnesty for the rest of the peasants. Muenzer encouraged his supporters by reference to biblical stories like that of Gideon, where the Old Testament judge aided by the power of God defeated the enemy with a small number of men in a holy war.[21] At the decisive moment of struggle a rainbow appeared in the sky, taken as a divine sign that the God of the New Covenant would give them victory. That Muenzer and the peasants believed that they were engaged in a holy war, the Last Battle, is confirmed by the evidence of their singing 'Veni Creator' according to Muenzer's arrangement, as they prepared for the final consummation. Any eschatological hopes were rudely shattered once the first cannon round had been fired. The peasants were routed. Muenzer escaped but was later captured. In a final letter to Muehlhausen he asked his friends to look after his wife and ensure she received his few possessions. He also warned them to learn the lesson of Frankenhausen, but enigmatically suggested that God's work can only be fully understood when complete (for Luther the defeat of the peasants and the death of Muenzer was ample sign of divine judgement). He was finally beheaded outside Muehlhausen along with Pfeiffer on 27 May, having recanted his theological 'errors'.

God within: visions and identification with the suffering Christ

It is Muenzer's political radicalism which has marked him as a forerunner of political theology. In fact very little is known about Muenzer's hopes for the New Age when it came. If we may trust the evidence of his confession after his arrest, he intended to promote an order in which 'all things were in common'. The outbreak of destructive revolutionary protest should not blind us to the real grievances which the peasants sought to have ameliorated.[22] But all the indications are that it was the pressure of the present critical moment demanding action which so preoccupied Muenzer's attention. 'If you will not do this, the Lord will let you be beaten by the Turk in the coming year', wrote Muenzer in the Prague Manifesto. As he reminded the princes in his sermon, they must respond by taking up the sword and destroying the impious, for it was a critical moment in the divine economy.[23]

There is in Muenzer's thought a conviction that the divine is there to be found in all persons and can be apprehended by those who are sensitive to 'the working of the Divine Order bubbling from his heart'.[24] Muenzer challenged the idea that only those who know the Scriptures intimately would be among the Elect. All nations under heaven given the right perception of the word within could find God without the Scriptures. Muenzer views all the Elect as having the Spirit already in their hearts: 'even if a man were born a Turk he might have the beginning of the same faith'.[25] This universalism is a feature of Muenzer's thought. God speaks directly to all; and many from the heathen lands will precede the so-called Christians into the Kingdom. Muenzer did not despise the Scriptures. What he inveighed against was book religion. That charismatic emphasis led him to draw heavily upon the contrast between Word and Spirit and to emphasize the latter at the expense of the former. The important thing is to respond to the promptings of the Spirit and subordinate the letter to the Spirit. In that way the common man will be able to understand without having to show deference to the intermediary powers of the academic scribe for whom the letter is all-important.[26] Some of the hostile comments hurled at Muenzer indicate the importance he attached to the inspiration of the Spirit.[27]

It is no surprise that with such an emphasis on the intuitive understanding of God Muenzer should be sympathetic towards dreams and visions as an important means of knowing the ways of God. There is evidence to suggest that he made a study of those passages in the New Testament which speak of visions being vouchsafed to the first Christians. In several places he compares himself with Daniel (in the Sermon before the Princes), John the Baptist and Elijah. There is little doubt that Muenzer had confidence in his election and his ability to function as a final prophet 'in the Spirit and power of Elijah before the great and terrible day of the Lord came'. He carried around with him volumes which included the early Christian apocalyptic tract, *The Shepherd of Hermas*, an indication of the importance he attached to such ideas.[28]

For Muenzer only the Elect can have a clear understanding of the difference between the Elect and the Wicked. The Elect knows by the prompting of the Holy Spirit within the mind of God. This emphasis on intuitive knowledge of God is a key to Muenzer's thought. Clearly the goal was:

> that we fleshly, earthly men shall become gods through the incarnation of Christ, and at the same time God's scholars, taught and made godlike by himself, utterly and completely transformed into him, so that our earthly life is taken into the heavenlies.[29]

In this type of religion there is no need for academic distinction to know the true meaning of Scripture:

> If a man had neither seen nor heard the Bible all his life, yet through the teaching of the Spirit he could have an undeceivable Christian faith, like all those who without books wrote the Holy Scripture. Even if you had swallowed the Bible whole, it is to no avail, you must suffer the sharp ploughshare, if you have no faith.[30]

This extract also indicates the importance of the cost of faith for Muenzer. He opposes the idea that the path of discipleship could be anything other than a stony one and castigates Luther for making faith seem an easy option. For Muenzer the whole process of becoming a disciple involved a period of trial and identification with the sufferings of Christ. It is only through the period of spiritual turmoil that true faith can come: 'then the heart of a man is so strangely captive with the true Spirit of Christ, the possessor of his soul, that it has a foretaste of eternal life'.

The inner turmoil of the radical who faces opposition and uncertainty, however strong the inner conviction may be of the rectitude of his cause, places the experience of Thomas Muenzer alongside better-known saints in Christian history. It is the same kind of inner conflict which drove Paul to speak of the close identity between the apostolic task and the sufferings of the messiah. Paul learnt that the mark of the spirit of the messiah was to bear the same kind of reproach as the messiah. Unadulterated triumphalism in the midst of an order where there was all too little evidence of the triumph of the God of justice was to be repudiated. Bearing witness to the new order in the midst of the old involved martyrdom, a costly witness: 'carrying round in one's body the death of Jesus', as Paul puts it. There was a price to be paid for the awful responsibility of being the agent of the critical moment. The sensitive soul could not remain impervious to the darts of opponents, particularly when they were directed at the deepest conviction concerning the divine basis of his calling. It is evident from Muenzer's writings that he felt deeply the inner turmoil which results from being part of the social upheaval. That turmoil became part and parcel of his own inner life. His writing enables us to catch a glimpse of the pain involved in the confident maintenance of the revolutionary task. Towards the end of his life Muenzer's actions may have all the appearance of fanaticism. Any flight from reality that there may have been cannot disguise the personal cost involved in seeking the way of the Spirit as he saw it. His career formed part of a wider protest against unjust social arrangements which constituted a blasphemy against the Holy Spirit.

Reformation or revolution?

That Muenzer's career was not marked entirely by destructive activity is indicated by his liturgical experiments with their concern to promote community building. Central to Muenzer's liturgy was the concept of a new covenant. There is evidence to suggest that he formed leagues of the Elect[31] which provided the backbone of his support as well as offering that remnant which is so typical of the millenarian outlook. This may offer evidence of a practical political strategy to ensure a hard core of support in time of difficulty. But Muenzer's plans seem to have been generally devoid of any coherent political strategy to consolidate the gains which his activity had brought. While appealing to certain strata of society he was not able to articulate the variety of discontents into a common front to bring about wide-ranging reform. At crucial moments he was deserted by various groups (the miners failed to support him after his participation in the Peasants Revolt and he was let down by members of the Council in Allstedt, and Pfeiffer went off ransacking monasteries, an easy target, at the beginning of the Peasants War instead of conducting a campaign which would have consolidated the support and military advantages accruing to the peasants). In Allstedt too the ongoing fiery anti-clericalism jeopardized the possibility of that town's becoming an alternative centre of the Reformation. It may have been sour grapes on Luther's part to complain about the abuse of the freedom gained by people like himself at the hands of hotheads like Muenzer; but it does give evidence of a turbulent spirit unable to recognize the constraints upon an individual within a specific social formation to initiate change.

Yet a stubborn bloody-mindedness is surely not the whole of the story. Unlike other revolutionaries it can be said of Muenzer that death and humiliation need not have been the final outcome. The liturgical experiments in Allstedt show an ability to articulate a pattern of reform which is innovative without being totally iconoclastic. His letters to the leading authorities often reflect a certain deference, evidence of a more diplomatic tone, which contrasts markedly with some of his uninhibited invective found elsewhere. This indicates a readiness to explore the possibility of seeking an umbrella of tolerance from the princes in order to pursue his programme of religious reformation in conformity with the Word of God.

Muenzer may have been able to recognize when the *Kairos* had come but he did not have the gift of recognizing when the *Kairos* was no longer propitious, at least for his more grandiose goals. The evidence suggests that he was a typical millenarian without any clearcut idea of what would happen when the Elect finally did triumph. We must suppose that he, like many of his radical millenarian predecessors, left detailed implementation of the final state in the hands of God once the Elect had done their bit. The pathetic sight of the motley army of peasants hoping for a miracle from the God whose covenant bow in the cloud seemed to offer a sign of divine deliverance is not the mind-set of the military strategist. It manifests faith in the God who had delivered the people in the past and would do so again, the kind of fanatic belief that inspired the prophet in the last hours of the city of Jerusalem in the year 70 and took the lonely idealists who wrote the War Scroll from Qumran to their death in a last battle against the Roman legionaries.[32]

After Muenzer's death a concerted attempt was made to blot out all the traces of 'the Devil of Allstedt' as Luther called him. His liturgical provision was banned from Allstedt (though the material continued to be used and to inspire others), and his memory vilified. But as with similar figures espousing such ideas, expurgation is not easy. Many of Muenzer's immediate companions may have fled dejected, with their beliefs in tatters; but the persistence of the convictions is indicated by the continuation of Muenzer's ideas, albeit in an attenuated form, in anabaptist circles. Within a decade a more virulent version of the revolutionary millenarian spirit manifested itself in Muenster, the new Jerusalem where an anabaptist millennium was set up under John of Leyden and Bockelson, inspired by the apocalyptic ideas of Melchior Hoffmann.[33] The events in Muenster with the prospect of an alternative society attracted anabaptist sympathisers from a wide area. The experiment ended in an orgy of antinomianism and a bloody suppression of a chaotic and enthusiastic messianism: a paradigm of reformation which friends and foes alike viewed with horror. It was out of the ashes of the Muenster debacle that one of the founding fathers of anabaptism, Menno Simons, offered a ministry of consolidation which enabled the refugees of the persecution of the Anabaptists to maintain their identity and their understanding of the radical implications of the Reformation which, in their view, were only inadequately appreciated by the reformers of the Lutheran tradition. However much later Anabaptists sought to distance themselves from the Muenster experiment and the radical reforming spirit of Thomas Muenzer, there is evidence of a link between South German Anabaptism and Muenzer. Thus in a celebrated letter of September 1524, only nine months before Muenzer's death, Conrad Grebel wrote to Muenzer at the very moment the nascent anabaptist movement in Switzerland was seeking to articulate its understanding of Christian discipleship. While acknowledging the difference between Grebel and Muenzer, the letter itself indicates the community of interest which existed between Muenzer's ideas and emerging Anabaptism.[34] The pacific tradition became typical of the various anabaptist groups. Muenzer's own theology facilitated an easy shift to radical inwardness whether of a personal or communitarian kind. As we have noted, Muenzer's own concern to stress the importance of the identification with Christ and his sufferings which derived from the mystical tradition could stand without any reference to the social transformation which inner transformation demanded.[35] Once belief in the arrival of the critical moment had gone, the edifice of Muenzer's theology did not disintegrate. That prophetic consciousness which gave Muenzer such a heightened awareness of the decisive character of the present moment as one demanding immediate and uncompromising action could easily be separated off without irreparable damage to the rest of his thought.

The story of the various anabaptist groups, persecuted and frequently forced to become refugees, yet clinging to their convictions about the radical alternative posed by the gospel is one that deserves to be better known. The Anabaptists were the subversives of the sixteenth century. Their attitudes to social ethics represented a direct challenge to the ideology of the powerful. They were ideas which were (from the point of view of those who wielded power) political dynamite. They showed up the iniquity of a political system based on inequality and private property. They posed a direct, though not active, challenge to the contemporary values. For that reason they were suspected, hounded out of the country and deprived of civil rights. But the vision was one that was entirely in tune with the gospel: 'The kings of the earth lord it over their subjects and their rulers are accounted benefactors; but it shall not be so with you.' This could be a mark of Anabaptism and the roots of its appeal even in those churches whose ancient formularies explicitly marginalize anabaptist ideas such as the community of goods (as is the case in Article 38 of the Articles of Religion of the Church of England).

Through the vicissitudes of persecution and social ostracism have emerged in the present century movements like the Hutterites and the Mennonites,[36] representatives of many of those ideals which we have been examining in this book. But we must now turn to another period of social and religious upheaval, this time in England. In the ideas of Gerrard Winstanley and his companions some of the vigorous protest and egalitarian spirit which we have just been examining emerge again. As we shall see, while there are some similarities with Muenzer's ideas, Winstanley was reluctant to engage in the kind of holy war of the elect supported by Muenzer. His commitment was to social action of a different kind in the pursuit of equality and justice. This places him closer in several respects to the patterns of community and pacifism being espoused in the anabaptist tradition.

Gerrard Winstanley: Christ rising in sons and daughters

Here is the righteous law; man wilt thou it maintain?
It may be, is, as hath still, in the world been slain.
Truth appears in light, falsehood rules in power;
To see these things to be is cause of grief each hour.
Knowledge, why didst thou come, to wound and not to cure?
I sent not for thee, thou didst me inlure.
Where knowledge does increase, there sorrows multiply,
To see the great deceit which in the world doth lie:
Man saying one thing now, unsaying it anon,
Breaking all's engagements, when deeds for him are done.
O power where art thou, that must mend things amiss?
Come change the heart of man, and make him truth to kiss.
O death where art thou? Wilt thou not tidings send?
I fear thee not, thou art my loving friend.
Come take this body, and scatter it in the four,
That I may dwell in one, and rest in peace once more.

'The Law of Freedom as a Platform', quoted from Hill *Winstanley: The Law of Freedom* p.389.

This heartfelt and bitter lament is the concluding words of the long utopian tract by Gerrard Winstanley[37] and among the last words now extant of that short and brilliant writing career of an English Christian radical. Even in a remarkably inventive and turbulent period for English religion the writings of Gerrard Winstanley stand out as a testimony both to the power of radical religious ideas at the height of the English Revolution and to the way in which those ideas could be the catalyst of a profound analysis of human nature and society. Their extraordinary critique of the contemporary order and passionate commitment to equality may explain why they have generally been ignored by Christians but have attracted widespread attention from those who are committed to political change *outside* the mainstream of Christianity. Like Muenzer before him Winstanley's writings have drawn to themselves historians within the Marxist tradition. But Winstanley cannot adequately be understood as a political writer who merely chose the language of religion as the vehicle of his message. Unlike the contemporary Levellers[38] whose championship of a wider franchise was more narrowly political in its scope, the bulk of Winstanley's writings indicate a subtle blend of biblical imagery, political reflection and call to action in which the former is clearly an essential catalyst for the power of the political ideas which he enunciates.[39]

Digging the common land

Winstanley was born in Lancashire in the first decade of the seventeenth century. He was apprenticed to a London tailor in 1630, and was driven out of business by the Civil War.[40] The pain of economic hardship and social dislocation may help us understand his dissatisfaction and nostalgic quest for the roots of his existence, when 'we should have good times again'.[41] He moved to Surrey where his wife's family had some property and worked as a herdsman. His writing career spans the years 1648 to 1652, the period from the second civil war to the last years of the Commonwealth, a time of intense activity and commitment on his part. Events conspired to make the present moment pregnant with the expectation of the imminent fulfilment of the biblical promises, for the years preceding this were a period of enormous turmoil in religious and political life. In 1645 there died William Laud, Archbishop of Canterbury, an upholder of autocratic ecclesiastical authority and privilege. In 1649 the decision was taken to execute Charles and the significance of the demise of the monarchy and the shaking of the foundations of the English establishment could not be lost on those who saw in it the embodiment of Antichrist.[42]

Winstanley's extant writings coincided with the loosening of restrictions on censorship which led to a surge of pamphlets from a variety of sects and eccentric viewpoints. From April 1649 to March 1650 Winstanley's career and writing were intimately bound up with the Digger commune set up in Surrey. As the term 'Digger' implies, the group of which Winstanley was a member was concerned to give practical effect to its members' convictions.

He was prompted by a revelation[43] that he and his companions should dig the common land, thus claiming what they regarded as their rightful inheritance. Winstanley and a few others moved to St George's Hill, Cobham on 1 April 1649, and their number grew to about forty (there appear to have been similar experiments taking place elsewhere at roughly the same time). Their action provoked hostility from local landowners and complaints to the Council of State. Fairfax, the army commander, looked into the Digger's activities, and appears to have seen in them a threat to private property and the social fabric. No immediate action was taken against the Digger commune, but there was a campaign of harassment by local landowners. The Diggers moved the site of their activities to the neighbouring parish of Cobham. But here too local landowners and the parish priest proved to be implacable opponents and they were finally driven off the land in the spring of 1650.

After the failure of the Digger commune Winstanley moved to Hertfordshire where he worked as a foreman for Lady Eleanor Douglas. He appealed to Cromwell in his last publication *The Law of Freedom as a Platform*, but this appears to have achieved nothing. There is some evidence that he may have subsequently become a corn chandler, though the precise details of his later life remain shrouded in mystery.[44] Whether the failure of the experiment as the result of harassment from local clergy and landowners backed up by the military left Winstanley in disillusionment is not clear. There is evidence which suggests that he considered the Civil Wars had left ordinary people 'in the kennel of injustice as much or more than before'.[45] Since there is a concern with individual change as a necessary prelude to structural change in all his earlier work, it is possible that the former could have become an end in itself and have led to a retreat into pietism and a rejection of social change.

Eat bread together: Overcoming the old Adam in self and society

Fundamental to the communal experiment of the Diggers was the belief that the earth was a common treasury, and as such the whole concept of the ownership of land as private property conflicted with this fundamental right. Winstanley was concerned to expose the way in which the preoccupation with private property reflected an inherent characteristic of humanity after the Fall of Adam. Winstanley's writings betray a remarkable understanding of the intimate link which exists between the internal struggle that goes on between human acquisitiveness on the one hand and altruism and sharing on the other, and the parallel struggle in society at large between the maintenance of private property and common ownership of the creation. For Winstanley this struggle in individuals and society is exemplified in the story of Adam:

(The First Adam) provokes 'tyranny, particular interest, buying and selling the earth from one particular hand to another, saying, This is mine, upholding this particular propriety by a law of government of his own making, and thereby restraining other fellow creatures from seeking nourishment from mother earth. So that though a man was bred up in a land, yet he must not work for himself where he would sit down'.[46]

Adam consented to the serpent covetousness, then he fell from righteousness, was cursed, and was sent into the earth to eat his bread in sorrow: 'And from that time began particular propriety'.[47] Private property is the curse, and those who possess it have gained it by oppression, murder or theft.[48] The first Adam is the cause of 'covetousness after objects, pride, self-centredness and lying', while the outward manifestation of this cancer brings about 'particular interest, and thereby restraining other fellow creatures from seeking nourishment from the earth'.[49] So there is a situation where 'he that had no land, was to work for those for small wages, that called the land theirs; and thereby some are lifted up into the chair of tyranny, and others trod under the foot-stool of misery, as if the earth were made for a few, not for all men'.

The rule of the Serpent manifests itself in four ways: a professional ministry; the kingly power; the judiciary; and the buying and selling of the earth. These correspond to the four beasts in the book of Daniel: the lion with eagle's wings is kingly power; the one like a bear is the power of selfish laws; the leopard is the thieving art of buying and selling; the fourth is clergy power and the little horn coming out of it is ecclesiastical establishment.[50] Christian tradition is used to suppress the just demands of the poor. If the poor quote the words of Scripture which proclaim their blessedness, 'the tithing priest stops his mouth with a slam and tells him that is meant of the inward satisfaction of the mind'.[51]

Winstanley rejected the received wisdom on original sin, though he was emphatic that the internal struggle to overcome the evil within was an essential part of the process of human emancipation. He makes contemporary the myth of the Fall by stressing that 'Adam is within every man and woman'. Winstanley would have subscribed to the view of the doctrine of the Fall which is to be found in a late first-century Jewish apocalypse, the Syriac Apocalypse of Baruch 54.19, which asserts that 'each has become the Adam of his own soul'.[52] The consequences of the Fall are appropriated by each human being and there is consequently the obligation laid upon each to retrieve the situation and overcome the sins of pride and covetousness which manifest themselves in the will to possess and dominate. Winstanley did not underestimate the power of evil; he certainly was no starry-eyed optimist about the benefits of structural change in society without individual, internal transformation.

Like others before and since Winstanley related the doctrine of the Fall to a particular event in English history, the imposition of Norman yoke on the English. The private property owned by the gentry was linked with the granting of manorial rights by William the Conqueror. Just as the Babylonian yoke was laid upon the people of Israel, so the Norman yoke with its monarchy and lords is laid upon the English and enforced by imprisonment, robbing and killing that holds the people in bondage.[53] But, in a return to his nostalgia for a lost golden age, Winstanley points out that it was not always the case. What appears to be a natural way of organizing society has in fact only been operative since the imposition of the Norman yoke. Thus the return to the pre-Norman period can be seen to be equated with a return to Paradise.

The triumph of righteousness comes as the result of the inward triumph of Christ in the struggle between two powers: 'propriety on the one hand, called the Devil or covetousness, and community on the other hand, called Christ or universal love.'[54] In the New Law of Righteousness there emerges the conviction that private ownership, inheritance and rents, the purchase and selling of land, and the system of hired labourers must all be abolished as part of the outward manifestation of the process of spiritual regeneration within. When this takes place peace will be ensured because private property has to be maintained by force, 'by prisons, whips and gallows', for 'we that work most have least comfort in the earth, and they that work not at all, enjoy all'. True living begins when the quest for self-advancement and personal possessions is set aside, for the attainment of these things always takes place at the expense of the well-being of others. Bruising the serpents's head will come about when the earth becomes once again a common treasury. Christ, the Second Adam, 'stops or dams up the runnings of those stinking waters of self-interest, and causes the waters of life and liberty to run plentifully in and through creation, making the earth one store house, and every man and woman to live in the law of righteousness and peace as members of one household'.

Winstanley's method of internalizing the struggle between good and evil is reminiscent of the way in which Paul's language about the contrast between the present age and the glorious age to come is concentrated on the individual and the need for liberation where the flesh is subdued to the Spirit, the old order to the new. In the Saints' Paradise the Devil is not a separate being but what he calls the King Flesh ruling in man. Salvation is not the consequence of some sacramental action performed by the clerical elite but lies within the grasp of all those who are willing to set out on that path which proceeds from the recognition of the true state of affairs in which humanity finds itself. Liberty or freedom is a process of spiritual or moral emancipation. The Saints are those in whom the Beast, 'magistracy out of joint', has been overthrown and who are thus pioneers for the rest of society in the coming of Christ's reign of righteousness, a kind of firstfruits of the new society in whom the Risen Christ truly dwells.

'Christ in us the hope of glory': Winstanley's use of doctrine

What is truly remarkable about Winstanley's analysis of the human condition is its unwillingness to remain at the level of subjectivity: 'all the inward bondages of the mind are occasioned by the outward bondage that one sort of people lay upon another'. In the New Law[55] the struggles between the Dragon and Christ are now linked to the advocacy of communism. Spiritual regeneration and structural change are initimately connected: when the earth becomes a common treasury as it was in the beginning, and the King of Righteousness comes to rule in everyone's heart, then he kills the first Adam; for thereby covetousness is killed.[56] The new heaven and earth are something to be seen here and now,[57] for kingly power is the old heaven and earth that must pass away. In the New Law Winstanley dismisses the view that the New Jerusalem is 'to be seen only hereafter' and asserts 'I know that the glory of the Lord shall be seen and known within creation, and the blessing shall spread within all nations'. The kingdom of God was very much a this-worldly kingdom.[58] Christ's second coming was the establishment of a state of community[59]: true freedom lies in the community in spirit and community in the earthly treasury, and 'this is Christ . . . spread abroad in the creation'.[60] A new creation will see a 'community of mankind which is comprised in the unity of the spirit of love, which is Christ in you, or the law within the heart, leading mankind into all truth and to be of one heart and mind'.[61] God is not far above the heavens; God is to be found in the lives and experiences of ordinary men and women: 'he that looks for God within himself . . . is made subject to and hath community with the spirit that made all flesh, that dwells in all flesh and in every creature within the globe'[62] whereas 'he that worships God at a distance . . . is . . . deceived by the imagination of his own heart'. God's kingdom comes when God arises in his saints. The perfect society will come when there takes place 'the rising up of Christ in sons and daughters, which is his second coming' and 'his rising . . . shall enlighten all mankind and cover the earth with knowledge . . . when flesh becomes subject to the reason within it, it can never act unrighteously or trespass against others'.[63] Jesus was the great prophet, a man taken up to live wholly in the Father, 'a meek spirit drawn up to live in the light of reason'. The same anointing which dwelt in him and the apostles can dwell in the saints. Winstanley stresses the centrality of the contemporary existential application of doctrine: 'you must feel see and know Christ's own resurrection within you if you expect life and peace by him'.[64]

The end of the saints' captivity: Winstanley and the apocalyptic tradition

As we have seen, Winstanley used the imagery of the book of Daniel, particularly the reference to the Beast, to understand oppressive state power. This reminds us of the importance of this symbolism in the formation of radical Christian positions. Jesus had identified his ultimate triumph with the eternal rule of the heavenly Son of Man which would take place after the destruction of the Beast, representative of state power. The book of Revelation itself takes up the idea of the Beast of Daniel and relates it to the experience of oppression and power exercised by the state in the apocalyptist's day. Similarly, Thomas Muenzer used the example of Daniel as one which he could fulfil in his own generation and pointed to the present as a time of crisis and necessary action. Winstanley used the apocalyptic imagery of Daniel and saw the present as a critical moment in the life of the nation. He offered no precise details about when the new age was to come and what exactly would be the signs of its arrival. Nevertheless he was convinced that Christ would reign and judge the world in and through his saints. In the Breaking of the Day of God he expressed the view that 'the saints' captivity under the Beast are very near expired'. In Truth Lifting up its Head[65] he can speak of the present as a moment when the reordering of society which is God's purpose is now imminent:

> Is the Father's time now come to rule the earth and fill it with himself? Yes: and shall have as large a privilege to fill the earth, as the first man had surely; and he will change times and customs, and fill the earth with new law, wherein dwells righteousness and peace.

By rejecting any identification with any literal fulfilment of the eschatological material Winstanley leaves no room for complacency. The identification of the Beast with some eschatological figure removes any immediacy of impact of the symbol whose import is confined to the eschatological times which are to come. But by linking the beast to *contemporary* institutions and live human passions Winstanley makes the present a time for action: 'But for the present state of the old world that is running up like parchment in the fire, and wearing away'.[66]

Winstanley himself had an acute consciousness of his own vocation which he describes with the sense of immediacy familiar to us from the apocalyptic tradition[67]:

> As I was in a trance not long since, divers matters were present to my sight, which must be here related. Likewise I heard these words, Work together, Eat bread together; declare this all abroad. Likewise I heard these words.

> Whosoever it is that labours in the earth, for any person or persons, that lifts themselves as Lords and Rulers over others and that doth not look upon themselves equal to others in the Creation, The hand of the Lord shall be upon that labourer: I the Lord have spoke (sic) it and I will do it; Declare all this abroad.

Indeed, it is evident that Winstanley believed that the prophetic spirit was again active and that the prophetic promises of the past were coming to fulfilment: 'all the prophecies, visions and revelations of Scriptures, of prophets, and apostles, concerning the calling of the Jews, the restoration of Israel; and the making of that people, the inheritors of the whole earth; doth all seat themselves in this work' (i.e. the Digger experiment).[68]

He considered that his insights were not merely the product of intellectual exercise but the proclamation of the True Reason dwelling within him. It was part of Winstanley's task to unmask the reality of contemporary society. He did this by contrasting the present 'normality' with the Paradise which God intended. Winstanley refused to accept as given the contemporary state of society. He judged the present by the criterion of that lost innocence before the Fall when private property was not present. The unmasking of reality is an important task of the prophet in order to expose 'What are the greatest sins in the world . . . for any man, or men, first to take the Earth by the power of the murdering sword from others; and then by Lawes of their own making, doe hang, or put to death any who takes the fruit of the earth to supply his necessaries'. Most are still in darkness but those who are no longer blind have the task of shining 'as lights in the dark world'. It is for them to expose the present state of iniquity and point to the remedy in each individual. It is not by resort to the teachings of those in authority, whether clergy or magistrates, but by attention to the spirit within that a true understanding of the reality of oppression can be obtained.

In his Watchword,[69] when the Digger project was under threat, Winstanley perceives that the removal of the monarchy has not in fact changed the basic structure of society: 'those that do imprison, oppress and take away the livelihood of those that rise up to take possession of this purchased freedom, are traitors to this nation, and enemies of righteousness: and of this number are those men that have arrested, or that may arrest the Digger'. The reality of English society is clear to him: 'England is a prison, the variety of subtleties in the Laws preserved by the sword, are bolts, bars and doors of the prison; the Lawyers are the jailors, and poor men are the prisoners'. Here appearances are shown to be a deceit, and the reality of oppression exposed.

The experience of the Spirit within

What stands out in Winstanley's theology is the repeated grounding of knowledge of God in the world of experience. Winstanley is quite clear that all people including the poor and ignorant can by experience know the ways of God: 'sharp punishing laws were made to prevent fishermen, husband-men and tradesmen from ever preaching God any more' but 'tradesmen will speak by experience the things they have seen in God, and the learned clergy will be slighted'.[70] Indeed, it is the poor who would be the saviours of the land;[71] God is on the side of the poor who are the true saints, because God made the earth for poor as well as rich.[72] For Winstanley prophecy is 'to give testimony or proof of such things to be true by experimental dis-coveries'.[73] Those who respond to the Spirit within have greater knowledge of God than the learned and the wise: 'for the People having the Scriptures, may judge by them as well as you (i.e. the professional clergy) . . . it is the Spirit within that must prove those copies true'.[74]

True knowledge of God means that intermediaries will no longer be necessary: 'when your flesh is made subject to him, he will teach you all things . . . so that you shall not need to run after men for instruction'. Even the poor and ignorant can become learned in the experimental knowledge of Christ. In this Winstanley validates the importance of what ordinary people see and hear: 'Nay let me tell you, that the poorest man, that sees his maker, and lives in the light, though he could never read a letter in the book, dares throw the glove to all the humane learning in the world, and declare the deceit of it'.[75] It is the inward testimony of the individual, the reading of the book within, that is most important. Religion, therefore, is not just for the experts, for God dwells in everyone, and it is open to any person by over-coming the old Adam within to become the Perfect Man: 'But when the Second Adam rises up in the heart, he makes a man to see heaven within himself. . . . This Christ is within you, your everlasting rest and glory.'[76]

His own conversion is offered by Winstanley as a paradigm of the way in which one may be set free from bondage:

> 'Though men speak the very words of Scripture but speak not with the mind of Him that gives life, they may be strangers or even enemies to the God of the Scriptures. But if the same anointing dwell in you as in the Apostles, you can see into the mystery of Scripture. . . . When God sets you free from bondage, you shall find the Spirit within you . . . God's righteous law is not the letter of the Commandment but the spirit in man that discovers to him his uncleanness and hypocrisy . . . 'as a result in these national hurly-burlies, though you lack riches and food and clothing . . . you can rest quiet in God'.[77]

Indeed, if any one has the anointing of God, it is possible to 'speak the mind of Scriptures, though you should never see, hear nor read the Scriptures from men'. When Christ rules in sons and daughters, then 'the writings of the apostles and prophets . . . are to cease, for they will be superseded by the indwelling spirit'.[78] The Spirit is superior to the letter; the Bible shall cease when the Lord rules in sons and daughters. The democratic character of the prophetic spirit poured out on all flesh is the prerequisite for this egalitarian approach to the understanding of the ways of God: 'the Spirit is not confined to your universities; but it spreads from East to West, and enlightens sons and daughters in all parts'.[79]

Raising the consciousness of rich and poor

It is worth noting that Winstanley picks up the important link between women and prophecy. It is an indication of his sensitivity to the gender issue manifest elsewhere in his work that he links the negative side of human nature with masculine powers, and the feminine with loving and sharing.[80] Likewise, he rejects the excesses of other sects at the time like the Ranters (who practised free love) by denouncing this as degrading to women because it treats them as property.[81] In the Digger commune there was common ownership of land though not of personal possessions; monogamy remained the norm as also did the traditional family unity.[82] As far as Winstanley was concerned, since God dwells in everyone, no one has an excuse not to know or serve God. But freedom from outward rules did not mean antinomianism as there was need to 'subject your flesh to this mighty governor, the spirit of righteousness within yourselves', for 'You are not to be saved by believing that a man lived and died long ago at Jerusalem, but by the power of the Spirit within you treading down all unrighteousness of the flesh'.[83]

A long and painful process was necessary for Christ's rising within his sons and daughters to be accomplished. Winstanley's emphasis on the need for personal inner transformation is a recognition of this. He does not look for some cataclysmic event when the rich and mighty will suddenly be changed. Rather, he is looking for a gradual transformation: 'when this son of righteousness and love arises in magistrates and people, one to another, then these tumultuous national storms will cease; and not till then'.[84] The gradual education of the landed gentry and their conversion would bring about a new recognition of the iniquitous character of private property. Thus he did not encourage expropriation of private property, for 'the Diggers have no intent of Tumult or fighting, but only to get bread to eat'.[85] Whereas Muenzer felt that it was incumbent upon the elect to initiate an immediate transition to the earthly Paradise by engaging in a holy war, Winstanley's approach recognized the importance of the growth of Christ within. What they have in common, of course, is the conviction that the

Paradise to come is one in this world which necessitates breaking the bonds of the existing order. Also, both are quite clear that any spiritual transformation must be replicated in the outer world of social reality. As Wilson has put it, 'it is not enough simply to understand the cause and consequence of oppression. Those who sincerely wish to change things for the better have to be willing to work hard under strict self-discipline'.[86] In this both Winstanley and Muenzer draw on that Joachite tradition which looks forward to a paradisical age in this world. Both part company with the Augustinian tradition promulgated by Luther which viewed the City of God as that perfect entity incapable of creation in this world.[87] But, as the experience of the Digger colony soon taught him, Winstanley had underestimated the institutional power of the Beast. Even in the face of this disillusionment Winstanley did not forsake his conviction that it was necessary to move towards the perfect society in this world. In his last extant work no refuge is taken in an otherworldly perfection, however much the disappointment of the failure of the Digger colony may have made him despair of seeing his hopes fulfilled.[88]

Hope in Utopia

The Law of Freedom, Winstanley's last extant work, is a document written with the pain of the demise of the Digger colony fresh in his mind and the disillusionment in the face of Cromwell's unwillingness to embark on a programme of radical change. This long utopian text in which a blueprint of a righteous society is offered accepts the need for safeguards and acknowledges human imperfection on the road to the kingdom of God. As with the law of Moses in the Pentateuch (particularly the book of Deuteronomy) so also with the law of freedom there is necessity for an arrangement to enable that transition to a libertarian society to take place.[89]

The contrast between this text and Winstanley's earlier tracts is obvious. The passion and urgency are replaced by a prosaic account of the righteous society. While it is necessary to make due allowance for the different genre of this work, the feeling one is left with is that the passion is almost spent and here is a last attempt to persuade the powerful of the need to act in defence of the society of the saints. That Winstanley himself saw it as a forlorn task is borne out by the pathetic and haunting words with which he concludes the *Law of Freedom*. Winstanley experienced the might of kingly power and its ideologists, priests and lawyers; he learned from experience that Christ rose only slowly in sons and daughters.[90]

One of the problems of utopianism is that it can lead the reader into construction of ideal worlds which distract him or her from the demands of the present. Utopianism can lead to an escape from reality however much its attempts betoken that yearning for something better. Writers who resort to utopianism do so as a compensation for the inability to do anything about the world as it is. However remarkable a writing it may be, the character of the *Law of Freedom* has about it the air of a last attempt of the disillusioned idealist to enable his hopes to come to fruition. It is not that regulations in all their detail are themselves incapable of fulfilment. Rather the writing of the tract itself betokens the fact that the demands of the present have been put on one side in favour of a precise blueprint about how things might be in a situation where justice flourishes. The poem with which the *Law of Freedom* concludes is the work of a weary and disappointed man. Now

> truth appears in light, falsehood rules in power. To see these things to be is cause of grief each hour. . . . To see the great deceit which in the world doth lie: Man saying one thing now, unsaying it anon, Breaking all's engagements, when deeds for him are done.[91]

In contrast, Winstanley's earlier works are full of challenge to action and to understand the times, with very little detailed speculation about the form of the society which was to come. Like many others of his generation who entertained hopes of a change in society, Winstanley experienced disappointment.[92] Milton was to express this in his later writing as the hopes for political transformation become muted, and Bunyan did so in *The Pilgrim's Progress* as the quest for individual salvation in a Promised Land beyond this world compensated for the disappointment of never seeing it in this.[93] That concern with inner transformation provided a resource for a new generation to seek for the light within and engage in an inner struggle when the prospects for struggling with the world at large seemed to lead only to defeat. 'The experience of defeat' was to be the lot of many who looked for a new order. That experience led some to political conservatism, political realism offering a more appropriate paradigm of the exercise of political power than the democratic egalitarianism of the millenarians. The egalitarian spirit of the Quakers was kept alive through the concern for inwardness and the eschewing of hierarchy and force.[94] The quietist, silent protest against the status quo became the only strategy available to those who sought to keep alive the flame of radical protest in the seventeenth century when the opportunities apparently on offer in the 1640s seemed to have disappeared for ever.

Although Winstanley's ideas remained buried for 250 years, there were torchbearers in the gloom, like William Blake. This visionary and engraver perceived the exploitative threat of the nascent capitalism of the industrial revolution and the inability of the rationalist liberalism of his day to offer hope. Compared with Wesley's religion,[95] Blake's was of a different temper. His protest against the oppression of capitalist materialism and his conviction that a new Jerusalem could be *built* in England's green and pleasant land did not lead merely to a retreat into a utopian fantasy but to a desire to transform through struggle what actually exists. Blake was the inheritor of the radical protestantism of Winstanley's generation and in the changed circumstances of the satanic mills he sought to grope amidst the oppression of the grasping materialism around him for that utopian goal.[96]

What we have in the careers of Muenzer and Winstanley are different understandings of radical discipleship. Both understood well the pain and suffering involved in following the way of the cross; both understood the meaning of defeat for a radical vision. For Muenzer, however, the struggle was one which involved him in encouraging followers of Christ to take up the sword and engage in a struggle like that undertaken by the people of God of old to establish the divine righteousness. Such drastic measures do not appear to have formed part of the understanding of the more pacific Winstanley. Christ's rising in sons and daughters involves the long process of the overcoming of those inner bondages which obstruct true perception of the divine will and cause the formation of satanic structures in society. The removal of these involves an inner and outer renewal to which there are no short cuts. Whether Winstanley found it impossible to live with the hope for radical change when defeat was a reality we shall never know. What both men provide us with are examples of different outworkings of Christian discipleship aimed at the same goal which have their parallels in the struggles of Christians in the contemporary world as they seek liberation. Many in our day would echo the hope of Gerrard Winstanley:

This great Leveller, Christ our King of Righteousness in us, shall cause men to beat their swords into ploughshares and spears into pruning hooks, and nations shall learn war no more; and every one shall delight to let each other enjoy the pleasures of the earth, and shall hold each other no longer in bondage.[97]

5

The Theology of Liberation

Proclaiming God as Father in a World that is Inhumane

The relationship between an insignificant group digging the common land on St George's Hill in Surrey (a much desired residential area among the wealthy upper middle class of late twentieth-century Britain), the fiery revolutionary who perished in the Peasants' Revolt centuries ago and contemporary Latin America is not immediately obvious. But both the quest for social justice for the poor and the participation of apparently insignificant ordinary people have formed the driving force behind the theology of liberation. The struggle for land and justice and the analysis of what maintains the bond of injustice bridge the gap of centuries between Winstanley and his Digger community and the rural peasants and the inhabitants of the sprawling shanty towns on the margins of the cities of the Third World. The same hope which fired Winstanley and led Muenzer to his death has inspired millions to work for change. Few may have wanted to follow Muenzer's revolutionary path but many more would sympathize with Winstanley's hopes and experience in the midst of the social turmoil of the English Civil War.

Brazil: crucible of liberation theology

Starting with reality

It would be very tempting in a discussion of liberation theology to start by giving some account of the developments in Roman Catholic theology since the Second Vatican Council. In particular one might concentrate on the consequences of the decision taken by the Latin American bishops at their meeting at Medellin, reaffirmed at Puebla, to take a 'preferential option for the poor'.[1] There can be little doubt that these decisions have been of central importance for the emergence of the theology of liberation in the churches of Latin America and for its ongoing influence on mainstream catholicism and increasingly on the smaller protestant churches in Latin America. They have offered a foundation within the episcopal teaching of the church, based ultimately on the Second Vatican Council and the encyclicals associated with it, for those Christians committed to the betterment of the poor to justify their task as part of the church's mission.

There are few exponents of the theology of liberation in Latin America who would want a consideration of this distinctive theological approach to start with a story of episcopal decisions. Rather, as they insistently urge, it should start with the 'reality' which confronts millions in the sub-continent: a reality of poverty, appalling living conditions, malnutrition and inadequate health care; all contrasting with the affluence not only of the First World, but, even more glaring still, with the wealth and splendour of the upper middle-class accommodation of Latin American cities. A visit to a *favela*, a shanty town, on the periphery of São Paulo in Brazil will give a glimpse of that reality which makes any semblance of a solution for the thousands living without proper homes and facilities seem light years away. By way of contrast there are luxurious apartments in the well-protected condominiums often standing cheek by jowl with a *favela* with facilities which put the life-style of the North American and European middle class in the shade. It is that discrepancy between the gross affluence of the tiny minority and the demeaning squalor which the majority have to endure that has prompted many Christians to think again about their apostolic task, and in so doing they have learnt the importance of living and working with, and above all learning from, the poor. The theology of liberation is the product of a subtle mix of tradition and experience of poverty and oppression for the majority which has enabled the riches of the Christian tradition to be looked at afresh and some of its hidden contents uncovered. Just as the leading bishops and theologians in the fourth century became more aware of the gap between rich and poor in the later Roman Empire and sought to respond to it in a way far more radical than had been evident in earlier social teaching, so the reality of life for the millions of poor has provoked a pattern of theological reflection which above all seeks to 'give a voice to the voiceless'.

It is impossible to give any adequate picture of what the reality is for the majority in Latin America. All that can be attempted is a description of situations in which the theology of liberation has taken root outside the walls of the seminaries and the basilicas, often far away from the nearest priest, though often with the encouragement of local bishops. We speak in Europe and North America about the theology of liberation in Latin America as if it manifested itself in a uniform way throughout the world. Liberation theology is not only a Latin American phenomenon. It is part and parcel of church life elsewhere in the Third World, though it has distinctive contours and emphases as it is practised in Asia and Africa. While Latin America will provide the focus for this discussion, the role of liberation theology in Christian theology elsewhere in the Third World should be noted. Similarly, in Latin America there are differences of emphasis, and the variegated character of the theology we shall examine below.

The implementation of the preferential option for the poor in the pastoral practice of the Roman Catholic church in Latin America has been patchy. Although the bishops decided at their meeting at Medellin (a decision ratified at a subsequent meeting at Puebla) that resources both human and material should be devoted to a mission to bring the hope of the gospel into the poverty-stricken slums and rural areas, there has not been any uniformity in the level of commitment to that goal. Despite the fact that Latin America has a reputation for a progressive theological tradition, the extent of the influence of the theology of liberation is actually quite small. Countries like Mexico, Argentina and Colombia which have conservative hierarchies are less renowned for the grassroots theology as found, say, in Brazil and Peru (though observers in Colombia stress that a significant network of grassroots Christian communities has grown up and taken advantage of space for work and development even under conservative bishops). The power of diocesan bishops is such that people attempting to get the grassroots movement off the ground when there is no episcopal support have found the going very tough indeed, even though the social conditions of large numbers of people may be every bit as bad as in other dioceses where the theology has taken root. Equally, in those dioceses where the bishop is supportive, that power can be used to push a diocese in a progressive direction far more quickly than would be possible in protestant churches.

That variety applies to the level of support given in different dioceses in particular countries also.[2] Even in Brazil, whose episcopal conference has been at the forefront of change and acted as a leader in initiating social programmes, the number of progressive bishops among the three hundred or so which make up the Conference is still a minority, however influential it may have been. It has been able to mobilize the support of the larger middle of the road block in favour of its proposals. As a result the views of the conservatives have hitherto not had much effect, even though there are now signs that the balance may be shifting as the conservatives begin to see the importance of preparatory organization to achieve their ends. The importance of what has happened in Brazil over the last thirty years makes it the obvious country to focus on in order to understand the theology of liberation. So important is it that there are rumoured to have been attempts from conservatives in the Brazilian hierarchy aided by other sympathetic bishops in Latin America and in the Vatican to lessen the effective role of the

Brazilian Bishops' Conference (CNBB) in promoting progressive pastoral strategies. Such is the importance both ecclesiastically and politically of what has happened in the Roman Catholic Church in Brazil, providing reason enough for concentrating on aspects of its contemporary mission in this attempt to outline the character of the theology of liberation.

A glimpse of contemporary Brazil

It is impossible to do justice in the space available to the complexity of Brazilian politics and culture and the role that church is at present playing. Some brief personal glimpses which, it is hoped, may give some indication of the context in which the theology of liberation is flourishing must suffice.

The north-east of Brazil is an impoverished and depressed region. The problems of the large *favelas* in São Paulo and Rio are enormous, but poverty and disease exacerbated by drought have caused massive problems for the millions of poor in the north-east of the country. For example, in the state of Bahia, about two hundred miles inland from Salvador, the old colonial capital of Brazil, there lies a little village called Mirandela, near the town of Ribeira do Pombal. This village with its three-hundred-year-old church and attractive houses surrounding it is the centre of the territory of an Indian tribe, the Kiriri.³ It has been estimated that there may have been as many as four million Indians in Brazil at the time of the conquest. Today there are fewer than a quarter of a million. The story of their decimation by disease and expulsion is one of the saddest tales of Brazilian history. The Kiriri have suffered the loss of their language and much of their culture. But their contact with the Portuguese has had one very important consequence. The Jesuits responsible for the mission and the church in Mirandela negotiated land rights on behalf of the Kiriri covering an area measured from the various corners of the church in Mirandela and marked by obelisks in the surrounding undergrowth. Despite the vicissitudes of history and the growing acculturation in language and life, the tribe has managed to keep alive its claim to its ancestral possession negotiated on its behalf by the Jesuit priests with the King of Portugal at the end of the seventeenth century. Today members of the tribe have a clear idea of the extent of their ancestral territory and regularly keep the obelisks which mark the boundary under inspection by making a narrow clearing around the boundary of their territory. The village of Mirandela is today occupied by non-indigenous people, themselves very poor, with whom the Kiriri have very bad relations. Indeed, one of the tribe was murdered near the church in Mirandela in 1986 and Indian homes are regularly marauded by incursions of the local white population. The tribe has in recent years been tireless in using all means at its disposal, including the services of the government body responsible for

Indian affairs, to pursue its claim to the land. The story of the resurgence of the tribe and its common life and work in the last twenty years is a fascinating one and is indicative of the belated recognition of the value of the indigenous culture of Brazil and its preservation. What this remarkable story shows is the centrality and power of the struggle for land whether in rural or urban areas.

In the same area, not more than fifty miles from the settlements of the Kiriri, outside Cicero Dantas, a group of peasants meet regularly in the house of a peasant farmer, and are visited from time to time by a nun from Cicero Dantas. A regular component of their meetings is the study of the Bible. Such meetings are organized by the peasants themselves and the worship and community activity are entirely in their hands. Elsewhere in the country such groups can form the basis of the ecclesiastical life of hundreds of thousands of Brazilians, the significance of which we shall examine a little later. Their regular meetings and organization enable members of a particular community to take responsibility for being the people of God in that place and exercise a full role in the mission of the church. That in turn is based on an understanding of mission which involves more than the conversion of an individual to assent to a list of doctrines, for it concerns the manifestation of the kingdom of Christ in this world and the prophetic denunciation of all that stands against it.

In the study of the Bible by such groups the text becomes a contemporary means of giving encouragement and casting light on the present circumstances of the reader. For example, when asked what biblical stories the group in Bahia found particularly relevant, the group leader, a woman (and it is worth noting the important role women are playing in the organization of these groups) mentioned the story of Ananias and Sapphira in Acts 5 and the healing of the lame man in Mark 2. The reason for the importance of the latter centred on the need for co-operation by the friends of the lame man in the struggle to get to Jesus to achieve a common goal, wholeness and health. This was seen as a paradigm for the life of the people of God in that place.

Fifteen hundred miles south in a diocesan conference centre in Nova Iguaçu, some miles north of Rio de Janeiro, there is a conference for representatives of basic communities in a new diocese of Duque de Caxias. Caxias is a notoriously violent town with massive social problems. An indication of this is that the new bishop asks how he is to respond when a man comes to him in tears with a gun saying that he is on the way to commit a robbery in order to get food to prevent his children from starving to death. The new diocese has only recently been carved out of neighbouring dioceses, and the bishop, formerly an auxiliary bishop in the archdiocese of São Paulo, is seeking to involve Christians in discussions to work out a pastoral plan for the diocese. He comes with no detailed blueprint of a parochial structure. He is seeking to facilitate discussion and reflection among the people of God to work out an appropriate structure to articulate their mission. It may be that there will be no parishes in the traditional sense, and instead the whole diocese will be based on the basic communities (*comunidades eclesiais de base* or CEBs) as the basic ecclesial unit. But that is what these representatives of various groups are here to decide.

The discussion groups, working towards a decision, meet to listen to a lecture on the meaning of baptism by a young theologian who works with grassroot communities and in a mainly protestant research institute in Rio de Janeiro. An outsider looking around the main room of the conference centre would not easily spot which of fifty or so people in the big lecture room is the bishop. It transpires that he has been one of the participants in the discussion on what baptism means for those who have committed themselves to be part of a new creation. But the episcopal style is hardly authoritarian. The bishop seems genuinely to want the people of his diocese to have their full part in the articulation of an understanding of discipleship specifically relevant to the situation in which they find themselves. Episcopal guidance is on offer; but his preferences are subordinated to the careful articulation of a pastoral strategy. Such conferences on a Saturday are not uncommon as representatives of the grassroots communities participate in the programmes of education which many dioceses offer. Some will be engaged in narrowly theological matters; others in more general pastoral problems concerned with human rights, land reform, health and welfare, even discussion about the role of the churches in pushing for particular items in Brazil's new constitution. We shall see a little later how another diocese, the enormous archdiocese of São Paulo, has consolidated a pastoral practice based on the theology of liberation during a period of repression in Brazil, but before that we must note briefly what role the grassroots movement feels it can play in the life of church and contemporary Brazil.

Basic Christian communities: lifeblood of the Brazilian church

Just as in that rural village in Bahia, so throughout Brazil thousands of small groups meet regularly in *favelas* or rural villages for worship, Bible study and reflection on the everyday realities which confront them in the light of the challenge of the Christian tradition. For thousands of ordinary Brazilians the dialogue between the reality of poverty and the hope and inspiration offered by the scriptures has engendered a commitment to social change at local and national level based on popular participation and insight. The basic communities in Brazil are a significant component of the contemporary political as well as ecclesiastical scene. One can gauge their importance from the fact that at the sixth meeting of the CEBs in Goiania in July 1986 fifty-one bishops attended, the Pope sent a message of support and the conservative Primate of the Netherlands, Cardinal Adrian Simonis was there as an observer. Indeed Cardinal Joseph Ratzinger has observed that the CEB's offer 'a new consciousness of Christian existence and the opportunity for the real renewal of the Church'.[4]

Over fifteen hundred representatives from the one hundred thousand CEBs attended. Regional meetings before the national meeting had brought together tens of thousands of participants. This remarkable exercise in democracy is indicative of the role of the CEBs and the weight that is attached to popular participation in the whole programme of mission and development. There is little suggestion of edicts being passed down from on high, though, equally, there is a recognition that in the church ordained ministers have a legitimate contribution to make to the development of understandings of contemporary discipleship. It was estimated that well over half the delegates were from the poorest fifty per cent of Brazilian society. The concerns of contemporary Brazil were at the forefront of delegates' minds, particularly the need to make sure that adequate note was taken of the poor and underprivileged in the drawing up of Brazil's new constitution. The sensitive issue of land was also high on the agenda (as it has been for Brazil's poor and Indian population for centuries): 'the land is more than a piece of soil. It is the gift of God, the place of life and work'. Such issues were reflected in the final communique, and some of the characteristics of this remarkable grassroots movement can best be gleaned from noting some of the elements in that communique.

In one paragraph participants describe the way in which the CEBs have been a forum for a variety of different ideas:

> The people's movement has many rivers – the river of the trade unions, the river of the political parties, the river of the neighbourhood groups, the river of the landless movement, of the slumdwellers, of marginalised women, of fishers, of the aged, of the physically handicapped, of children, of women, of blacks, of the Indian nations. . . . But the struggles recounted here show that they are growing all over Brazil; struggles of resistance are becoming struggles of conquest. The people's political project will channel the waters of all these rivers into one great river that will finally do away with the society of wealth and oppression and lay foundations for the kind of society God wants.

It published nine proposals:

- to the Brazilian bishops, asking the bishops to propose that CEB representatives participate in the preparation of the synod in Rome on the laity, and that they be invited to be present at that event;
- to the church that a debate on women's participation in church life be opened up at once;

- to bishops and priests, religious and theologians, that they take up the cause of the oppressed and unambiguously support the new way of being the church;
- to the CEBs that they involve themselves in the process of writing the new constitution, representing the people's interests;
- to bishops and priests, that they be present pastorally to Christians who have made commitments to political parties 'so that they can bring these parties the liberating ferment of the gospel';
- to the CEBs that they pursue the struggle for land reform, participating peacefully in actions such as resisting land expulsions, occupying unused land, communally organised occupation of lands, pressurising government agencies, accompanying landless workers, and encouraging the church to set an example of a people's land reform;
- to the CEBs that they use all possible pressure to make sure that those who have committed crimes against the people should be brought to justice;
- to the local churches to identify and offer protection to those in the local churches whose lives are in danger because of the land struggle;
- to the whole church: 'On the occasion of the celebration of 500 years of evangelization in Latin America the historical memory of the victims of colonisation should be recovered, be they Indian, blacks or other oppressed peoples, to allow for a new and courageous liberating evangelization of the whole continent'.[5]

We can see in these statements some of the distinctive characteristics of the theology of liberation. First and foremost, it arises out of the specific needs and concerns of the poor. The story of the Exodus and God's covenant with his people based on the land is one that frequently enables a direct link between the present circumstances of many peasants and the biblical narrative.[6] The land is a pressing issue in contemporary Brazilian politics. Hundreds of thousands of peasants have found themselves ejected from land they have farmed for generations because of the interests of the growing agrobusiness, so important is this for economic growth and the servicing of the foreign debt. The new government of Brazil has been seeking to pass land reform legislation (though much watered down)[7]. Even if such legislation were enacted, the problem for many poor people is how to obtain redress from the courts without adequate legal support. As the Kiriri themselves have found under the present legal system, fine-sounding words and phrases in state legislation are no substitute for the ability to implement that legislation on the ground.

Secondly, the problem of the indigenous people is particularly sensitive. Nowhere else is the tension between justice for the possessors of land and the economic needs of contemporary Brazil so starkly put. These people were the first to experience eviction from their land when it was despoiled by the

Spanish and Portuguese conquests. The concept of liberation itself in its more obvious Old Testament guise of the liberation or deliverance of the people of God from oppression and their journey to a promised land is a potent story which relates directly to the experience of the people, particularly when many of them have engaged in their own exodus and wanderings, seeking better things in Brazil in waves of emigration from the poor north-east to the big cities of the south.

Finally, the scene at the conference of the new diocese of Duque de Caxias reminds us of the understanding of hierarchy which is emerging. It is difficult to drive a wedge between the so-called 'popular church' and mainstream catholicism, at least in Brazil. Certainly there are tensions, particularly in those dioceses where there is less sympathy towards the CEBs (a factor which is particularly evident in the ecclesiastical situation in Nicaragua). But Brazilian catholicism is characterized by a widespread acceptance of the CEBs and their central role in being the church in contemporary Brazil, a fact which is evident from the episcopal support of the CEBs' assembly in 1986.[8] Nowhere is that more evident than in the pastoral practice that has emerged in the archdiocese of São Paulo under the episcopacy of Cardinal Paulo Evaristo Arns.

The archdiocese of São Paulo

One of the most important centres of the practice of the theology of liberation within the Roman Catholic Church is the archdiocese of São Paulo in Brazil, where the episcopacy of Dom Paulo Evaristo Arns has witnessed a high profile for the church in the struggle for a more just society. The story of the church in that city revolves round three issues.

The first is the mushrooming of internal immigration within Brazil, particularly from the impoverished north-east, to cities like São Paulo during the period of the economic boom.[9] The conditions facing those uprooted from rural Brazil were awful. Drawn by the promise of a better life as the economy expanded, those who were desperately trying to keep body and soul together drifted to the big cities, particularly in the prosperous south-east of the country. Those who arrived at the bus station with only those possessions they could bring with them resorted to making makeshift homes on any piece of spare land available or under motorway arches. It was this desperation which led to the mushrooming shanty-towns (*favelas*) where the majority of São Paulo's population live. Even in the *favelas* rents are extortionate: $60 a month for a wooden shack is quite common in 1987. That is quite beyond the means of those who are without any work. Those who do occupy land and build their rudimentary dwellings there are harassed. Private security firms are hired by land speculators to evict even those who have gained title to the land; squatters are harassed by the police, this provokes violence, and deaths are all too frequent an occurrence in some areas. Recourse to the courts is often difficult, despite the growth of law surgeries. Even with the return to democracy in Brazil the situation of the homeless in cities like São Paulo continues to deteriorate. Now immigration from the countryside has slowed down, even though the plight of millions there has not improved. During the time of the economic boom there was work: men could participate as labourers in building projects, constructing luxury homes for São Paulo's elite, for example, while the women could get work as maids for that same group. In a time of economic recession work is not so plentiful, but that has made women's work essential for existence. In situations where it is not possible for friends and relatives to look after children, thousands of them are left to join hundreds of thousands more children in São Paulo to roam the streets and increase the already alarming problem of 'the street children'.

Secondly, close links were forged between the churches and other groups struggling for human rights during the dictatorship of the late sixties and seventies. The development of popular movements covers a wide range of positions and the CEBs offer one expression of it. Grassroots participation during the period of the military dictatorship (1964–1985) was focused on church-based bodies which provided an umbrella for individuals from different backgrounds to meet and work for common goals. It was perhaps that experience above all which has laid the foundations for the fruitful dialogue and co-operation between the churches and various groups struggling for justice for the majority of São Paulo's population. The community of interest in this goal, the shared experience of persecution, led Christians and politicians and trade unionists on the left to sink their differences in search of a more humane environment for ordinary people to live in. Throughout the period of the military dictatorship the church in São Paulo was tireless in defence of human rights, and Christian people themselves suffered torture and even death. This led to a long official campaign of vilification of leaders and basic communities as crypto-communist. During the early seventies, a time of political repression in Brazil, graphically portrayed in *Brasil Nunca Mais*,[10] the church continued its promotion of human rights. During this period there was the massive influx of hundreds of thousands who formed the *favelas* which grew up on the periphery of the city with terrible living conditions and massive exploitation by unscrupulous landlords. This situation demanded a response from the church which put many resources human and financial in the support of the development of the people on the periphery: the archdiocese of São Paulo's response to Medellin's preferential 'option for the poor'. Gradually a pastoral plan emerged after a process of consultation involving the bishops and priests and taking place at grassroots level also, with discussions and assemblies leading to the emergence of priorities for mission focused on the following:

1 the engagement of the whole church in the defence of human rights;
2 the defence of the right to work and the rights of workers;
3 the defence of the poor on the outskirts of the city;
4 the organization of the people of God into CEBs.

Finally, in the last six or seven years that pastoral programme has been consolidated with programmes of development in education, health and human rights in which the political dimension of Christian mission is very much to the fore, evident in a variety of educational projects. The consequence of all this is that the life of the Church is primarily focused on the CEBs. In them the capacity of the people to unite and to promote justice and human rights has probably had a not insignificant role to play within the gradual and fragile return of Brazil to a more democratic form of government. Still there are pressing problems stemming from the appalling economic conditions in Brazil. In São Paulo there are severe inner-city problems resulting from the overcrowding in the tenement buildings, increasing urban violence and the growing abuses of human rights in the poor areas. Two major issues in which the CEBs are involved are the discussions about a Constituent Assembly and the character of the new constitution and the issue of land reform. In the cities land speculation has driven many into the *favelas* and into creating more *favelas* in any empty space the poor can find. As one priest has put it:

> The challenge of the church in the next decade will be her capacity to announce the gospel of the promised land. Our rural workers dream of a 'terra sem males', that is a land where there is no evil. They long for a land marked by the presence of the Kingdom of God which is the inheritance of the poor and the disinherited of this world (Matthew 5.5).[11]

Explaining liberation theology in Latin America

While liberation theology[12] takes its start from the experience of exploitation and poverty which is the lot of the vast majority of the population of Latin America, the approaches to the Christian tradition manifest in the writings of its various exponents cannot easily be reduced to a single system.[13] Of course, there are recurrent patterns which can be discerned in much liberation theology (stemming from the option for the poor taken by the Latin American bishops at their conference at Medellin), and some of these common elements we shall examine in a moment. But liberation theology is being carried out in many different situations varying from war-torn countries like El Salvador and dictatorships like Chile via the emerging democracies of Brazil and Uruguay to the post-revolutionary situation of Nicaragua. Thus, there are important distinctions to be made between the various theologians of liberation, a fact recognized by the Brazilian conference of bishops in a recent document.[14] In it distinctions are made between the work of theologians like Hugo Assmann on the one hand and the Boff brothers on the other. Assmann's explicit consistent espousal of a Marxist hermeneutic contrasts with the more restrained and nuanced usage in the writings of the Boff brothers.[15] As we shall see, the enthusiastic support of Uriel Molina for the Sandinista revolution and the ready transference of theological language to the experience of the revolution contrast markedly with the more subtle and cautious path being taken by Jon Sobrino in El Salvador. In Molina's case we have some at times uncritical equations of the revolution with the kingdom of God, whereas in the case of Jon Sobrino we see the creation of space for development amidst the armed conflict to exploit openings promoting the development of projects to assist the poor and enable those suffering from the counter-insurgency campaign to build new lives and communities for themselves.

Liberation theology can be briefly described as a form of contextual theology, in which the experience and circumstances of the interpreters are given a prime importance as the first step in seeking to be a disciple of Jesus. Thus there is no blueprint from the tradition, from the theologians or for that matter from the bishops, which is going to offer unambiguous guidance independent of the circumstances in which the people of God find themselves struggling for justice amidst oppression and want. A theological assumption undergirding this approach is that God does not come from outside the reality of that situation but is to be found primarily there and only secondarily in the tradition. Action for justice in the face of a reality of oppression is the prime step in theology. The poignant words of the Son of Man in the story of the last judgement in Matthew 25.31ff provide a clue to the first step of this theology: Inasmuch as you have done it to one of the least of these you have done it to me.'

We may understand something of what this may mean if we look at the outline of the liberation theology perspective sketched by Gustavo Gutierrez, a Peruvian priest and the founding father of liberation theology:

> The theology of liberation seeks to understand faith from within this histori-
> cal praxis. . . . this is the fundamental hermeneutical circle: from humanity
> to God and from God to humanity, from history to faith and from faith to
> history . . . from the love of one's brothers and one's sisters to the love of the
> Father and from the love of the Father to love of one's brothers and one's
> sisters, from human justice to God's holiness and from God's holiness to
> human justice . . . theology in Latin America is an understanding of the faith
> from an option and a commitment. It will be an understanding of the faith

from a point of departure in real, effective solidarity with the exploited classes, oppressed ethnic groups, and despised cultures of Latin America. . . . It will be a reflection that starts out from a commitment to create a just society.[16]

Gustavo Gutierrez has contrasted the approach of the theology of liberation with some of the concerns of European and North American theology in the following way:

The question in Latin America will not be how to speak of God in a world come of age, but rather how to proclaim God as father in a world that is inhumane. What can it mean to tell a non-person that he or she is God's child? These were questions asked after their own fashion by Bartholomé de las Casas and so many others in their encounter with native Americans. The discovery of the 'other', the exploited one, led them to reflect on the demands of faith in an altogether different way from the approach taken by those on the side of dominators.[17]

The emphasis on the prior commitment which is the result of identification and action with and on behalf of the poor is a distinctive mark of the theology of liberation. Theology is not the articulation of a set of ideas worked out in isolation from the pressing realities which confront millions in Latin America. Rather, theology emerges from the experience, the reflection on and action to change that reality of oppression and injustice which is the daily lot of millions. Thus it is not content to accept certain 'truths' from those 'experts' at the top of the pyramid of church or state. The discovery of truth is something found on the journey of life (a metaphor which is very popular in liberation theology). In this process all can share in their own experiences of reality. As the Brazilian Jesuit João Libanio has put it:

the first step of the theology of liberation is to grasp reality, not in an immediate fashion, but through 'scientific' tools chosen in accordance with the option of the theologian against injustice and in favour of the poor. . . .
. . . the second step is theological. It consists in confronting this reality, analysed in a scientific way, with the revelation learnt in the heart of the church community. . . . There is a dialectical relation between the given revelation and social reality. Social reality is interpreted in the light of this 'Given'. . . . We are face to face with a theology, because social reality is yet read in the last analysis in the light of Revelation (i.e. the Christian scriptures and tradition). . . . The third step consists in orienting reflection towards action. Thus it is theology geared to providing reflection on certain issues in the light of faith for Christian action. . . . It does not envisage mere reflection as such. . . . Theology of liberation ought to be done by those who are either directly involved in liberating action, or at least linked with it. . . . If theology

of liberation does not help the committed Christian community to grow in its
pastoral practice . . . it is not good theology.[18]

So the theology of liberation follows the structure of 'seeing, judging,
action'.[19] That means using appropriate tools to help in the understanding
of the oppressive reality which confronts the majority of Latin America's
population – usually Marxist tools of social analysis which are thus an
important means of analysing 'reality' before turning to the Christian tradition and the reflection on appropriate action. But care needs to be taken to
avoid giving the impression that the whole method of liberation theology is
shot through with Marxism. The way in which the CEBs function indicates
a variety of different perspectives intermingling and contributing to their
understanding of discipleship. What they do share is an acknowledgement
of the reality of oppression and poverty as a common datum which is an
affront to humanity. To the charge that they have sold out to atheistic
communism many liberation theologians would echo the words of the
Peruvian bishop at the meeting of Latin American bishops at Puebla. When
conservatives accused liberation theologians of being Marxists thinly disguised as Christians he responded: 'Let him who is without ideology cast the
first stone'.[20]

It is precisely that charge which is at the heart of its most pungent challenges to theology. Liberation theologians question the use made of certain
doctrines and ask in whose interests they have been utilized: for the ruling
class or the poor? It is important, therefore, to question the dominance of
some items on the theological agenda set by First World theology when the
pressing concerns of the poor in the Third World demand very different
priorities. The emphasis on the contextual nature of all theology has led
liberation theologians to question the absolute character of theological pronouncements from the past as well as the present and to a theological
unmasking of the reality. The task can be exemplified by the following
words from the Brazilian Franciscan Leonardo Boff:

> Theologians do not live in clouds. They are social actors with a particular
> place in society. They produce knowledge, data, and meanings by using
> instruments that the situation offers them and permits them to utilize. . . .
> The themes and emphases of a given christology flow from what seems relevant
> to the theologian on the basis of his or her social standpoint. . . . In that sense
> we must maintain that no christology is or can be neutral. . . . Willingly or
> unwillingly christological discourse is voiced in a given social setting with all
> the conflicting interests that pervade it. That holds true as well for theological
> discourse that claims to be 'purely' theological, historical, traditional, ecclesial
> and apolitical. Normally such discourse adopts the position of those who hold
> power in the existing system. If a different kind of christology with its own

commitments appears on the scene and confronts the older 'apolitical' christology, the latter will soon discover its social locale, forget its 'apolitical' nature,
and reveal itself as a religious reinforcement of the existing status quo.[21]

These words echo those of Ernst Bloch quoted at the start of this book.
Boff reminds us that all our theological preferences and orthodox constructions need to be subjected to careful, critical scrutiny. Liberation theology forcibly reminds us that we need to look critically at the way in which
theology has come to focus on specific issues. Thus the contemporary theological enterprise cannot escape the need for critical reflection on its own
assumptions and preferences. This is more than a theoretical issue. The
clear preference shown by liberation exegetes for the teaching of Jesus on the
reign of God rather than the Pauline or Johannine theologies manifests its
own wish to identify with the gospel as good news for the poor and the quest
for social justice. Liberation theologians want to remind us of the other
strands of the tradition with daring convictions about a new order in this
world, open to abuse and disappointment, which have continued throughout
the history of Western Christianity to be a potent resource for those who have
been unwilling to cope with the kingdom by confining its demands and its
impact to a sacred sphere. Liberation theology has reminded us, if nothing
else, that when viewed from the underside of history, from the standpoint of
the poor and the marginalized, the message of the kingdom looks rather
different from the way in which it has been portrayed by those who have had
the power to write the story of the church and formulate its dogmas and its
social concerns.

But the Achilles heel of the Latin American liberation theologians might
be the difficulties they find in dealing with the social conservatism manifest
in some of the Pauline corpus.[22] They have shown up the signs of unease *we*
feel with other parts of the canon, notably the synoptic gospels and the book
of Revelation. Emphasis on the individual and his/her internal state which
has loomed so large in Western Christianity derives in large part from a
concentration on *certain aspects* of the legacy of Paul and John. Few liberation
theologians would want to deny the importance of attending to the need for
the liberation of the individual from the demons and bonds which prevent
the growth to maturity in Christ. Indeed, Gustavo Gutierrez has always
insisted that the inner struggle for liberation must go hand in hand with the
transformation of the world. If liberation theology's emphasis is on the
social and the political, that is because the pressing reality of existence with
the dehumanizing demands made on the poor make the need for space in the
social sphere a pressing priority to achieve even a modicum of personal
human growth. Perhaps more than some recent First World writers on
spirituality who want to take the political seriously, they would want to

stress the importance of seeing this personal liberation as part of a communal rather than an individual spiritual pilgrimage.

The use of the Bible in liberation theology

What is particularly fascinating is the method of biblical reading adopted in the CEBs. In their reading the text becomes a catalyst in the exploration of contemporary issues, so that the historical preoccupation with the original meaning of the text which so often characterises the bulk of our reading of Scripture is nothing like so important. There is an immediacy in the way in which the text is used in the CEB's as this comment from a woman in one of the *favelas* of São Paulo indicates:

> Why did Jesus choose to be born poor and humble? I think that God chose his Son to be born like us so that we can realise that we are important. It is not just to show the bosses; it's to show us too.[23]

There are superficial similarities between this and the approach of that form of protestant Bible study which goes straight to the text with no concern to ask questions about its original historical context or meaning. But while it may be true that the lay character of the CEBs and their resort to the Bible as a collection of paradigms of contemporary discipleship is akin to what we find in much evangelical reading of Scripture, the major difference is at once apparent. While there is a lack of concern for the more 'distanced' approach of the historical exegesis (with its concern to ascertain what the text originally *meant*), the difference from the naive fundamentalist reading is the communitarian setting and the avoidance of a narrowly individualist 'religious' reading. The setting for the reading is seen not primarily as the inner life of an individual Christian but as a world of poverty, disease and death in which good news comes to offer hope and a path to life.

Carlos Mesters, a Brazilian Carmelite priest, who has spent all his life working with the poor in both urban and rural areas of Brazil has spoken in the following way about the use of the Bible by the poor:

> The emphasis is not placed on the text's meaning in itself but rather on the meaning the text has for the people reading it. At the start the people tend to draw any and every sort of meaning, however well or ill founded, from the text . . . the common people are also eliminating the alleged 'neutrality' of scholarly exegesis . . . the common people are putting the Bible in its proper place, the place where God intended it to be. They are putting it in second place. Life takes first place! In so doing, the people are showing us the enormous importance of the Bible, and at the same time, its relative value – relative to life.[24]

As Mesters puts it elsewhere: 'the principal object of reading the Bible is not to interpret the Bible but to interpret life with the help of the Bible'.[25] Mesters' approach to Scripture is one that never devalues the contribution of the apparently unsophisticated reading. That experience of poverty and oppression is for the liberation exegete as important a text as the text of Scripture itself. The poor are blessed because they can read Scripture from a perspective different from most of the rich and find in it a message which can so easily elude those who are not poor. Yet Mesters himself does not disparage traditional exegetical concerns with the original setting and meaning either. Indeed, he regards them as an important antidote to a self-centred reading which binds the text too firmly to the world of the immediate present, just as historical exegesis can allow too great a preoccupation with the past meaning of the text at the expense of reflection on the present interpretative activity.

To enable the poor to read the Bible has involved a programme of education using the contents of the biblical material so that it can be a resource for thousands who are illiterate. In such programmes full recognition is taken of the value of the primary text, experience of life. Therefore, the poor are shown that they have riches in plenty to equip them for exegesis. This is balanced with the basic need to communicate solid information about the stories within the Bible, of which many remain ignorant. This is evident in the programme of Bible studies based on the parables of Jesus published by a team from the Archdiocese of São Paulo. These centre on slide sequences in which stories from the experience of CEBs are linked with biblical parables as a way of enabling discussion of the biblical text and the utilization of the Bible within the development of a community's understanding of its discipleship.[26] Full account is taken both of the 'text of life' and the text of Scripture, together with all the insights that have been offered by modern exegetes.

The kind of fruitful dialogue between the exegesis of mainstream biblical study and the use of the Bible in the CEBs is nowhere better illustrated than in that remarkable collection of peasant reflections on the gospels edited by priest and Nicaraguan Minister of Culture, Ernesto Cardenal. What is so interesting for the biblical scholar is the contrast in styles between the priest's interpretation and those offered by the *campesinos*. As one would expect, Ernesto Cardenal is very anxious to bring out the liberative quality of the text, but his approach is primarily concerned with *what the text originally meant*. It contrasts with the immediate and sometimes startling application of Scripture to contemporary issues as the following reflections on Jesus's 'manifesto sermon' in Nazareth in Lk. 4.16ff indicate:

Ernesto Cardenal comments: In the time of Christ the word (gospel or good news) was a political term associated above all with the cult of the emperor. . . . Just by using this word, Christ was indicating that his announcement was the announcement of a new kingdom.

And others comment: And his good news is for the poor because this new kingdom is the triumph of the poor and the humble.

One of the women says: What we read in the book of that prophet is a prophecy of liberation. And it's a teaching that a lot of Christians haven't learnt yet, because we can be in church singing day and night tra-la-la-la, and it doesn't matter to us that there are so many prisoners and that we're surrounded by injustice, with so many afflicted hearts, so many people without education who are like blind people, so much unfairness in the country, so many women whose eyes are filled with tears every day. And if they take somebody else prisoner, what do we lose? Maybe he did something, they say, and that's the end of the story. . . .

. . . And another: And if we talk about this they say it's communism. That's what the radio says hour after hour. It's communism. What they mean is that they like keeping us in slavery.

Ernesto comments: I explained that the year of grace that Isaiah speaks of and that was also called the 'holy year' was a year of general emancipation of people and goods, which Yahweh had ordered to take place in Israel every seven years. Bought slaves should then be freed, all debts should be abolished, and lands that had been sold should be returned to their original owners. The aim of this measure was to guarantee equality and freedom, to prevent the monopolising of lands. The law later decreed that the year of grace should be fifty years (the jubilee), and it was really a law that was not carried out. The prophecy of Isaiah was that the Messiah was going to announce a Lord's year of grace that would be definitive.

William comments: And the holy or jubilee year now means that people go to Rome to pray in the churches and receive a papal blessing. But the holy year should be agrarian reform and the socialization of all means of production.

Another comments: A holy year is what's been done in Cuba.[27]

A popular book with peasants and the poor is the book of Revelation. This is not only because it speaks in graphic terms about the kinds of conflicts which are so real to the poor and oppressed. (Indeed conflict – *luta* – is a word which seems to be frequently on the lips of many poor people.) As we have seen, what Revelation offers is the unmasking of reality. The experience of the state as an oppressor and the enormous concentrations of wealth in the hands of the powerful make the imagery of Revelation 13 and 17–18 particularly apposite. In these passages the demonstration of the state's diabolical role and the injustices of a society that has grown rich on the basis of oppression and exploitation chime in with the experience of millions of poor. Those who have protested have frequently paid the price with their lives. The graphic crucifixes in many churches are redolent of the sufferings of the people of Latin America for centuries. Washing one's robes and making them white in the blood of the Lamb[28] is no abstract image. When martyrs like Oscar Romero, the Archbishop of San Salvador, can be assassinated because of their stand for justice, the promise to those who hold fast to the testimony of Jesus is a living word to those who are in the midst of 'the great tribulation'. In the continuing struggles of the poor for basic facilities, of *campesinos* in rural areas to hold on to their land in the face of the ever-expanding arm of agro-business and multi-national development, suffering and death are a reality which Revelation illuminates and in doing so helps those in the struggle to hold on to hope.

Also, the book of Revelation appeals to the imagination, the heart rather than the head. This makes it more readily understood by those whose approach to the world is not primarily via the kind of rationality of the academy (though it needs to be stressed that Revelation *does* have its own distinctive rationality). Like the newspaper cartoons which make a political comment more tellingly than any editorial, however skilfully written, the resources of apocalyptic imagery can conjure in the imagination a grasp of reality and offer an instrument to understand reality with the result that the reader is stimulated to change it.

The focus of liberation theology on the synoptic gospels rather than the writings of Paul, and on the coming of the Reign of God, reflects the preoccupations and emphases of Bible study in the CEBs. Of course, the concentration on the Reign of God is not particularly distinctive. It is hard to imagine a lecture on Jesus or on the church and politics in Europe which does not resort to that particular theme. In a similar way to their European predecessors, the theologians of liberation have taken up the quest for the historical Jesus as a means of criticizing a preoccupation with the Christ of ecclesiastical confession. The concern of Jesus with the poor and the outcast, their interpretation of his challenge to the authorities of his day and his persecution by them are an attractive paradigm. In emphasizing the Jesus of history over against the lord of faith, theologians like Sobrino and Boff[29] are following in the footsteps of the historical critics since the rise of critical biblical scholarship. The fragility of that quest itself, of course, must be stressed. If the theology of liberation (or for that matter any other theology) is based primarily on the shifting sands of historical research, then changes in the perception of the historical Jesus will also affect the importance which can be attached to the Jesus of history as a basis for a politically committed discipleship.

An interesting development in some recent liberation exegesis has been the recognition that an approach which is more sensitive to the fabric and detail of the text and the responses it provokes is necessary. Thus in the work of Fernando Belo and Michel Clévenot (whose writing is widely read by theologians of liberation) there is a complicated but fruitful recognition that the New Testament texts are themselves social products.[30] Belo's sensitive reading of Mark which relegates concern for the *precise* historical context to a secondary level exposes the way in which the text of Mark is itself a combination of a story of radical change which is mingled with and to an extent interrupted by an emerging preoccupation with theological reflection involving an escape from issues of justice. That mixture, he argues, is itself a product of a situation of political powerlessness when the space available continually cuts short the reading and living of a subversive, radical story whether in the past or the present. What is referred to as a socio-structural reading of the text is being developed by theologians in Brazil who are seeking to be sensitive to the ways in which texts as a whole or in part have developed and reflect the struggle between different economic groups.

The approach to Mark's Gospel which focuses on the mighty *deeds* of Jesus in the first part of the narrative as the primary thrust of the messianic proclamation contrasts starkly with trends in First World interpretation of Mark. In the latter, there has been an influential view which has regarded the emphasis on the necessity of the suffering and the death of Christ in the second half of the gospel of Mark as a corrective to the optimism and activism which the dynamic account of Jesus' deeds in the first half seem to promote. For the First World exegete, then, it is the idea of the suffering messiah which is primary for the understanding of salvation: believe in this and you will be saved. In contrast the liberationist perspective puts the emphasis on Jesus' *praxis*, with the reflection as a secondary stage. This corresponds closely to the priorities of the liberation theologians where practical identification with the poor takes precedence over, though it does not exclude, theological reflection. Nowhere are the epistemological undergirdings of the two exegetical worlds better seen than in their approach to Mark's gospel.

Despite its complexity and sophistication Belo's exegesis is in some respects closer to the reading of Scripture in the CEBs than is the exegesis of Boff and Sobrino. We have noted that when we talk of the theology of liberation we are not just speaking of the works of the theologians but of a theological approach which gains its inspiration from the activities of the CEBs in many countries in Latin America. As we have seen the Bible is being used as part of the reflection by the poor on their circumstances as they seek to work out appropriate forms of response and action. In that process the reading of Scripture often bypasses the dominant methods of the First World. To those of us brought up on the historical–critical method the interpretations can often appear cavalier. Third World readers often have little regard for the historical circumstances of the text, its writer and its characters. There is frequently a direct identification of the poor with biblical characters and their circumstances, with little concern for the hermeneutical niceties invoked in applying the text to our own circumstances. The resources of the text are used from their perspective of poverty and oppression, and a variety of meanings are conjured up in a way reminiscent of early Christian and ancient Jewish exegesis.

The understanding of the theology as a second-order task, namely one of critical reflection on life and practice, is not new to Christian theology. That subtle dialectic between the 'text' of life, viewed in the light of recognition and non-acceptance of unjust social arrangements and the other 'text' of Scripture and tradition is the kernel of a lively theological, or for that matter any, interpretative enterprise.[31] The world of the poor as well as their imagination provides shafts of light which can often throw into the sharpest possible relief the poverty of much First World interpretation.

A distinctive theological voice from the Third World?

The history of Latin America over the last four hundred years has been one of the export of its material wealth and the import of European culture. The imposition of European culture in all its forms, including Christianity, has over the centuries produced a mutation of that culture as the peoples of the sub-continent have sought an accommodation with ideas and values which they inherited. That should always be borne in mind whenever we are tempted to suppose that the phenomenon of liberation theology is merely a pale reflection of the theology and culture of Europe.[32] That it is in part a reflection of European theology cannot be denied. This is evident when we read the translations of the books of the liberation theologians which evince that same concern to reproduce the academic genre which so characterizes the theological scholarship in Europe and North America. Many priests have received a European education not only in their theology but also in other areas of academic life. The academic influence of Louvain in Belgium, Munich and the École Biblique in Jerusalem is to be found in seminaries of both traditional and radical hue throughout Latin America.

While the education and the ideas are European in origin, however, the use made of them is of a different order. It is a well-known fact that the Christianity which came with the Spanish and Portuguese conquerors did not remain unaffected by contact with the indigenous populations and those brought from West Africa to work the plantations. In Brazil, cosmopolitan as it is today, the area around Salvador in Bahía still bears the marks of the era of slavery. Hundreds of thousands were brought from West Africa to work the sugar plantations, hence the obviously much higher proportion of Brazilians of African origin in this region of Brazil today. The emergence of what are termed Afro-Brazilian religions (Umbanda, Macumba and Candomblé) is a manifestation of the kind of mutation of traditional catholicism which has taken place.[33] Like Rastafarianism in Jamaica [34] in this century it has offered a symbolic universe to millions who have lost their bearings and long for their roots. This is something which is particularly important for the millions in Brazil who have left their ancestral homes in that country as part of the vast internal emigration within Brazil to become 'exiles in their own land'.[35]

Afro-Brazilian religion is a religion of the oppressed, displaced and dispossessed. It manages to accept outward devotion to the traditional saints of catholicism by identifying them with the gods and goddesses of the African religions which the Africans brought with them. The persistence and vitality of that religious tradition is exemplified by the continued popularity and widespread influence of this folk-religion even among those who are not themselves initiates into the rites of the various cults. This classic example of the fusion of religious traditions allows the oppressed subtly to subvert the content of the religion of the masters. The oppressed can give new meanings to the devotions in which they are asked to participate, thereby rejecting what is offered from above and replacing it with something into which their personal story is injected. For example, the Virgin Mary was identified with the goddess Yemanjá, and Christian feasts in January and February, particularly in Salvador, Bahía, the old colonial centre of Brazil, offered the opportunity to evoke those memories of an African past. There was only a limited amount of space for the expression of that identity within the life of slavery, but the Afro-Brazilian religions have exploited that space to the full.

Afro-Brazilian religion is a powerful force in Brazilian society. Women are offered a prominent role within them, and the ecstatic states which the drumming and dancing induce offer a temporary release from the squalor and degradation of the surroundings of the *favelas*. It is contact with 'home' for those who have left the drought-stricken north-east and sought refuge in the large cities. But that home is ultimately the far-off shore of West Africa and the Yoruba rituals. The beat of the drums can be heard down in the valley in middle-class Botofogo in Rio from the Santa Marta slum perched precariously on the hillside above.

The attraction of the power of spirits when there seems to be little human resource to nourish and defend is understandable. Today the rituals attract all levels of Brazilian society. It is no longer merely a religion of the oppressed, and there is big money to be made in selling artefacts for the rituals. The costly devotion is well exemplified by the flowers and gifts devoted to Yemanjá at Candlemas in Salvador and New Year's Eve in Rio. The mutation of the Christian religion by the slaves has become part and parcel of Brazilian society at all levels. In the light of this it is hardly surprising that Pentecostalism with its strange tongues, ecstatic states and, more importantly, promise of divine healing of the body, offers hope to those who are otherwise without hope.

This disgression on Afro-Brazilian religion has been necessary to indicate the vitality and ingenuity of the Latin American mutation of the European culture. Similarly, whatever ideas might have been channelled into the Christianity of Latin America by priests trained in Europe have not remained unaffected by the people and circumstances of the various countries. In liberation theology we are not dealing with a simple transference of the political theology of north European universities. Of course, that theological background is important and has had its part to play in the systematic presentation of liberation theology most familiar to North American and European readers of Boff, Sobrino, Segundo and Gutierrez. But the main thrust of the theology itself has not come from the political theology of Europe, which is a rather different theological phenomenon as found, say, in the writings of Moltmann and Johannes Baptiste Metz.[36] Liberation theologians working closely with grassroots communities in Latin America stress that the inspiration for their work of biblical interpretation has been the way in which the Bible is being read and used by such communities.[37]

The influence of priests and religious touched by political theology has rubbed off on these groups, particularly in those dioceses where there has been a well-organized pastoral programme. Similarly, the understanding of evangelization rooted in the Second Vatican Council,[38] 'the bringing of good news into all strata of humanity and making it new', has doubtless had its part to play in the understanding of mission in today's world. Nevertheless the character of the biblical exposition and the particular issues which concern members of Basic Christian Communities is firmly rooted in the experience of poverty and oppression and the hope of the gospel for a better world when God's reign appears on earth. Yet it would be a mistake to suppose that CEBs are always explicitly political in orientation. In those dioceses where there is less sympathy for the approach of the theology of liberation (the Archdiocese of Rio de Janeiro is an example often quoted) there has sometimes been a break in the extent to which Basic Communities have been able to explore much beyond what has traditionally passed as 'religious'. Sometimes the ethos of the CEBs can be pietistic. As we have noted, Pentecostalism has its attractions in Latin America and is a rapidly growing social force in the sub-continent. This has sometimes led to an evaporation of support away from the Basic Christian Communities to pentecostalist and other protestant groups rooted in poor areas. But there are few short-cuts offered in the long road to justice. Miraculous interventions and escapism offered by tongues of ecstasy cannot change the social fabric which is so deleterious to the poor. The rapidly growing influence of Pentecostalism and its appeal because of its apparently 'supernatural' character is a matter which is disturbing leaders of the CEBs as also are the steady inroads made by US-backed fundamentalist Christian groups with their allegedly 'apolitical' stance.[39] Such developments are a timely reminder that the story of Christianity in contemporary Latin America is incomplete without reference to the surge of support for a variety of fundamentalist groups.

The theology of liberation is only one strand of a complicated tapestry of religious life, however attractive it may be to those in the First World seeking social change. But as such, like the mutations of European culture and religion which have happened in the past, it is an example of that distinctive appropriation and transformation of tradition which is typical of so much that has happened in Latin America since the end of the fifteenth century. But even more significant from the point of view of the whole history of Christian theology, the evolution of political theology into liberation theology deserves to stand alongside other theological developments in Christian history; it is, in short, a gospel of hope for the third millennium.

Liberation theology and the millenarian tradition

Frequently, New Testament exegetes have wanted to separate politics from eschatology and to assert that the *content* of the Kingdom as preached by Jesus and the early church has little, if anything, to do with this world. We noted that one of the consequences of Johannes Weiss' discussion of the eschatological element in the teaching of Jesus was a rejection of human agency in the bringing about of a transcendent kingdom. That view has been a cornerstone of discussions of the future hope in the New Testament among many First World exegetes.[40]

As we have seen, the concentration on Jesus' proclamation and inauguration of the Kingdom of God and the widespread use of Revelation are typical of the liberation theology perspective. The description of Jesus as a prophet of a new age is frequently found in New Testament scholarship. The expectation of the Kingdom of God on earth which was dominant in early Christian eschatology, even if it was for various reasons marginalized in later centuries, parallels the main stream of Jewish eschatological expectation at the end of the Second Temple period as well as the Joachite tradition. Also the key conviction that this coming Kingdom could be established in part in this present age and is not wholly of the future has its echoes in the communitarian practice which undergirds the theology of liberation. It has stressed the material, this-worldly character of the future hope in the New Testament. This is most evident in the writing of Leonardo Boff, where the language of millenarianism and utopianism is frequently used:

> The determining element in the Latin American person is not the past, our
> past is a European past, one of colonization, but the future. Herein lies the

activating function of the utopian element. Utopia ought not to be understood as a synonym for illusion and flight from present reality . . . utopia is born of the springs of hope. It is responsible for models that seek a perfecting of our reality, models that do not allow the social process to stagnate nor society ideologically to absolutize itself, models that maintain society permanently open to ever increasing transformation. Faith promises and demonstrates as realized in Christ a utopia that consists in a world totally reconciled, a world that is the fulfilment of what we are creating here on earth with feeling and love. Our work in the construction of a more fraternal and humanised world is theologically relevant: it builds and slowly anticipates the definitive world promised and demonstrated as possible by Jesus Christ.[41]

According to Boff, the struggle of the disciples of Jesus Christ is to be centred on a goal which is not beyond this world, however difficult and far-removed from present realities that goal may appear. Boff clearly regards the utopian horizon as a constant source for a critique of the present order and a hand beckoning forward to transformation. The springs of hope are based in Christ. But these are not just a promise, for in him there is *already realized* a utopia. In his person is the embodiment of that *shalom*, or universal harmony, which will characterize a world in which God is all in all. Meanwhile that future hope lays an obligation on those who are in Christ to begin to 'create it with feeling and love', as an anticipation of the messianic kingdom on earth still to come.

Something of that utopian mentality can be glimpsed in the importance attached to the CEBs. They are viewed as microcosms of that equality, popular participation and mutual support which characterize 'a more fraternal and humanized world'. There is a clear indebtedness in the ecclesiology of the Basic Communities to Vatican II and its emphasis on the people of God.[42] So in the CEBs a considerable degree of autonomy has been given to lay people for the organization and instruction of the community. Many priests have welcomed the opportunity to work out new roles as the Basic Communities take more and more responsibility for their own lives, even in fields which in the past might have been expected to be reserved for priests and nuns. Boff gives a glimpse of what this sort of ecclesiology might mean in the book which provoked the suspicion of the Vatican, *Church: Charism and Power*:

> the church is the people of God. There is fundamental equality in the church. All are people of God. All share in Christ, directly and without mediation. Therefore, all share in the services of teaching, sanctifying, and organising the community. All are sent out on a mission; all are responsible for the unity of the community.[43]

and in the following quotation from a more recent book:

> We in Brazil and Latin America are confronted with a new concretization of the church without the presence of consecrated ministers and without the eucharistic celebration.[44]

Behind these words there lies the experience of a significant part of the Brazilian church born of an acute shortage of priests and of a rejection of an outmoded view of hierarchy. It attempts to articulate a new way of being the church which seeks to do justice to the church's tradition. That Boff's views of the role of the hierarchy are not mere fantasy is apparent when one looks at ways in which some of the more progressive bishops in Brazil are relating to their dioceses. An example is Dom Mauro Morrelli in Caxias whom we examined earlier. He believes that the church should be a microcosm of the reign of God, a foretaste of what is to come, in which every member including priest and bishop has his/her role and in which office is based on service rather than power. This has been perceived as a direct challenge to the practice of most churches whether catholic or protestant.

In such ideas there is more than a passing resemblance to the utopian millenarian tradition within Christian theology to which we have alluded earlier: the vision of a perfect society which is inevitably at variance with the imperfections of existing society and which includes a critique of social institutions.[45] Liberation theology's concern for practice makes it conform in some respects to Mannheim's definition of the utopian frame of mind as a type of orientation which breaks the bands of the existing order.[46] In other words liberation theology is engaged in change in the present and is not merely dreaming about a better world.

While in liberation theology the specific means of analysing existing society can involve tools borrowed from Marxism, the basic critique is one inherited from a utopian tradition which has a long pedigree in the Judaeo-Christian tradition. To suggest this might immediately confirm the worst suspicions of many that the theology of liberation is after all bent on the fragmentation of the church and a division between the utopian elite and the rest. But such a conclusion would be precipitate, for it ignores the care with which liberation theologians have in the main sought to balance utopian enthusiasm with devotion to the Catholic Church. This was evident in Leonardo Boff's acceptance of the restrictions put on his activities after the inquiry instigated by the Congregation for the Doctrine of the Faith encapsulated in the following words:

> the utopia of the kingdom anticipated in the community of the faithful, a community of more human ties, more lively faith and more profound communion of members, never died in the church . . . the basic community constitutes . . . a bountiful wellspring of renewal for the tissues of the body

ecclesial, and a call and a demand for the evangelical authenticity of ecclesial institutions, so that they may come more closely to approximate the utopian community ideal. . . . In the church the institutional may be allowed to predominate over the communitarian. The latter must ever preserve its primacy. The communitarian, for its part, must always seek adequate institutional expression . . . the basic church communities cannot pretend to constitute a global alternative to the church as institution. They can only be its ferment for renewal.[47]

Ecclesiologically, the practice of the basic communities is not too far removed from the kind of pattern set out by Paul in 1 Corinthians, where the need for the people of God as a whole to take responsibility for their governance is accepted with the apostle in an essentially supportive, non-directive role. There is a tendency in some liberation theology towards naive idealism, sometimes approaching a kind of theocracy in the repudiation of structures. But the gentle routinizing process which is evident in 1 Corinthians is not untypical of the creative institutionalism found in many CEBs as they seek to articulate their catholic faith while at the same time affirming their peculiar identity as the people of God within specific social contexts.

Of course, one of the problems with millenarianism is that it all too easily becomes exclusive and provokes a reaction in which a much harsher process of routinization takes place, effectively removing the power from the people of God. The tension between the freedom given to the CEBs in their use of Scripture and their organization and obedience to the teaching authority of the bishops seems to me to be a contemporary example of that problem, but one that so far at least has been negotiated with a surprising degree of success by all concerned. In Brazil, there is no rift between the hierarchy and the popular church. We have noted the important role the CEBs are playing in the emergence of the new diocese of Caxias, just north of Rio de Janeiro. Even more telling, of course, is the example of São Paulo where Cardinal Arns has presided over the most complete institutionalization of liberation theology in Latin America. When Leonardo Boff went to Rome in 1984 to answer the charges laid against him, he was accompanied by Cardinals Arns and Lorscheider of Fortaleza, so that every indication was given that it was not just an individual who was on trial but a church and its pastoral practice. More recently, the Brazilian bishops have been summoned to Rome, and there are signs that the importance of the theology of liberation within the practice of the Brazilian church is being recognized. It is the implementation of the vision of the theology of liberation over the years by the Brazilian Conference of Bishops (CNBB) which has made it very difficult to argue that there is a split between the Catholic Church and the popular church in Latin America.

Those opposed to the theology of liberation, therefore, might be expected to do all in their power to reduce the influence both of the CNBB in the Conference of Latin American Bishops (CELAM) and of the influential minority of progressive bishops in Brazil. With the retirement of influential figures like Dom Helder Câmera as Archbishop of Recife and Olinda and the appointment of more conservative successors, it is possible that this strategy may succeed or that the Basic Communities might be provoked into a position of opposition to the hierarchy and thus confirm all the worst fears of the critics. At present in Brazil that does not seem to be the case.

There is evidence, however, that the rather strident tone and misleading assessment of the character of the theology of liberation in some Vatican pronouncements may be giving way to a more understanding approach to its centrality in the pastoral practice of some Latin American dioceses. This is evident in the Pope's recent letter to the Brazilian bishops where he says that 'liberation theology is not only opportune but is useful and necessary'.[48] The most recent statement of the Congregation for the Doctrine of the Faith is one indication, a document which, in Leonardo Boff's view, serves to strengthen all those initiatives taken from a liberation perspective and which Gustavo Gutierrez regards as 'a new moment opening'.

Nicaragua and South Africa: the churches and revolution

Nicaragua[49] has become something of a political and ecclesiastical *cause célèbre*. Few countries can have provoked such diverse reactions from Christians. On the one hand there are those who see its government as the embodiment of Marxist–Leninist atheism and as such a threat to the freedom of religion. Others see its revolutionary process as a sign of hope for Latin America (and, indeed, other parts of the world as well).

For over forty years the Somoza dynasty ruled this small Central American republic. Standards of living were low, and there was widespread corruption, culminating in the confiscation by the Somoza regime of large quantities of money donated for relief and rebuilding after the earthquake in Managua in 1972. The centre of the capital city remains a wilderness fifteen years later. After a long civil war the Somoza dictatorship was overthrown in 1979 by the Sandinista Liberation Front. The economy was in ruins, yet an immediate response was made to achieve a modicum of change for the poor majority of the population. That heralded a determination to rebuild the country in the interests of the majority of the population. To this end there were literacy and health campaigns. The Literacy Crusade dramatically reduced the national rate of illiterarcy from over fifty per cent to 13 per cent, and the nationwide health promotion campaign won wide acclaim. The

World Bank's first post-Triumph report on the country predicted that *given sufficient foreign aid*, the prospects for the economy were good in spite of the enormous costs incurred during the long civil war.

However, the years after the revolution have seen the establishment of a terrorist movement (the 'Contra'), based in neighbouring Honduras and Costa Rica, to which the USA has given financial and logistical support – so much, in fact, that many observers wonder whether the Contras would have any cohesion at all without US co-ordination. Nicaraguans have been involved in a costly war against the Contra which has caused enormous suffering and has left the economy in ruins. This has been made worse by a US trade embargo. The US views Nicaragua as a threat to its national security and as an intrusion of Soviet Marxist–Leninist totalitarianism into the mainland of Latin America. The present US administration is determined to seek the overthrow of the present Nicaraguan government as it believes that the Nicaraguan revolution is a threat to US interests in the region. In pursuit of its policy goals the US administration was prepared to resort to a variety of covert actions to subvert the Nicaraguan government. The mining of Nicaraguan ports by the CIA in 1983 led to the condemnation of US intervention in Nicaragua by the International Court of Justice in the Hague in June 1986, but the US government refused to accept the court's ruling. Nicaragua has been accused of seeking to export its revolution to neighbouring countries, particularly El Salvador. This has never been proved. What is not in doubt, however, is that the democratically elected government (in elections which were widely regarded as being conducted in a free and fair manner) is socialist in complexion and does contain several Marxists. But it is committed to a non-aligned foreign policy and its recently agreed constitution commits the country to a mixed economy and a participatory form of democracy in which the leaders are regularly subjected to questioning from ordinary Nicaraguans.

There have been mistakes and shortcomings in the last eight years by the Sandinista government. A major problem has been the resentment of the Miskito Indian population in the north of the country about the forced migration policy; but there are now signs that this problem is in the process of being resolved. Still a contentious issue is the split within the churches between those Christians who give general support to the government and its programme of social and political change and those who have become steadfast critics and opponents. Among the latter is the Roman Catholic hierarchy which is convinced that the government is engaged in persecution of the church and its priests. Indeed, two leading members of the Roman Catholic church were expelled, though at the time of writing (September 1987) there are indications that a successful implementation of the Central American Peace Plan might lead to a relaxation of restrictions. Initially,

there was a sympathetic attitude towards the post-revolutionary government on the part of the Roman Catholic church reflected in the Nicaraguan
bishops' first pastoral letter after the Triumph. But since then relations
between church and state have deteriorated quite markedly. The so-called
'popular church' in Nicaragua and the hierarchy are polarized, in large part
because of attitudes to the Revolution. The close identification of the revolution process with movement towards the reign of God and the intimate links
between Sandinista rhetoric and Christian theology in some quarters have
been disturbing to many Christians. For example, in the El Riguero church
in Managua, where Franciscan priest Uriel Molina ministers, there are vast
murals in which revolutionary images are closely woven with biblical
imagery of liberation. The death of young Nicaraguans in the war agains the
Contra-terrorists is seen as nothing less than Christian martyrdom. Suffering for the sake of 'the new humanity' is an idea frequently found in progressive Christian circles with regard to the war. For Molina the coming of the
kingdom of God is an event in human history, and the opportunity to have a
hand in its coming is offered in the shape of the revolution. God's reign is not
an abstract entity but is intimately bound up with contemporary struggles to
bring about justice:

> New signs of Christ's presence have to be set up in the midst of a people
> mobilised for war, or picking coffee or cotton. . . . We must also celebrate the
> faith in ways which take up the life and suffering of our people, and especially
> we must not wound them by refusing mass for their heroes and martyrs. To
> celebrate the memory of a hero or martyr is the same as celebrating the
> revelation of God in his act of liberation, because we could not remember
> heroes if there had not been revolution. The commemoration of a hero is the
> evocation of the liberating act of God in revolution. It is the celebration of the
> cause of an entire people. . . .
>
> The challenges presented to the Nicaraguan Church by this revolution are
> so numerous and of such a kind that we shall never be able to respond to them
> from rigid positions. . . . We need to open our doors to the Spirit, who is
> blowing everywhere but has not yet succeeded in finding a chink in the house
> of bishops. . . . There is need of . . . much freedom of spirit to understand the
> signs of the times, and above all much humility and love, so as not to condemn
> what is pejoratively called 'The People's Church' but is in fact the innovatory
> sign of a new way of being the Church.[50]

The problems are not by any means all on one side. Hard feelings still
exist among many Nicaraguan Christians about the Pope's unwillingness to
show sympathy for the mothers of Contra victims during the mass in
Managua and the reluctance of the Nicaraguan bishops to condemn the
Contra atrocities and to recognize the progress made in the standard of
living of ordinary Nicaraguans since the revolution.

The acute tensions between hierarchy and government in Nicaragua culminated in the censorship of the Church-controlled newspaper and radio station by the government for ignoring various restrictions placed upon them because of the war. There are signs that the acute tension between church and government may now have eased somewhat. The Cardinal Archbishop, Obando y Bravo has considerable support among many Nicaraguans, which has made it very difficult for ordinary citizens to have to choose between loyalty to the Archbishop or support for the revolution. As a result the vibrancy of the CEBs has diminished somewhat of late as positions have become more polarized. But it would be dangerous to explain this as a growing exclusion of the 'religious' element in the revolution. There is abundant evidence of what Philip Berryman has called 'the religious roots' of the Nicaraguan revolution.[51] There are four Roman Catholic priests in the government. All four have sought, in two cases unsuccessfully, to maintain their opportunity to fulfil their vocations as priests along with a full participation in the revolutionary process.

Fernando Cardenal, Minister of Education, has been excluded from the Jesuits (though he still lives with them in Managua). This is a direct result of the new code of canon law whose regulations on the limits of priestly duties were specifically drawn up with the priests serving in the Nicaraguan government in mind. He is quite clear about the compatibility of his priestly vocation with the necessity for his involvement in the government, and speaks of his understanding of his apostolic ministry in Nicaragua in the following way:

> I thought that I could nourish the hope that the church would see in my work a missionary type of apostolic service along the lines of the gospel presence . . . in a new historical process which has taken an option for the poor. . . . In all sincerity I consider that before God I would be committing a serious sin if in the present circumstances I were to abandon my priestly option for the poor, which is presently being concretised in Nicaragua through my work in the Sandinista People's Revolution.[52]

In addition, the main protestant ecumenical organization, CEPAD, offers 'critical solidarity' to the government and has frequently called upon the USA to end the war. For this it has been described as a front organization for communist subversion by right-wing organizations. Post-revolutionary Nicaragua has attracted support from progressive Christians and it has succeeded in bringing the issues confronting Central America before a wide audience throughout the world. Nicaragua is a symbol of hope and of resistance to colonialism and imperialism. Dom Pedro Casaldaliga, bishop of São Felix in Mato Grosso, Brazil, was not untypical of many progressive Christians when he spoke, at a Sevice for Peace in Managua in

September 1985, of Nicaragua and its revolution as a cause to which he has committed himself 'as a man commits himself to his wife'. His moving re-reading of the prophecy from Micah quoted in Matthew 2 gives some indication of the enormous investment many throughout the world have made in the Nicaraguan revolution:

> And you, little Nica, shall not be the least of my cities, says the Lord, for out of you has been born my daughter, freedom, and my son the new man. Woman who fights for our freedom, girded with tenderness, flower of liberty, paraded before us, sacrament of the New America. NICARAGUA.[53]

South Africa: the Kairos Document

Nicaragua is a country which has undergone a revolution. Political, economic and military power have passed from the aristocracy to a government which has a popular mandate for reform. The problems posed for progressive Christians there are are different from those facing Christians in dictatorships (though the return to civilian rule in Brazil has necessitated a different pastoral practice there). In Nicaragua it is a question of the limits of identification with the revolution. 'Critical solidarity' is a phrase often used to express the sympathetic attitude to the Sandinista government. That means the need to retain some distance from government policy while keeping a degree of commitment and involvement in the difficult process of implementing social reform. Solidarity enables the Christians' voice to be heard within the revolutionary process; but criticism is an indispensable part of maintaining the need to subordinate all human projects to the standards of the reign of God. That course differs from those strategies which either give uncritical support to the government or involve total opposition to all that the revolution stands for.

Polarization of ecclesiastical opinion is also evident in South Africa. Whereas in Nicaragua the challenge to progressive Christians is connected with the extent of involvement in the revolutionary process, in South Africa they are excluded from power which would bring about social change and are in the main a voice of protest and denunciation. The names of Archbishop Desmond Tutu and Allan Boesak are well known around the world for their opposition to apartheid. Such opposition needs little justification in Europe, and it is not my concern to detail Christian involvement in the maintenance of a racialist system and in the long struggle against it. In the context of this study, however, mention should be made of two remarkable documents which have emerged from South Africa in the last two years. The first is the Kairos Document and is described as a Christian, biblical and theological comment on the political crisis in South Africa.[54] It is the product of meetings and discussions by a large number of concerned theologians and the character of the churches' response to the present crisis. The second is closely related to it and comes from a group of 'concerned evangelical' pastors and theologians. The evangelical document is more muted in its political radicalism than the Kairos Document but is no less brave for that. Its constituency is one which has a history of political quietism and support of the status quo, and has been concerned to provide sufficient space for the church's missionary and liturgical activities 'as understood by them'. Despite the lack of the same political commitment that is found in the Kairos Document *Evangelical Witness in South Africa*[55] represents a solid reminder to conservative, evangelical Christians about the challenge of the biblical basis of their faith and the need to be aware of mouthing slogans of state security and anti-communism as if they were the Word of God. In what follows I shall concentrate on the Kairos Document as a sample of recent attempts at theology within Christian witness in South Africa.[56]

The Kairos Document starts with the arresting words of Jesus at the opening of his ministry in Mark 1.15: ' "the time has come"; the moment of truth has arrived. . . . It is the *Kairos* or moment of truth not only for apartheid but also for the church'. The document recognizes the splits among the churches over the issue of apartheid and proceeds to subject to critical scrutiny 'state theology' and 'church theology' either for support of the government or for being too restrained in its critique. There is a concerted 'unmasking of South African reality', particularly in the ideological use made of certain biblical texts by the state and conservative churches.

The critique of state theology concentrates on an analysis made of Romans 13. It rejects the idea that Paul presents an absolute doctrine about the state, and argues that the text must be interpreted in its context. That context was a situation in which Christians were arguing that they were exonerated from obeying the state because Christ alone was their king. While Paul insists on the necessity of some kind of state until the reign of God comes, that does not mean that all that the state does is approved of by God. Thus, it is to passages like Revelation 13 that one should turn instead when a state does not obey the law of God and becomes a servant of Satan. The use made of a divine sanction for the apartheid system in the constitution of South Africa is said to be idolatrous: 'the god of the South African state is not merely an idol or false god, it is the devil disguised as Almighty God – the Antichrist.'

Christian churches do not escape condemnation. They are particularly taken to task for advocating reconciliation as 'an absolute principle that must be applied in all cases of conflict or dissension'; whereas 'in our situation in South Africa today it would be totally unChristian to plead for reconciliation and peace before the present injustices are removed. . . .

That is not Christian reconciliation; it is sin.' Neutrality, therefore, is nothing but a means whereby the status quo of oppression can continue.

The peace which the churches should pursue is God's peace, for there can be no real peace without justice. The document rejects the gradualist approach to reform as being demonstrably ineffective: 'God does not bring his justice through reforms introduced by the Pharaohs of this world'. Appeals by the church to the leaders of the apartheid regime are ineffective. Instead they should appeal to the oppressed to stand up for their rights. The document rejects non-violence as an absolute principle and exposes the violence perpetrated by the security forces as part of the problem of violence in South Africa. It poses the question: 'how can acts of oppression, injustice and domination be equated with acts of resistance and self-defence?' Referring to the biblical tradition it points to the use of violence in the struggle of Israel for liberation and rejects the idea that Jesus said Christians should never use violence in self-defence. In other words, it affirms that there *are* circumstances in which limited violence may be legitimately used. The document explains the church theology as a consequence of naivety and lack of discrimination in its social analysis. It also considers the dominant spirituality with its other-worldly and individualistic air to be an important factor in creating an apathetic attitude towards oppression. It criticizes the view which advocates quietism: Christians may look for change, but that must come in God's time; 'that leaves very little for human beings to do except to pray for God's intervention.'

The document then puts forward some suggestions for what it calls 'a prophetic theology'. Firstly, this involves social analysis, 'what Jesus would call reading the signs of the times'.[57] That would mean an awareness of the interests of those maintaining the present system and the exploitation of those who labour to keep in affluence the privileged minority. Secondly, the document challenges the churches to take action, first of all by taking sides with 'God who is always on the side of the oppressed' and to participate in the struggle (campaigns, consumer boycotts etc. are offered as examples). The churches are urged to identify with popular organizations and not be a 'third force' between oppressor and oppressed. Those who share common goals should work together. Churches are told that they cannot collaborate with tyranny, and civil disobedience is suggested in order to avoid giving any moral legitimacy to the regime, 'for it is an enemy of the people, opposed to the well-being of the oppressed and an enemy of God.'

Thus 'there are two conflicting projects and no compromise is possible'. Either Christians respond to the biblical teaching about liberation from oppression and use Christian criteria for assessing what is a tyrannical regime or they connive in maintaining the status quo. For the writers of the document 'the most loving thing that we can do for both the oppressed and for our enemies who are oppressors is to eliminate oppression, remove the tyrants from power and establish a just government for the common good of all people.'

Finally, the writers call on the churches to offer the oppressed a message of hope, though they recognize that suffering will be a necessary prelude to resurrection:

> the church of Jesus Christ is not called to be a bastion of caution and moderation. The church should challenge, inspire and motivate people. It has a message of the cross that inspires us to make sacrifices for justice and liberation. It has a message of hope that challenges us to wake up to act with hope and confidence. The church must preach this message not only in words and sermons and statements but also through its actions, programmes, campaigns and divine services.

In a polarized situation of manifest tyranny this tract for the times breathes a greater urgency than is found in much of the material produced by many liberation theologians, though it has its parallels with some of the pastoral letters issued by bishops in times of repression, most notably from the assassinated Oscar Romero.[58] The political situation in southern Africa is so fluid that it is not possible to predict what the outcome of a Christian radical stand is going to be. What the Kairos Document offers is a supreme example of contextual theology manifesting in particular the critique of ideology which is such an important part of the theology of liberation and at the same time urging the course of costly prophetic witness to the righteousness of God.

Liberation theology has come to stay, and its impact on First World churches where injustice is becoming more widespread within society, albeit for a minority of the population, is growing.[59] In Latin America at least there are signs that the immediate fears of reprisals against the theology of liberation from the ecclesiastical authorities are not to be fulfilled, at least for the moment. This movement, which draws deeply on the wells of the Christian tradition, in the light of the severe social problems of Latin America, will hopefully be able to be retained within the life of the church at large as a vital and invigorating stream of Christian spirituality.[60] Too often the history of all our churches has been marked by an inability to make room for and learn from those renewal movements which have sprung up, appealing to the tradition itself as the inspiration for radical change in church and society. To allow it room would be a true mark of catholicity and would show that at the end of a turbulent century the church has learnt something about the breadth of the Christian tradition and the radical and reforming instincts deeply imbedded within it.

Concluding Reflections

At the outset of this study a contrast was drawn between what are popularly held to be monuments of the divine glory, the cathedrals and chapels of Christendom, and the stark simplicity of the challenge of Jesus' life and message. It is difficult to resist the temptation to return to that theme, because it underlines discussion of the character of the Judaeo-Christian understanding of religion. While the importance of the communal celebration of God's mighty acts in history can give focus to the conviction that God's presence is at work in human history, it is easy for that celebration to become an end in itself. The place and the medium of celebrating the triumph of God's justice become central and the pursuit of that justice in human affairs is subordinated to a secondary role. Then we find ourselves in the position of seeking to reconcile the contradiction between the environs of the celebration and the message which it exists to proclaim.

In ancient Israelite society the Temple in Jerusalem provided the focus for an ideology of a quality and sophistication still admirable today. Nowhere in the laws of Moses do we find a reference to regulations for the Temple. The centralizing of the cult in a building of brick in Jerusalem stands in stark contrast with the portable, temporary phenomenon of the tabernacle which accompanied the people on their journey to the Promised Land. The political purpose which led to the centralizing of religious activity in Jerusalem and the downgrading of other (older) places of worship is widely recognized. Its implications for the character of the religion were immense. The establishment of the Temple in Jerusalem linked with a dynastic succession of the house of David was the political triumph of David and his son Solomon. The ideology supporting dynasty and city was to have a pervasive influence on Jewish thought.[1] Their legacy was to be an enduring one. The picture of Zion's invincibility lauded in the Psalms was one that was deeply rooted in the ancient Jewish culture. Even opponents of the moral quality of the dynastic regime like Isaiah used its language, and a prophet of doom like Ezekiel was so attached to the violability of Zion that the vision of the removal of the divine glory from the Temple and the emptiness of its splendour was a prerequisite for his understanding of the hollowness of its religion and the absence of the divine from its practice. It was left to Jeremiah to subject the myth of complacency and confidence to ruthless criticism in his famous condemnation of the Temple,[2] words that were echoed by Jesus of Nazareth when he cleansed a later Temple at the end of his life.[3] The absence of a Mosaic sanction for the Temple was recognized by a later critic of the prevailing ideology, Stephen, who also paid for his outspoken critique with his life.[4] In Jesus' day memorials were built to the prophets even though they had been reviled during their own lives.[5]

Contemporary churches erected to the glory of God as places of celebration of the divine justice are marked with the trappings of political power and thereby sanction oppression of the poor by the mighty; in them are tombs of kings, and memorials to military prowess and chauvinism. The keepers of the modern Temples are dedicated men and women who would be appalled to find any disjunction between what they are maintaining and the tradition of the founder for whose glory these buildings were erected. But these artefacts are memorials to oppression and exploitation, memorials to human greed and power. The point is most easily made when one looks at the baroque churches of Latin America. In Salvador in Bahía, Brazil, for example, the gold leaf which decks the walls of the Franciscan church (something which would surely have bewildered Francis himself) is a salve to the conscience of conquest and oppression, a memorial to the oppression and despoliation of millions in Latin America. In the Franciscan church in Recife a reminder of the cost is found not only in the bleeding crucifix and the relics of the saints but in the haunting pictures of Franciscans and Jesuits round the walls being crucified by the conquistadores. As Revelation 11.8 puts it, 'their dead bodies will lie in the street of the great city which allegorically is called Sodom and Egypt, where also their Lord was crucified'. But the same is true in the great cathedrals and buildings of Europe. If the divine glory is to be found, it is to be seen in the humanity and wisdom which produced such beauty, the talented men and women whose experience of oppression and the constraints of whose circumstances produced those monuments. The God who sides with the poor and the marginalized was with those who sought to express their humanity in the fractured existence of their world and with the limited space available to them as they expressed that humanity.

Above all else the fragmentary story of hope and protest which I have been telling is a witness to the conviction that the arena of divine justice will be human history. It is that conviction which resounds clearly through the pages of the Old Testament and which undergirded the hope of the nascent messianic movement that was to become Christianity. It is part of Christianity's ambivalence towards the Old Testament that it has been uneasy about its concern for history and the material world as the focus of salvation. As a result it has been all too ready to retreat into a hope which centres primarily on the individual and heaven beyond, rather than on a community of people in this world and their liberation. There is little to suggest that Jesus and his first followers unravelled the fabric of convictions about the divine justice and liberation in human history. The individuals whose ideas have been surveyed have clung to this conviction, and their wisdom casts fresh light on much reading of Christian eschatological hope so eloquently expressed in biblical prophecy and narrative.

Throughout this book we have seen examples of the conviction that the divine indwells the human and the process of human history, a conviction particularly strong among those on the margins of society, who like Jesus were rejected and died 'outside the city' (Hebrews 13.12). Many must have understood what it was like to bear the reproach of Jesus of Nazareth in their witness to God's righteousness. The experience of the everyday world was an essential part of the knowledge of God. In the theology of liberation the primary text is 'reality': the reality of oppression, poverty and dehumanizing attitudes and circumstances. Knowledge of that primary text makes theologians out of all God's people. The professional exegetes are not afforded a privileged position in the understanding of God's word. The invective of Winstanley and Muenzer against the preachers and theologians of their day finds an echo in the emphasis on the liberating potential of the poor as interpreters of the Word of God in reality and tradition. It is they, not the scribes, who have the key to the knowledge which will enable them to enter the Kingdom of God.[6] Theologians have an important role as participants in the dialogue of the whole people of God rather than jealous possessors of the keys of knowledge.

We can discern a use of the tradition which refuses to be content with the letter but pierces to the real meaning of the text. At times this attitude may manifest itself as a rejection of the priority of Scripture and a subordination of it to the inner understanding which comes through the Spirit. From Paul's letter to the Galatians, where the reading of Scripture is subordinated to experience of the Spirit, to the use of the Bible in the Basic Christian Communities, the emphasis is on the understanding of reality as a prior 'text' which must inevitably condition the way in which Scripture and tradition are read. In that situation the voice of those who had been told that their task was merely to listen begins to be heard. It is not that their message is substantially different from the tradition they have learnt. What they find in it is there for all to read and to use; but they are the ones who find in the challenges to the status quo and the hope for a better world a message which is not easily heard by those who already have enough and to spare.

Frequently, claims are made to renewed knowledge of God which is in some sense more immediate. This is seen as the continuing activity of the immanent God through the Spirit in the world who has inspired the prophets of old. That inner prompting of God enables the believer to know what the mind of God is in a particular matter and to which the written text acts as confirmation of that intuitive knowledge of God:

> But this is the covenant which I will make with the house of Israel after those days, says the LORD: I will put my law within them, and I will write it upon their hearts; and I will be their God and they shall be my people. And no longer shall each man tell his neighbour and each is brother, saying, 'Know the LORD', for they shall all know me, from the least of them to the greatest, says the LORD.[7]

This text is alluded to from time to time in Jesus' words at the Last Supper when he speaks of a 'New Covenant' being ratified by his death, and Paul contrasts his ministry with the ministry of Moses on behalf of an obsolescent covenant. Muenzer in the Prague Manifesto refers to the inwardness which characterizes that knowledge of God enabled by the Spirit within,[8] and Winstanley in the New Law of Righteousness quotes Jeremiah 31: .

> For every one shall know the Law, and every one shall obey the Law; for it shall be writ in every one's heart; and every one that is subject to Reason's law shall enjoy the benefit of Sonship. And that is in respect of outward community; to work together, and eat bread together; and by so doing, lift up the creation from the bondage of self-interest, or particular propriety of mine and thine; which is the Devil and Satan, even the God of this world, that hath blinded the eyes of covetous, proud flesh, and hath bound them up in chains of darkenss. Acts 4.32

Those who have true knowledge of the world as it really is recognizes the divinity dwelling within them:

> perfect man shall be no other but God manifest in flesh; for every manifestation of this power in any creature, shall be seen, known, rejoiced in, and be declared of by man. Jeremiah 31.34; John 8.22; Romans 8.22.[9]

The excitement of the immediacy and freshness of the millenarian spirit cannot shield us from the destabilizing effects of its convictions. Problems are posed by radical social movements which do not stop at analysis but embark on a programme which enables 'the absolute to interfere with the world and conditions actual events', to quote Mannheim's words. What can be lacking in them is any assessment about the realistic possibility of achieving these goals, so that there can occur what Engels terms 'communism by fantasy'.[10] In this the writing or the ideas become a means of fulfilling what turns out to be impossible within history. Thus Muenzer, according to Engels, anticipated in the form of a communist myth a stage of social development – communism – which would become possible only after the due process of social evolution, the bourgeois revolution, to which Muenzer was in fact opposed. In the circumstances, Muenzer's religious reading of the political struggles in which they were engaged had an effect which 'can be positively reactionary as events, although as ideas they were as revolutionary as may be: which goes to show that their character as events (whether revolutionary or reactionary) is not determined by their character as ideas'.[11]

Similarly, Turner[12] points out:

> Winstanley's communism is unambiguous in its recognition of the class character of political, economic, legal and religious oppression. But his capacity to identify the class character of the new social order which was emerging in the mid-seventeenth century owes more, one suspects, to the prophetical and the millenarian religiosity of his character than to any well-supported empirical analysis. It is unsurprising that Winstanley's work disappears . . . it was written far in advance of its time.

That sympathetic view of Winstanley's insights cannot protect this kind of position from the criticisms of those who consider that such individuals and movements are incapable of a creative development into a post-revolutionary phase. A recurring criticism of millenarianism and the anabaptist tradition is the inability to manage routinization.[13] Certainly there were difficulties surrounding the failure of the *Kairos* to mature, whether because of the destructive outbursts of revolutionary zeal or massive disappointment at failed expectations. Nevertheless, often there was little opportunity for the management of a transition to arrangements which would keep the cutting edge of the original millenarian spirit alive. There are signs in several millenarian movements that recognition of what we now term routinization *was* on the agenda at some point in the history of the group, but that an opportunity never arose for it to be explored fully. Consequently, it is a backlash rather than a creative routinization which takes place, all too often at the expense of the millenarian spirit, a fact that has been borne out by the history of Anabaptism.[14]

Of course, there is always a temptation for a movement which expresses dissatisfaction with the present and is in search of an unrealizable perfection never to engage in the difficult task of interim arrangements in the transition to the new age; it may treat routinization as a symptom of decline (a fact well illustrated in the yearning for the pristine perfection of the past in several movements). Because it fails to recognize that the age of perfection has not arrived, it cannot cope with the impossibility of maintaining a consistently high level of messianic enthusiasm. Its nostalgia for a better age can involve it in a stubborn rejection of *all* developments and compromises. That must be a counsel of perfection; few can avoid making some accommodation, however strongly held their views. As Stephen Sykes has pointed out, what such a group can legitimately challenge is the *costs* of the process of routinization and institutionalization rather than the necessity of such a development.

The reason for the continued manifestation of the revolutionary and subversive spirit within the Christian tradition is easily explained. The canon of the New Testament may tell the story of progressive routinization, but, as we have seen, in the canon are texts which act as the basis for upsurges of charismatic-millenarian protest against hierarchy. The millenarian spirit is an essential part of the process of *ecclesia semper reformanda*. Routinization channels charisma; it is not in the business of stemming its flow. As a result, it enables its power to be a resource for future movements of protest and change. An ideology of the powerful (in the case of the church, the triumph of Christian orthodoxy) did not achieve its dominant position and partial reading of the tradition by complete subjection of opposing views. Rather, it developed a process of the legitimation of the opposing viewpoints by incorporating them within the framework of the prevailing way of reading the canonical scriptures. A process of neutralization of the subversive ideas which threatened the status quo took place. This helps explain how a religion like Christianity which has its roots among the rural population of Galilee could be transformed into a buttress of an imperial system whose earlier supporters had murdered its founder. All this is not to suggest that the canon is a collection of texts simply expressing incompatible ideologies. Certainly those differences can be discerned when texts are compared, but it is also apparent within a single text which will not usually offer a minority ideology of an oppressed group in a 'pure' form. Any given text's relation to that struggle may well be ambiguous. It will not necessarily stand unerringly on one side or another. It is part of the task of interpretation to lay bare the ambiguities and contradictions that are inherent in all texts as they form part of struggles between groups and classes in the present as well as in the past.

The messianic group erupted from the seething cauldron of an expectant society, developed its beliefs and practices and indeed found itself at odds with those outside its circle (a situation the nascent Christian movement certainly found itself in). But in its evolution the heady enthusiasm which characterizes the initial outburst can be quenched by disappointment or the need for consolidation and accommodation. Alternatively it may find new expression in institutional form which enables that first flush of messianic enthusiasm to be preserved as a resource for change in generations to come. When a messianism moved to different settings and into different social strata, there was bound to be an effect of the socio-economic reality on those ideas. One of the fascinating things about the formation of ideologies is the subtle way in which language can undergo significant shifts of meaning in different social contexts. The radical political thrust of millenarian beliefs means that rapid shifts in the core meaning of dominant ideas can take place, and then they can be accommodated into a dominant ideology with their cutting edge blunted. But the startling fact about Christianity is the way in which a religion which has so frequently become a means of supporting the position of the powerful offered the instruments which enabled that apparently secure ideological structure to be undermined and toppled. As we can see in contemporary use of apocalyptic imagery, the promise of the millennium and the message of doom on an unrighteous society are viewed very differently by different groups. On the one hand there are those who find in these symbols signs of renewal and catalysts in the struggle for justice. On the other are those who see only a means of escape for those whose hearts are right with God. It is a division which cuts across the boundary between rich and poor, not least because the resources at the disposal of the rich have enabled religion to become merely an opium of the people in the shanty towns of the Third World, when in the same area there are those for whom it is not the heart of a heartless world but a catalyst for change.

The story of Christianity in this and every age is in part a story of the ways in which its symbols have been used by different groups and classes but partly also the extraordinary ambivalence of its scriptures with regard to change in society. In the very process of taming its radical symbols by their incorporation into a collection which also included injunctions to political quietism and social conservatism, these potent symbols of change were preserved to be used by those who saw the Beast at large in their own day and needed the encouragement of the foundation documents of the faith to continue the struggle even if it did mean that they would have to follow their own Way of the Cross like the Messiah.

One of the consequences of millenarian movements is the reaction to their failure and the anathematizing of their views and their excesses. It is easy to understand why this should happen, though it is not always clear that the views which are stigmatized as heretical really are so. But the weaknesses of the heretics are often little removed from the weaknesses of the saints. That dividing line between constructive promotion of change and a destructive fanaticism is a fine one. What is assumed to be diabolical may be little, if at all, different from the sublime teaching. The point is well made by the sane Franciscan, William of Baskerville in Umberto Eco's *The Name of the Rose*. In contrast to his fellow-Franciscan, Ubertino's, confidently expressed ability to distinguish between what is of God and what is of the Devil, William maintains a tolerant recognition of the divine wisdom to be found in those who had been denounced as heretics and who paid the ultimate penalty in torture and death. William confesses that he is no longer able to distinguish between those on God's side and those on the devil's, for, 'often the step between ecstatic vision and sinful frenzy is very brief'. It is precisely because it has been difficult to distinguish, and because the movements we have been examining have sometimes tended to fall into a fanaticism destructive of themselves and others that it has not been difficult for opponents of those who transgress into sinful frenzy to pour scorn on the inspiration. Such a reaction is usually itself a product of the challenge to vested interest in the face of the painful truth of the gospel which the dispossessed and margin-alised have glimpsed. If that challenge had been met with a degree of tolerance, it could have proved edifying for the mass of humanity. Instead of that, the millenarian spirit is channelled into inward-looking groups who can find no outlet for their frustrations except in a destructive outburst on those bastions of power which refuse to recognize the spark of divine truth in their message.

A recurring theme in many of these texts has been nostalgia for a golden age of the church. Such nostalgia is by no means the property of groups committed to egalitarian change in society. Harking back to what things were once like is an appeal which elicits a ready response among those who find only 'change and decay in all around I see', to quote H.F. Lyte's famous words. Such appeals have often provoked a sympathetic reaction at times of decay. It is important, therefore, to distinguish between this reac-tionary nostalgia and the kind of nostalgia which has emerged in the texts we have been examining. This latter has its focus not on the attempt to put the clock back but on the need to recapture that openness to the activity and creativity of the prophetic spirit which was found in the past and should characterise the present as well. So creativity and the prophetic challenge are to be seen as the mark of the golden age and of the present, a feature which the church has lost in its quest for consolidation and compromise.[15]

It is that nostalgic quest for the spirit of Jesus and the apostles which may enable us to offer an initial reflection on the criterion for separating ecstatic vision from sinful frenzy. The belief that Christianity must be about a contemporary replication of the way of Jesus takes radical Christianity back to the gospel story of non-violent protest and the implementation of the reign of God on earth as the paradigm by which all that claims to be

Christian should be judged. Those who have sought an alternative pattern in which violence, whether physical or psychological, is repudiated and there is instead a recognition of a common humanity created in God's image and the provision of that freedom for the development of the peculiar talents of each, have glimpsed the way of Jesus set out in the gospels. It is a challenge to articulate an alternative vision of human relationships:

> You know that those who are supposed to rule over the Gentiles lord it over them, and their great men exercise authority over them. But it shall not be so among you; but whoever would be great among you must be your servant, and whoever would be the first among you must be slave of all. For the Son of man also came not to be served but to serve, and to give his life as a means of liberation for many.

Such sentiments seem far removed from the aggressive pursuit of change by violent means in the promotion of the reign of God on earth which occurs from time to time in radical Christian movements. The issue of violence in the pursuit of liberation remains a pressing problem, as the Kairos Document reminds us. We have noted in Muenzer's case that the recognition of the *Kairos* provoked the promotion of a struggle culminating in his ignominious defeat outside Frankenhausen. The proclaimers of the present as a critical moment are not united in support of the solution of Thomas Muenzer, however. As far as we can ascertain, Jesus went to Jerusalem without expecting to take the initiative himself in overthrowing the might of the hierarchy by the force of arms. The reading of the gospel narrative in this book suggests that resort to violence as an instrument of change is rejected as a strategy by Jesus, though that should by no means lead us to suppose that it involved a passive attitude to the circumstances which confronted him. Violence should be excluded as an option by those who seek to offer hope and change for all people in conformity with the mind of Jesus Christ. The pursuit of the millennium and the use of violence may seem inextricably intertwined. Yet it is part of the misapprehension of contemporary religious movements pressing for change that it is not widely recognised that non-violence is an important component in the quest for an 'alternative' style of life. Such people would want in addition to point out that those who are critical of the use of force to bring about social justice are frequently those who themselves depend on violence to preserve their wealth and power.

This is a particularly sensitive issue for the theologians of liberation. Churches have not objected (and the majority still do not object) to involvement in a war against tyranny (there is a coherent doctrine of the just war to which recourse can be made). Nevertheless there is a difficulty in deciding exactly what constitutes tyranny and whether there is a reasonable possiblity that the tyrant may be deposed. According to those criteria, however, Nicaragua in 1979 offered the most obvious attempt to apply the just war theory in the practice of revolution. It is a mark of the variegated character of the theology of liberation that pacifism can sit side by side with those who feel that the armed struggle is essential in the promotion of righteousness. Nicaragua presents a major problem for those who want to promote peaceful action for change. The hope offered by its revolution places those who renounce violence in the most awkward position. It is part of the facile approach to the theology of liberation that it has been depicted as a cipher for Christian support of violent social change. Its commitment to social change is not in doubt, but it is by no means the case that its exponents all consider violence to be the means of achieving the 'evangelical insurrection',[16] to borrow a phrase of Leonardo Boff. As long as that insurrection remains 'evangelical', it will have to take account of the patient process of bringing to awareness the challenge of the reign of God and of the need for a present response: exactly what the parabolic teaching of Jesus set out to do. Gerrard Winstanley's emphasis on the important links between combating the Devil within and the societal structures without is a theme which would be echoed by many in Latin America. Influenced by educationalists like Paulo Freire, the education about the proper perceptions of reality and responses to it is an essential prerequisite to the whole movement of social change. 'Christ rising in sons and daughters' and the overcoming of the covetous flesh which promote private property and instruments of oppression are as much part of the pedagogy of the oppressed today as they were in Winstanley's day. The road to the 'evangelical insurrection' is both long and difficult.

The writing of a book like this depends on an ease of environment which seems to sit uneasily with the urgency and constraints placed on most of the figures discussed in this book. For those who seek to espouse egalitarian views in a hostile political and economic environment, writing becomes a safety valve and can become 'communism by fantasy'. The quest becomes an end itself and as a result there is a constant temptation to use this as a means of avoiding the hard political realities of practical change to alleviate the burden of oppression which seems to be growing at the end of the second millennium. To those who say that instead of writing about change I ought to be changing the world, a response is difficult and not entirely convincing. Involvement in a wide range of movements for change is essential, but the sustenance of the inner resources to persevere in the struggle for justice and the quest for utopia is as important as the practice itself. Part of the process of the sustenance of one's inner resources must come through the reflection on those who have sought to tread the same path before, to be inspired by their actions and to learn from their mistakes. But the example of Gerrard Winstanley stands as a reminder of the vulnerability to feelings of desolation that are ever present.

The cries of protest and the movements for change in Christian history are an eloquent testimony to the fractured existence of life in a fallen world. The quest for a perfect society to which early Christianity was committed is reflected in a fragmentary way in its textual production, evidence of the constraints on the pursuit of millennium. The eager longing for change and frustrated expectations manifest in the outbursts of vengeful anger in the songs of triumph over the fall of Babylon in Revelation are expressions of that fractured existence. Resolution is offered in the vision of hope as a necessary means of overcoming the tensions inherent in an oppressive society. The dangerous visions of a messianic age speak a language different from the prevailing culture which is madness to the world.

It is this alternative tradition which seems to be madness, and it is this to which the apocalyptic and millenarian tradition has borne witness. It has protested against those arrangements which have the appearance of order but which in reality have brought about the prosperity and progress of some at the expense of others. It is frequently those who have to bear that suffering who can see the fragility of those structures which appear to offer peace and security. Those whose lives are fragmented and who live at the margins can discern the signs of the times in ways which are frightening to those of us who cannot see from what is apparently a more favoured vantage-point. Their cries of protest and their aspirations for liberation are expressed in that longing for the manifestation of God's righteousness: 'Your reign come on earth as it is in heaven'. It is hardly surprising that such powerful statements should be domesticated or branded as eccentric or, worse, anathematized and repressed.

Has the radical inheritance of Christianity any signposts to help in the construction of a better world, or must the story of its proponents be written off as romantic illusion? Is it so preoccupied with the goal of perfection that it is incapable of offering us any means of getting there? To write sympathetically of its ideals and its failures indicates that I believe it must remain at the very centre of any Christian quest for justice. What is most encouraging about trends in Latin American liberation theology is that it is aware of the importance of remaining as part of the larger church, however impatient it may be to see greater change and more unequivocal commitment to justice and liberation. There will always be a danger of enthusiasts losing patience and moving out on the way of perfection, leaving behind those they believe are compromisers and unwilling to pay the full cost of discipleship. What they can learn is the lesson of the past, when the reaction to the failure of projects has been detrimental to the poor. It is the concern for human beings and their impoverishment both spiritually and materially that has prompted cries of protest and hope for a better world. As such the ideals and the commitments are too important to be allowed to be written off as destructive fanaticisms, for they are a simple response to injustice and a demand for attention to basic human need. Indeed, it is that conviction that faith must be primarily about *doing* something which runs like a thread throughout the previous pages. The struggle against injustice remains at the heart of those committed to the good news of Jesus Christ and that means the need to embark on a course of action, however inadequate it may seem, to remedy it. Those who refuse to remain spectators of the panorama of injustice or disputants about its cause and course will expect to be victims in conflicts with those who have most to lose in the removal of injustice. But it is they who will inherit the kingdom, for they were the ones to hold on to the 'dangerous vision . . . of the kingdom of justice which enables the suffering people to take off their bonds and to keep moving along the road to liberation'. The radical saints have shared with millions of little people throughout history the 'tribulation and the kingdom and patient endurance in Jesus' and in hope have longed for a time when 'the whole world shall see the salvation of our God'.

Notes

Introduction

1 For an important introduction to the socio-political factors at work in the formation of the Old Testament see N. Gottwald *The Hebrew Bible*.
2 *Marxism and Religion*.
3 On this see David Martin *The Breaking of the Image* especially pp. 160ff.
4 K. Mannheim *Ideololgy and Utopia*, especially pp. 190ff and N. Cohn *The Pursuit
   of the Millennium*.
5 Mannheim, *Ideology and Utopia* pp. 190ff.
6 See B. Wilson's 'A Typology of Sects' (summary in Bocock and Thompson
   Religion and Ideology).
7 From A. Mojtabai *Blessed Assurance*.
8 Hall 'Religious Ideologies' in Bocock and Thompson *Religion and Ideology* p. 273f.
   On this theme see also the introductory chapter of P. Worsley *Three Worlds*.
9 Weiss *Jesus' Proclamation of the Kingdom of God* p. 129f.
10 See E. Ullendorff *Ethiopia and the Bible*.
11 Particularly J. Weiss *Jesus' Proclamation* and A. Schweitzer *The Quest of the Historical Jesus, The Mystery of the Kingdom of God* and *The Mysticism of Paul the Apostle*.
12 Schweitzer deals with this in *The Mysticism of Paul* and the whole subject of the
   transformation of Christian doctrine in the light of the Delay of the Parousia was
   explored in detail by M. Werner in *Die Entstehung des christlichen Dogmas* translated and abridged as *The Formation of Christian Dogma*. See also below pp. 41ff.
13 See Rowland *Christian Origins* pp. 87ff and 113ff and see below pp. 17ff.
14 For an introduction to his philosophy see W. Hudson *The Marxist Philosophy of
   Ernst Bloch*. Cf. L. Kolakowski *Main Currents of Marxism*. 'Ernst Bloch: Marxism
   as a Futuristic Gnosis' pp. 421ff and now McLellan *Marxism and Religion*. See
   also E. Hobsbawm 'The Principle of Hope' in his *Revolutionaries*, and for an
   excellent introduction to this area see J. Bentley *Between Marx and Christ* especially
   p. 89f. In addition to Bloch influential figures like Karl Barth and Gershom
   Scholem were influenced by eschatlogy and apocalyptic, see Bentley *Between
   Marx and Christ* and D. Biale *Gershom Scholem. Kabbalah and Counter-History*.

15 See *Atheism in Christianity* pp. 163ff.

16 See Moltmann's *Theology of Hope*, R. Bauckham Moltmann. *Messianic Theology in the Making* and Hudson *Marxist Philosophy* and see Moltmann's correspondence with Bloch discussed in J. Bentley *Between Marx and Christ* pp. 94f (published in *Revolution, Religion and the Future*). On utopianism see below p. 11.

17 A good example in comparative religion is the work of Mircea Eliade. On topics relevant to the subject of this book see particularly his *Myths, Dreams and Mysteries* and *Cosmos and History. The Myth of the Eternal Return*.

18 On this see Rowland *Christian Origins* pp. 75ff and 113ff. For an illuminating introduction to the character of Second-Temple Judaism see E.P. Sanders *Paul and Palestinian Judaism*.

19 See e.g. the work of Christopher Hill, particularly *The World Turned Upside Down*, E.P. Thompson *The Making of the English Working Class* (and further H. Kaye *The British Marxist Historians*; also Keith Thomas *Religion and the Decline of Magic* and B.W. Ball *A Great Expectation*).

20 See Radford-Ruether and McLaughlin *Women of Spirit* and below p. 174 n. 97.

21 See Lavinia Byrne *Mary Ward. A Pilgrim Finds Her Way* and her *Women before God*.

22 See further Rowland *Open Heaven* pp. 1ff.

23 K. Mannheim *Ideology and Utopia* p. 35.

24 See the useful summary in Gager *Kingdom and Community*. There are important contributions on the ideas and practice of millenarianism in the collection ed. S. Thrupp *Millenial Dreams in Action*, particularly the essay by Y. Talmon 'The Pursuit of the Millennium: the Relationship between Religions and Social Change' and S.R. Isenberg 'Millenarism in Greco-Roman Palestine' and a more recent bibliography in R. Bloch *Visionary Republic*. See further Stark and Bainbridge *The Future of Religion* especially pp. 506ff.

25 There are useful comments on the variety of ways eschatological language is used in G.B. Caird *The Language and Imagery of the Bible*.

26 B. Goodwin and K. Taylor *The Politics of Utopia* and J.C. Davis *Utopia and the Ideal Society*. The book of Deuteronomy offers an example of biblical utopianism. Its setting is the very moment of entry into the Promised Land. It offers a blueprint of the way the holy nation should live if it wants to maintain its relationship with Yahweh. There is a frank recognition of the need for restraint but an idealistic quality about its rhetoric and some of its provisions.

27 Goodwin and Taylor *Politics of Utopia* pp. 72ff.

1 Radical Christianity
Roots and Branches

1 Lk. 1.46ff.

2 On this see e.g. A. Kee *Constantine versus Christ*. For the most up-to-date discussion of Constantine see T.D. Barnes *Constantine and Eusebius*. There are important discussions of the seeds of accommodation in K. Wengst *Pax Romana and the Peace of Jesus Christ*.

3 On this term and its importance for the study of the sociology of religion see Max

Weber *Economy and Society* pp. 1151ff and for a survey M. Hill *The Sociology of Religion*.

4 On this see A. Grillmeier *Christ in Christian Tradition* pp. 219ff.

5 H. Maccoby *Paul the Mythmaker* and earlier S.G.F. Brandon *The Fall of Jerusalem and the Christian Church*.

6 His writings are conveniently collected in ed. A. Louth *Early Christian Writings* and with the original Greek in ed. Kirsopp Lake *The Apostolic Fathers*.

7 On the centrality of these ideas see Rowland *Christian Origins* pp. 111f.

8 e.g. 1 Cor. 15.20 and Phil. 3.21.

9 1 Cor. 6.2ff and Matt 19.28.

10 1 Cor. 1.7; 1 Pet. 1.7; Mk. 8.38 and Jude 14.

11 Acts 3.21.

12 Ro. 13.11 and Rev. 22.20.

13 Mk. 13.32. Cf Mk. 9.1; 1 Thess. 5.1; 2 Thess. 2.2f.

14 See the summary of the Jewish material in J. Jeremias *New Testament Theology* pp. 76ff.

15 Ro. 8.18ff especially v. 23.

16 On the shift to Hellenism see e.g. J. Daniélou's three-volume work on early Christian theology: *The Theology of Jewish Christianity; The Gospel and Hellenistic Culture* and *The Origins of Latin Christianity*.

17 See further G. de Ste Croix *The Class Struggle in the Ancient Greek World* pp. 427ff, D.J. Kyrtatas *The Social Structure of the Early Christian Communities* pp. 87ff, and G. Theissen *The First Followers of Jesus*.

18 See further below pp. 51ff and the books cited there.

19 On the social setting of Paul's missionary work see the survey in W. Meeks *The First Urban Christians*.

20 1 Cor. 14.16ff and 34ff.

21 Survey of material in E. Schweizer *Church Order in the New Testament* and H. von Campenhausen *Ecclesiastical Authority and Spiritual Power in the Church of the First Three Centuries* and ed. E.P. Sanders *Jewish and Christian Self-Definition*. For a more sociological approach see Meeks *First Urban Christians* pp. 74ff and the literature cited there.

22 See Rowland *Christian Origins* pp. 254ff.

23 The account of the prophet in the last days of Jerusalem and of Jesus son of Ananias is taken from Josephus, *Jewish War* vi. 281ff and vi. 300f respectively and of the unnamed prophet from *Antiquities* xx. 167f. The account of the prophecy of Jesus son of Ananias is taken from *Jewish War* vi. 300f (translation from the Loeb edition edited H. St. J. Thackeray). The version of the crucifixion of Jesus is Mk. 15.22ff. On such movements see R.A. Horsley 'Popular Prophetic Movements at the Time of Jesus', *Journal for the Study of the New Testament* 26 (1986), T. Rajak *Josephus* and Isenberg 'Millenarism in Greco-Roman Palestine', *Religion* 4.

There is a wide divergence of approach to the historicicty of the gospel narratives. My view is that they are a window onto the life of Jesus and that, though there were inevitable changes in the tradition of Jesus' sayings in the course of transmission, there was a sufficient interest in the history of Jesus within early

Christianity to ensure that we are not offered a completely distorted picture (see
B. Gerhardsson *Memory and Manuscript*). In saying this I would want to make two
points. First of all, I recognize that any writing is a product of a particular social
setting, and it would be naive to suppose that this window onto Jesus gives us
access to the totality of the history of Jesus. The very fragmentation of the
tradition and the story is itself a reflection of the distortion of the social situation
in which any writer finds him/herself (see F. Jameson *The Political Unconscious*).
Secondly, while it has to be admitted that what follows in these pages is the barest
of summaries, the outline of Jesus' ministry followed here coincides in general
terms with the critical scholarly consensus on Jesus research, as examplified e.g.
in E.P. Sanders *Jesus and Judaism* and E. Rivkin *What Crucified Jesus?* Finally,
what is also important is the fact that the narratives of Jesus, once they were
received into a canon of Scripture, have become themselves initiators of ideas
and so their authoritative status as expositions of the life of the messiah could
then continue to stimulate imitation and thereby challenge attempts to establish
and petrify the religion.

24 Many Zealots finally died in the hill-top fortress of Masada in 73 CE where the
Zealots made their last defiant stand against the Roman legionaries and preferred suicide to ignominious capture; see Y. Yadin *Masada*.

25 Matt. 6.9. The familiar words of the Lord's Prayer are full of eschatological
ideas, see J. Jeremias *New Testament Theology* pp. 193ff.

26 Lk. 17.21. Cf. 7.21ff.

27 For a discussion of Jesus' ministry see Sanders *Jesus and Judaism* and Rowland
Christian Origins; for a summary from a liberationist perspective see J.L. Segundo
The Historical Jesus of the Synoptic Gospels and in the context of Roman imperial rule
K. Wengst *Pax Romana and the Peace of Jesus Christ*.

28 On this see the suggestive comments of G.B. Caird *Jesus and the Jewish Nation*.

29 This is something which readers of Mark are expected to know about, see
Mk. 15.7.

30 For Josephus' use of this word see Rajak *Josephus* and Schuerer *History of the
Jewish People* vol. ii p. 500f.

31 Jn. 18.33.

32 Mk. 10.42 Cf. Lk. 22.25.

33 Mk. 12.13–17. In Matt. 22.19 Jesus is shown a coin for the tax (a Matthaean
change as compared with Mark), thus indicating that the issue is about paying
taxes rather than the whole economic system of which the coin is but a symbol.
Cf. Ro. 13.7 where Paul probably alludes to the Matt. version of the story.

34 Lk. 23.2.

35 E.g. Mk. 12.15; Lk. 11.17; 11.54.

36 Deut. 5.8.

37 Mk. 6.37f.

38 Mk. 6.8.

39 Mk. 12.43.

40 Mk. 11.15.

41 Mk. 14.11.

42 On this saying see further F. Belo *A Materialist Reading of the Gospel of Mark*;
Wengst *Pax Romana* pp. 58ff; R. Eisler *The Messiah Jesus and John the Baptist*

pp. 196ff. Cf. Bammel and Moule (eds.) *Jesus and the Politics of his Day* pp. 32ff and 249ff.

43 Lk. 13.31ff and Schuerer, Vermes and Miller *The Jewish People in the Age of Jesus Christ* vol. i pp. 330ff.

44 That probably underlies the obscure saying in Matt. 11.13 and its parallel in Lk. 16.16.

45 On the *kairos* see Mannheim's suggesive comments noted above pp. 3ff.

46 Mk. 1.15.

47 Cf. Ez. 1.1; Is. 6.1ff and Jer. 1.1ff. The importance of the prophetic element is well brought out by W. Brueggemann in his *Prophetic Imagination*.

48 On this see Rowland *Christian Origins* pp. 175ff.

49 Isaiah 64.1.

50 Lk. 4.16ff and see further J.H. Yoder *The Politics of Jesus*, T. Hanks *God So Loved the Third World* and R.B. Sloan *The Favorable Year of the Lord. A Study in Jubilary Theology of the Gospel of Luke.*

51 Jn. 6.14f.

52 Lk. 6.20ff. The gospel for the poor is a sign offered to the imprisoned mentor of Jesus, John the Baptist, that the reign of God has drawn near. See Lk. 7.20ff.

53 Lk. 11.20.

54 Lk. 10.18.

55 Mk. 1.22, Mk. 3.6 and Mk. 3.22ff. See further E. Stegemann 'From Criticism to Enmity' in Schottroff and Stegemann eds. *God of the Lowly.*

56 Lk. 12.51f; Matt. 10.34f.

57 Mk. 5.1ff. See Wengst *Pax Romana* p. 66 and Theissen *Miracle Stories* p. 250. The destruction of the hostile powers in the lake of fire can be found in Rev. 19.20 and 20.10.

58 Mk. 3.27.

59 Mk. 4.26ff.

60 Matt. 6.25ff.

61 See Belo *Materialist Reading* pp. 139ff.

62 Mk. 4.9.

63 Mk. 2.27f; Mk. 3.35; Mk. 10.21.

64 Mk. 16.1ff; Lk. 7.39. Also note Mk. 14.9 and see Elizabeth Schuessler Fiorenza *In Memory of Her.*

65 Mk. 10.43f.

66 Lk. 13.34.

67 Mk. 10.29.

68 Mk. 8.34f. Cf. Mk. 10.33ff.

69 Mk. 4.18f.

70 Mk. 10.21.

71 Mk. 3.22ff.

72 Matt. 5.21ff.

73 Mk. 2.23ff and Mk. 10.11.

74 Lk. 11.49.

75 Hos. 2.14f; 13.4f.

76 Matt. 8.11.

77 Mk. 10.6f.

78 Mk. 8.33f.

79 Lk. 9.51 and 13.33.

80 1 Kings 18–19 and Jer. 15. Jesus is identified with Jeremiah and Elijah in Matt. 16.14.

81 See further, for a cogent and concise presentation of the factors which led to Jesus' execution, E. Rivkin *What Crucified Jesus?*

82 Jn. 1.29 and on the death of Christ in the New Testament see F. Young *The Sacrifice and Death of Christ* and M. Hengel *The Atonement.*

83 Jn. 11.54 and 57. Cf. Mk. 11.11.

84 Lk. 7.22f.

85 Mk. 14.22ff. Cf. 1 Cor. 11.23ff.

86 Cf. 1 Peter 2.21f.

87 L. Boff in *Martyrdom Today. Concilium* vol. 163 (1983) pp. 12ff.

88 Mark 11.1ff.

89 On the significance of the Temple see Sanders *Jesus and Judaism* pp. 61ff and Belo *Materialist Reading* pp. 178ff.

90 See Schuerer *History of the Jewish People* vol. I pp. 338ff and H. Hoehner *Herod Antipas.*

91 Jn. 11.47–49.

92 Mk. 13.2ff for the eschatological discourse, on which see L. Hartmann *Prophecy Interpreted* and D. Ford *The Abomination of Desolation in Biblical Eschatology*; for other evidence of Jesus' predictions against the Temple see Mk. 14.58. Cf. Jn. 2.18f and Acts 6.13f.

93 Mk. 14.2. Cf. 14.10.

94 This passage is the basis of John's unmasking of the reality of the Roman state in Revelation 13 and 17; see below pp. 66ff.

95 Lk. 23.2.

96 Mk. 15.34, quoting Ps. 22.1.

97 On the resurrection see P. Perkins *Resurrection* and P. Carnley *The Structure of Resurrection Belief* and on the antecedents G. Nickelsburg *Resurrection, Immortality and Eternal Life.* The relationship between resurrection and christology is explored by W. Pannenberg *Jesus God and Man.* On christological development and eschatology see Rowland *Christian Origins* pp. 244ff and J.C. Beker *Paul the Apostle.*

98 Heb. 6.4 and 2 Cor. 5.17 and see above pp. 16ff.

99 Literature on Paul is immense. The most important recent studies on Paul's thought are E.P. Sanders *Paul and Palestinian Judaism* and J.C. Beker *Paul the Apostle. The Triumph of God in Life and Thought.* There has been enormous interest in recent years in Paul's social world, conveniently summarized in W. Meeks *The First Urban Christians* and G. Theissen *The Social Setting of Pauline Christianity.* There are important comments on Paul's relationship to the Roman social and economic system in K. Wengst *Pax Romana and the Peace of Christ* pp. 72ff and further de Ste Croix *The Class Struggle in the Ancient Greek World* and J.L. Segundo *Paul's Humanist Christology.*

100 On questions of authorship see W.G. Kuemmel *Introduction to the New Testament.*

101 Suetonius *Life of Claudius* 25.4 (printed in C.K. Barrett *New Testament Background. Selected Documents* p. 3f).

102 There are helpful comments on this in Bammel's essay on Ro. 13 in eds. Bammel and Moule *Jesus and the Politics of his Day* and E. Kaesemann *Commentary on Romans* pp. 354ff and see Wengst *Pax Romana* pp. 72ff.

103 For suggestive comments on Paul's strategy and social situation see F. Watson *Paul, Judaism and the Gentiles*.

104 E.g. Gal. 1.12 and 1.16.

105 There had been a long history of proselytes and there was probably also a large group of Gentiles loosely attached to the synagogue who kept some of the Jewish laws without becoming full proselytes. For a discussion of some of these issues see J.J. Collins *Between Athens and Jerusalem*, Esler *Community and Gospel* p. 36 and the dissertation of M. Diffenderfer *Membership of the People of God* (Durham Ph.D. 1987).

106 1 Cor. 10.11.

107 2 Cor. 3 and see further Sanders *Paul, the Law and the Jewish People* and Watson *Paul, Judaism and the Gentiles* pp. 85ff.

108 Lk. 10.23f. Cf. 1 Pet. 1.12.

109 Heb. 6.5 and on the intuitive understanding of the will of God by means of the Spirit see 1 Cor. 2.9ff.

110 Ro. 5.12ff and 1 Cor. 15.47ff.

111 Ro. 8.19ff.

112 2 Cor. 6.2.

113 1 Cor. 10.11 and 1 Pet 1.11f and the important comments in D. Allison *The End of the Ages has Come*. On the consequences of messianism see Taubes 'The Price of Messianism' and W.D. Davies 'From Schweitzer to Scholem'.

114 E.g. Gal. 5.1ff and see on this J. Barclay *Obeying the Truth*.

115 Gal. 5.16ff.

116 Gal. 3.28.

117 Gal. 3.27 and Ro. 13.14.

118 Ro. 8.9; Gal. 2.21f.

119 This is evident in passages like 2 Cor. 4.10 and 1 Cor. 4.11ff. Cf. Gal. 3.1.

120 See e.g. G. Theissen *Social Setting* and J.C. Hurd *The Origin of 1 Corinthians*.

121 7.1; 8.1, 12.1.

122 1 Cor. 10.23 and 8.4.

123 1 Cor. 14.22ff.

124 1 Cor. 11.2ff and chapter 7.

125 See e.g. A.C. Thiselton 'Realised Eschatology at Corinth', *New Testament Studies* vol. 24 pp. 510ff.

126 1 Cor. 7.17ff; 7.26; 7.31.

127 1 Cor. 14.23f.

128 E.g. 2 Cor. 1.8; 1.17; 2.3ff; 10.9ff; 11.7ff; 11.22ff.

129 See Meeks *First Urban Christians* and Theissen *Social World and First Followers of Jesus* pp. 11ff and on the sociology of authority and community in the Pauline churches see B. Holmberg *Paul and Power*. Cf. the different social strategy opened up in the Gospel of Luke and the Acts of the Apostles where the

boundaries of the house-church were being breached (see further P. Esler *Community and Gospel in Luke–Acts*).

130 E.g. 1 Cor. 7.17ff.

131 On these J.E. Crouch *The Origin of the Colossian Haustafeln* and on the development of 'patriarchalism' see Schuessler-Fiorenza *In Memory of Her* pp. 243ff.

132 1 Cor. 3.16 and 6.19.

133 1 Cor. 12.4ff and Ro. 12.3ff.

134 2 Cor. 5.17.

135 See the survey by R. Bauckham in *Aufstieg und Niedergang der roemischen Welt* ed. Haase II.28.3. On Paul see Schweitzer *Mysticism* and Werner *The Formation of Christian Dogma*. For a brief consideration see Rowland *Christian Origins* pp. 285ff.

136 2 Tim. 1.6.

137 1 Tim. 3.

138 1 Tim. 2.11ff.

139 2 Tim. 2.20.

140 Titus 3.1ff.

141 1 Tim. 6.10.

142 1 Tim. 6.17f.

143 The fundamental study is that of L. Festinger *When Prophecy Fails*. It has been applied by John Gager (*Kingdom and Community*) and Robert Carroll (*When Prophecy Failed*) to the New and Old Testaments respectively. Other studies on Third-World millenarian movements on which Gager bases his work include K. Burridge *New Heaven New Earth* and P. Worsley *The Trumpet Shall Sound*.

144 See Gager *Kingdom and Community*.

145 E.g. Matt. 13.24ff and 24–25.

146 Rev. 22.7 and 22.20.

147 *Ideology and Utopia* pp. 190ff. On Paul's eschatological strategy linked to the collection see J. Munck *Paul and the Salvation of Mankind*.

148 Mannheim, *Ideology and Utopia* pp. 192–3 and 195.

149 On the delay of the Parousia in the Johannine literature see R. Brown *The Gospel of John* vol. i pp. cvff and C.K. Barrett *The Gospel of John and Judaism*. Cf. Rowland *Christian Origins* pp. 285ff.

150 14.21.

151 14.23.

152 14.2. cf. 14.23.

153 14.19.

154 Is. 52.3ff.

155 Rev. 1.9. Cf. Mk. 14.62.

156 Rev. 22.3f.

157 Jn. 17.24.

158 Jn. 14.17ff; 15.26.

159 See W. Meeks 'The Man from Heaven in Johannine Sectarianism' printed in ed. J. Ashton *The Interpretation of John*.

160 Jn. 14.15ff and on the independent activity of the Spirit as the witness to the divine righteousness after Jesus' departure see Jn. 16.7ff.

161 R. Bauckham, 'The Delay of the Parousia', in *Tyndale Bulletin* vol. 31 1980.

162 See Rowland *Open Heaven* and A.T. Lincoln *Paradise Now and Not Yet*.

163 Geza Vermes *The Dead Sea Scrolls. Qumran in Perspective*. See also D. Aune *The Cultic Aspect of Realised Eschatology in Early Christianity*.

164 1.21. Cf. 3.5ff.

165 Heb. 6.5.

166 2 Cor. 4.10. Cf. Gal. 2.20 and see above p. 40.

167 Ro. 15.14ff; 1 Cor. 4.14ff; 1 Cor. 5.3ff; Phil. 2.12. See R. Funk in Farmer et al. *Christian History and Interpretation*. Peder Borgen has demonstrated the importance of the sending formula in the christology and ecclesiology of the Fourth Gospel but the same is also true of Paul ('God's Agent' reprinted in ed. J. Ashton *The Interpretation of John*).

168 1 Cor. 4.16 and 11.1.

169 See Rowland *Christian Origins* pp. 272ff.

170 See Irenaeus *Against the Heresies* v. 25.35. There is no history of interpretation of the book of Revelation though material may be found in W. Bousset *Die Offenbarung des Johannes* and in the excellent chronological bibliography in Patrides and Wittreich *The Apocalypse*. See further W. Bousset *The Antichrist* and also the material discussed in K. Berger *Die griechische Daniel-Diegese*.

171 See H. Chadwick *Priscillian of Avila*. Note the reference to a bishop in Syria who led his congregation into desert (Hippolytus on Daniel 4.10, quoted in Lietzmann *History of the Early Church* vol. ii p. 196).

172 *City of God* Book xx. 7 and 9. See further R.A. Markus *Saeculum*.

2 Themes of Protest and Prohecy
'It shall not be so among you'

1 Lk. 9.58.

2 Matt. 6.19; Lk. 22.25; Matt. 6.25.

3 Mk. 10.21f.

4 Matt. 5.48.

5 See further, A. Kreider *Journey into Holiness*.

6 On this tradition in the earliest church see H. Chadwick's article *enkrateia* in *Reallexikon fuer Antike und Kirche* and the second volume of M. Foucault *Histoire de Sexualité* which deals with this issue and on the important Syriac-speaking tradition A. Vööbus *The History of Asceticism*. There was an opposite 'libertine' tradition in which antinomianism flourished, see Irenaeus *Against the Heresies* i.6.4, *Excerpta Theodoto* 52, Hippolytus *Refutation* v. 8.33f and M. Smith *Clement of Alexandria and a Secret Gospel of Mark* pp. 254ff. On later antinomianism see e.g. Hill *The World Turned Upside Down*.

7 e.g. Deut. 14. Cf. Lev. 11.2ff.

8 Lev. 19.2.

9 On this period see V. Tcherikover *Hellenistic Civilisation and the Jews* and M. Hengel *Judaism and Hellenism*.

10 The main outlines of Pharisaism are conveniently summarized in Schuerer

History of the Jewish People vol. II pp. 388ff and J. Neusner *From Politics to Piety*. Cf. E. Rivkin *The Hidden Revolution*.

11 This is the earliest written collection now extant of detailed laws relating to the main elements of Jewish life, derived from the scriptural principles, though in large part a product of custom which evolved over centuries. There is an English translation by H. Danby (*The Mishnah*). There are interesting anthropological issues raised in B. Malina's *New Testament World*.

12 E.g. 1 Sam. 15.3 (See G. von Rad *Studies in Deuteronomy* pp. 45ff) and on the period D. Rhoads *Israel in Revolution*.

13 See G. Vermes *The Dead Sea Scrolls: Qumran in Perspective*. On the Therapeutae see Philo's *De Vita Contemplative* 10 and his *Quod omnis probus liber* sit 75f.

14 *Jewish War* ii. 214ff.

15 See H.W. Kuhn *Enderwartung und gegenwaertiges Heil*.

16 There is an English translation by J. Maier but the best edition of the text together with translation and introductory study is by Y. Yadin who has also written a popular introduction to the Scroll (See also Dimant in Stone *Jewish Writings of the Second Temple Period* pp. 526).

17 *De Vita Contemplativa* 28. For a survey of Philo's writings see P. Borgen's essay in M. Stone *Jewish Writings of the Second Temple Period* and on Egypt see J. Collins *Between Athens and Jerusalem*.

18 *De Vita Contemplativa* 11f.

19 Jer. 35.

20 Dan. 10.2ff.

21 Acts 10.10.

22 Rev. 14.4.

23 Deut. 23.9f (and see also above n. 12).

24 Mk. 12.25.

25 Cf. *The Letter to Rheginos* (ed. M.L. Peel) 49.15f (published also in ed. J.M. Robinson *The Nag Hammadi Library*).

26 On Origen's castration for the sake of the kingdom: Eusebius *Ecclesiastical History* vi. 8, also Lane Fox *Pagans and Christians* p. 355f.

27 Cyprian *Epistle* 4. See further Lane Fox *Pagans and Christians* p. 369f.

28 1 Cor. 7.33.

29 1 Cor. 7.36ff.

30 Novatian *On Purity* 7.

31 Col. 2.18f and see further Rowland 'Apocalyptic Visions and the Exaltation of Christ' and F.O. Francis and W. Meeks *Conflict in Colossae*.

32 1 Tim. 4.3.

33 On Elchesai see G.P. Luttikhuizen *The Revelation of Elchesai*.

34 See Lane Fox *Pagans and Christians* pp. 336ff, Murray *Symbols of Church and Kingdom* and Vööbus *History of Asceticism*.

35 Ps. Clem. Pseudo-Clement *On Virginity* 1.10; 2.1ff. Lane Fox *Pagans and Christians* p. 738 n. 35.

36 On the Carpocratians who practised communism (they were the 'Ranters' of the second century), see Irenaeus *Against the Heresies* 1.25-6; Epiphanius *Heresies* xxviii.1.1 and Hippolytus *Refutation* vii. 34.1.

37 Matt. 6.25ff; 10.5ff; Mk. 6.8ff.

38 See G. Theissen *The First Followers of Jesus*.

39 Meeks *The Moral World of the Early Christians* p. 106. Cf. Isaiah 20.3.

40 On the beginnings of monasticism see D. Chitty *The Desert a City*; D. Knowles *From Pachomius to Ignatius*. There is an account of the 'millenarian' spirit of monasticism and its antecedents in Essenism in J. Möhler *The Heresy of Monasticism*. Something of the spirit of the solitary movement can be glimpsed in the collection of aphorisms by B. Ward *The Wisdom of the Desert Fathers* and for important background survey see C.H. Roberts *Manuscripts, Society and Belief in Early Christian Egypt*.

41 See P. Rousseau's biography *Pachomius. The Making of a Community in Fourth-Century Egypt*.

42 Mention should be made of the opportunity offered to women by emerging monasticism, see Ruether and McGaughlin *Women of Spirit*.

43 On the social significance of monasticism see Peter Brown *The Making of Late Antiquity*.

44 Hos. 2.14.

45 On the community of goods in the Jerusalem church see B. Capper in *Journal for the Study of the NT* vol. 19 and further on the links with the Dead Sea Scrolls see ed. K. Stendahl *The Scrolls and the New Testament*.

46 On the significance of sayings like Lk. 14.26 see Theissen *First Followers*. For an assessment of the varying ethical worlds of early Christianity see W. Meeks *The First Urban Christians* and his *The Moral World of the First Christians*.

47 Ro. 15.25ff; 1 Cor. 16.1; 2 Cor. 8-9; Gal. 2.10. On Paul's collection and its significance see D. Georgi *Die Kollekte* and K. Nickle *The Collection*.

48 Outline in J.N.D. Kelly *An Introduction to Early Christian Doctrine*.

49 See above.

50 See R.A. Greer *Broken Lights and Mended Ways*, E.R. Dodds *Pagan and Christian*, W. Meeks *Moral World* and P. Brown *The Making of Late Antiquity*.

51 There is a useful introductory survey in M. Hengel *Property and Riches in the Early Church*.

52 Mk. 10.21.

53 See further R. Murray *Symbols of Church and Kingdom* and Vööbus *History of Asceticism*.

54 See further G. de Ste Croix 'Early Christian Attitudes to Property and Slavery', D.J. Kyrtatas *The Social Structures of the Early Christian Communities* and Avila *Ownership* (for material on Augustine of Hippo, Clement of Alexandria, Basil of Caesarea, John Chrysostom and Ambrose of Milan).

55 *Quis dives salvetur* 13. Cf. the Pelagian *De Divitiis* 12.1.

56 See Avila *Ownership* p. 33ff.

57 On martyrdom see W.H.C. Frend *Martyrdom and Persecution in the Early Church* and Lane Fox *Pagans and Christians* pp. 419ff.

58 Matt. 19.21.

59 The quotation is taken from de Ste Croix *Class Struggle* p. 438.

60 Ibid.

61 Eph. 4.13.

62 Text and translation Haslehurst *The Writings of Fastidius*. The text is mentioned

by de Ste Croix *Class Struggle* p. 438. I am grateful to Anthony Waterman for reminding me of the importance of this text.

63 There is a reference to the practice of community of goods in the Jerusalem Church, *De Divitiis* 10.5.

64 *De Divitiis* 3 and 17.

65 Ibid. 7.2.

66 Ibid. 17.2.

67 Ibid. 8.1.

68 Ibid. 8.2f.

69 Ibid. chs 9–10.

70 Ibid. 18.10.

71 Ibid. 18.1.

72 Ibid. ch. 16.

73 Ibid. 19.1.

74 Ibid. 19.

75 Ibid. 6–7.

76 Ibid. 12.2.

77 Peter Morris in 'Pelagian Literature', *Journal of Theological Studies* vol. 16 (1965) p. 50f.

78 Acts 2.17ff; 1 Cor. 12.13; Gal. 3.27f.

79 For an outline of the history of the period see W.H.C. Frend *The Rise of Christianity* and H. Lietzmann *History of the Early Church* vol. ii pp. 196ff.

80 History in P. Labriolle *La Crise montaniste* and sources in Labriolle *Les Sources de l'histoire du Montanisme.*

81 Jn. 16.13.

82 Epiphanius *Heresies* xlviii.4 (see R.M. Grant *Second Century Christianity* p. 95).

83 On Montanism and the emerging ecclesiastical order see H. von Campenhausen *Ecclesiastical Authority and Spiritual Power* pp. 178ff.

84 Epiphanius *Heresies* xlix. 1 (Grant *Second Century Christianity* p. 95).

85 See A. Strobel *Heilige Land.*

86 See L.W. Barnard *Justin Martyr* pp. 157ff.

87 On this see W. Schepelern *Der Montanismus und die phrygische Kulte.*

88 See W. Ramsay *The Letters to the Seven Churches* and Rowland *Open Heaven* pp. 403ff.

89 *Contra Celsum* 7.4f.

90 See G. Dix, ed. H. Chadwick *The Apostolic Tradition* p. 5.

91 Lev. 12; 15.19ff. Cf. Lev. 22.

92 Rev. 2.20, though we may note the glorification of virginity and holiness elsewhere in the book, e.g. Rev. 14.4 and 21.8.

93 1 Cor. 11.5. Note also the positive picture of Huldah the prophetess in 2 Kings 22.14ff.

94 The text may be found in Hennecke-Schneemelcher *New Testament Apocrypha* vol. II pp. 332ff. On the element of control in ascetic practices see the suggestive comments of S. Orbach *Hunger Strike.*

95 1 Tim. 2.15f and note the way in which this text was quoted against Margery Kempe when she was confronted by ecclesiastical authorities in the fifteenth century (see *The Book of Margery Kempe*).

96 See also Rowland *Open Heaven* pp. 395ff, Dodds *Pagan and Christian* pp. 47ff, and Lane Fox *Pagans and Christians* pp. 438ff.

97 On this see *Women of Spirit: Female Leadership in the Jewish and Christian Traditions* eds R. Ruether and E. McLaughlin. The work of Elizabeth Schuessler Fiorenza (e.g. her *In Memory of Her*) is also important in showing the kind of sensitive handling of the material that is necessary in order to extract information about the activities of oppressed minorities whose existence is suppressed by a dominant ideological perspective. See also now S. Heine *Women and Early Christianity*. I am grateful to Catherine Ogle for making available material she has collected on women in the early church.

98 Prov. 29.18.

3 The Apocalypse
Hope, Resistance and the Revelation of Reality

1 On the Montanists see above pp. For Cerinthus see G. Bardy 'Cerinthe' *Revue Biblique* 20 (1921) pp. 344ff. The texts are collected in Klijn and Reinink *Patristic Evidence for Jewish-Christian Sects*. On the use of Revelation in the Reformation period see Patrides and Weittrich *The Apocalypse* and R. Bauckham *Tudor Apocalypse*.

2 Bultmann *Theology of the New Testament* vol. ii p. 175.

3 See especially the Kairos Document below pp. 146ff.

4 Rev. 3.14ff. For an example of contemporary North American usage of Rev. see A. Mojtabai *Blessed Assurance*.

5 An example of an exegetical approach which takes these points into consideration is that of Carlos Mester *Esperança de um povo que luta. O Apocalipse de São João: uma chava de leitura*. See also below pp. 130ff.

6 On this see the literature cited in Rowland *Open Heaven* pp. 403ff.

7 Rev. 5f.

8 1 Cor. 15.20 and Ro. 8.22.

9 See A. Voegtle *Das Neue Testament und die Zukunft des Kosmos*; O. Cullmann *Salvation in History* and *Christ and Time*.

10 The crucial passage is 1 Cor. 15.23ff which Schweitzer *Mysticism* interpreted as a reference to the millennium. Cf. W.D. Davies *Paul and Rabbinic Judaism* pp. 286ff.

11 Ro. 13.1ff cf. Rev. 12.12 and 13.5.

12 1 Cor. 15.28.

13 1 Cor. 15.24.

14 Matt. 5.5.

15 Lk. 6.22-4.

16 Mk. 14.25.

17 Matt. 8.11. For an attempt to spiritualize Jesus' hopes see Jeremias *New Testament Theology* p. 248.

18 Ro. 8.18ff. See J.P. Miranda *Marx and the Bible* pp. 274ff.

19 See article *chilioi* in *Theological Dictionary of the NT* (eds G. Kittel and G. Friedrich) in vol. ix pp. 466ff.

20 See Irenaeus *Against the Heresies* v. 33.3 and Daniélou *Theology of Jewish Christianity* pp. 377ff.

21 Ro. 13, 1 Pet. 2.14 and Titus 3.1.

22 See O. Cullmann *The State in the New Testament*.

23 Mk. 13.14ff and 13.26.

24 e.g. Mk. 3.22ff and W. Winle *Naming the Powers*.

25 See Rowland *Open Heaven*.

26 1.10 and 4.2.

27 Acts 2.17ff; 11.27ff; 1 Cor. 2.6ff.

28 1 Cor. 14.12 and 26.

29 Acts 9.1ff. Cf. 22.6ff and 26.12ff.

30 Acts 10.11.

31 Mk. 1.10.

32 Ro. 11.25; 16.25; 1 Cor. 2.1; 2.7; 4.1; 13.2; 15.51.

33 See E.R. Dodds *The Greeks and the Irrational* and *Pagan and Christian in an Age of Anxiety*; also Lane Fox *Pagans and Christians* pp. 375ff and Rowland *Open Heaven* pp. 9ff.

34 On this subject see Rowland *Open Heaven* and M. Stone's article on the apocalyptic literature in *Jewish Literature of the Second Temple Period*.

35 P. Vielhauer in Hennecke, Schneemelcher *New Testament Apocrypha* vol. 2 pp. 608ff.

36 As Martin Hengel has described it in *Judaism and Hellenism* vol. 1 p. 210.

37 Rev. 13 and 17.

38 On the major themes of Rev. see further Rowland *Open Heaven* pp. 423ff, E. Schuessler-Fiorenza *The Book of Revelation. Justice and Judgement*, Wengst *Pax Romana*.

39 Rev. 9.20 and 16.21.

40 Rev. 13. Cf Rev. 12 which speaks of the descent of the Devil from heaven; the juxtaposition of Rev. 13 with ch. 12 suggests that the consequence of the fall of the Devil from heaven is the demonic inspiration of the power of the state.

41 13.8.

42 13.15f.

43 Rev. 11.10.

44 Rev. 14.10.

45 Rev. 17.16 and note the graphic description of the fall of Babylon the Great in chs. 18–19 (on which see now Allan Boesak *Comfort and Protest*).

46 Rev. 22.10 and 18ff.

47 7.14 and 14.9.

48 In 2.14 and 2.20 and see Wengst *Pax Romana* pp. 120 and 132f.

49 Mk. 10.43.

50 Wengst *Pax Romana* p. 133f. See also A.Y. Collins 'The Political Perspective of the Revelation to John'.

51 Rev. 1.5 and Rev. 19.10.

52 Leonardo Boff in 'Martyrdom: An Attempt at a Systematic Reflection', in

Martyrdom Today Concilium vol. 163 (1983) eds Metz and Schillebeeckx p. 13.
53 Matt. 24–5; Mk. 13 and Lk. 21.
54 Mk. 10.35–45.
55 E.g. 2.7.
56 There are helpful comments on the climax of the book in M. Rissi *The Future of the World*.
57 Jn. 1.1ff. On the relationship see Rowland *Christian Origins* p. 252ff.
58 Jn. 1.14.
59 Jn. 1.10.
60 22.4.
61 Note similar themes elsewhere: 1 Jn. 3.2 and 1 Cor. 13.12.
62 Ro. 8.9.
63 2 Cor. 5.17.
64 1 Cor. 3.16; 1 Cor. 6.19. Further on this theme see Rowland *Christian Origins* p. 255.
65 1 Cor. 2. 10–13.
66 Ro. 8.19ff.
67 See von Campenhausen *The Formation of the Christian Bible* pp. 215ff and B.M. Metzger *The Canon of the New Testament*.
68 Cf. Eusebius' comments on Papias of Hierapolis in his *Ecclesiastical History* Book iii. 28.2.
69 Norman Cohn *The Pursuit of the Millennium* p. 58f.
70 See Friesen *Reformation and Utopia* pp. 17ff.
71 See McGinn *Visions of the End* p. 135. Cf. pp. 186ff.
72 Marjorie Reeves *Joachim of Fiore and the Prophetic Future* p. 8 and her *The Influence of Prophecy in the Later Middle Ages: A Study in Joachism*; also D.C. West *Joachim of Fiore in Christian Thought*; ed. B. McGinn *Visions of the End*, a selection of medieval eschatological material and also his *Apocalyptic Spirituality*. There is a review of scholarship on Joachim by M.W. Bloomfield in ed. Williams *Prophecy and Millenarianism. Essays in Honour of Marjorie Reeves* pp. 21ff.
73 Translation from McGinn *Visions of the End* p. 133f.
74 See McGinn *Apocalyptic Spirituality* p. 100.
75 See above p. 49.
76 From Joachim's *Exposition on the Apocalypse* printed in McGinn *Visions of the End* p. 130.
77 See Marjorie Reeves 'The development of apocalyptic thought: medieval attitudes', in C.A. Patrides and J. Witreich eds *The Apocalypse in English Renaissance Thought and Literature* p. 51.
78 On this see Cohn *The Pursuit of the Millennium* passim, McGinn *Visions of the End* pp. 203ff and 226ff, Leff *Heresy to the Later Middle Ages* vol. i pp. 51ff and Reeves *Joachim of Fiore* pp. 29ff.
79 See H. Kaminsky *The Hussite Revolution*, Kaminsky 'Chiliasm and the Hussite Revolution' *Church History* 26 (1957) pp. 43ff, McGinn *Visions of the End* pp. 259ff, Goldstein in ed. Williams *Prophecy and Millenarianism* and M. Reeves *Joachim of Fiore and the Prophetic Future* p. 141f, Leff *Heresy* vol. ii pp. 606ff and McGinn *Visions of the End* pp. 196ff.

80 Rupp *Patterns of Reformation* p. 257.
81 See W. Hayes *Winstanley the Digger* pp. 97 and 146.

4 Muenzer and Winstanley
Two Models of Radical Discipleship

1 Literature on Muenzer is now immense and is the subject of considerable controversy particularly over his role within the Peasants Revolt (survey in Scribner and
Benecke *The German Peasants War* 1525) and his place in the evolution of society
and the transition from feudalism. Some of the background is discussed by
A. Friesen *Reformation und Utopia*. The importance of Muenzer for Ernst Bloch
may be gauged by his *Thomas Muentzer als Theolog der Revolution*. The main work on
Muenzer is in German, e.g. W. Elliger *Thomas Muentzer, Leben und Werk*. The
critical edition is by G. Franz *Thomas Muentzer. Schriften and Briefe* and earlier
O. Brandt *Thomas Muentzer. Sein Leben und seine Schriften*. In English Gordon
Rupp's masterly survey in *Patterns of Reformation* offers a concise introduction, and
there is material in G. Williams *Radical Reformation* and A. Gritsch *Reformer without
a Church*. There is a useful survey of issues in eds H.J. Goertz and A. Friesen
Thomas Muentzer and Stayer and Packull *The Anabaptists and Thomas Muenzer*. On
Muenzer's eschatology see R. Schwarz *Die apokalyptische Theologie Thomas
Muentzers und der Taboriten* and T. Nipperdey *Reformation, Revolution, Utopie*. On the
Twelve Articles see P. Blickle *The Revolution of 1825. The German Peasants' War from
a New Perspective*.
2 See Rupp *Patterns* pp. 200f.
3 On Luther's attitudes to Muenzer, the peasants and the Jews see the study by H.
Bornkamm *Luther in Mid-Career 1521–1530* pp. 143ff, H. Loewen *Luther and the
Radicals* and M. Edwards *Luther and the False Brethren* pp. 36ff.
4 See F. Engels *The Peasants Revolt* and Friesen *Reformation und Utopia*.
5 See e.g. the survey in Rupp *Patterns* and Goertz and Friesen *Thomas Muentzer*. On
the relationship between the inner and outer world see H.J. Goertz *Innere und
auessere Ordnung in der Theologie des Thomas Muentzers*.
6 Tauler was a fourteenth-century Dominican mystic who emphasized divine
indwelling and personal suffering as a mark of holiness. Muenzer carried works
by Tauler with him (Rupp *Patterns* p. 255).
7 See further Goertz and Friesen *Thomas Muentzer* p. 115.
8 Some of the antecedents of such ideas are sketched by Cohn *The Pursuit of the
Millennium*.
9 Muenzer spent some time in Bohemia where the ideas of Wycliffe had been
appropriated by John Huss who in turn had become a catalyst for social critique
of church and society (see the brief survey in G. Leff *Heresy in the Later Middle Ages*
and A. Kenny *Wycliff*). On Taborite influence, see Cohn *The Pursuit of the
Millennium* p. 228 and Rupp *Patterns* pp. 228 and 259. On Hussite influence see
Rupp *Patterns* p. 258 and above p. 176 n. 79.
10 Malachi 4.5.

11 A version of the Prague Manifesto may be found in Rupp *Patterns* pp. 169ff.

12 On Muenzer's experiments, ibid., pp. 305ff.

13 See Tom Scott 'The "Volksreformation" of Thomas Muentzer in Allstedt and Muehlhausen', *Journal of Ecclesiastical History* 22 (1983).

14 Dan. 2. English translation of the Sermon before the Princes by G. Williams in ed. Williams *Spiritual and Anabaptist Writers*.

15 Dan. 2.35.

16 Dan. 2.44.

17 Dan. 2.47.

18 On the relationship between Luther and Muenzer see the article by E.G. Rupp ' "True History": Martin Luther and Thomas Muentzer', in *History, Society and the Churches* eds D. Beales and G. Best, also Goertz and Friesen *Thomas Muentzer* p. 74f and Bornkamm *Luther in Mid-Career* pp. 143ff.

19 Ro. 13.4.

20 Matt. 5.17.

21 Judges 6–7.

22 See the Twelve Articles (printed in Kidd *Documents Illustrative of the Continental Reformation* p. 174f) and Bornkamm *Luther in Mid-Career* pp. 360ff. On the social setting see Scribner and Benecke *The German Peasants War 1525* and P. Blickle *Die Revolution von 1525*.

23 Rupp *Patterns* p. 293.

24 Ibid. p. 269 and see below for a similar theme in Winstanley's work 'The True Levellers' Standard Advanced' (Hill *Law of Freedom* p. 88f).

25 Rupp *Patterns* p. 266.

26 Cf. Winstanley below pp. 110ff.

27 Rupp op. cit. p. 163.

28 See Rupp *Patterns* p. 257f. Muenzer's *vade mecum* included Ps.-Joachim's Commentary on Jeremiah.

29 Rupp *Patterns* p. 273.

30 Ibid. p. 284.

31 See Scott 'Volksreformation'.

32 See above pp. 20 and 49.

33 On the Muenster 'experiment' see Cohn *The Pursuit of the Millennium* pp. 261ff. On the part played by Melchior Hoffmann see Rupp *Patterns*, K. Deppermann *Melchior Hoffmann. Social Unrest and Apocalyptic Visions in the Age of the Reformation* and Deppermann in Goertz *Profiles of Radical Reformers*.

34 The letter is translated in G.H. Williams *Spiritual and Anabaptist Writers* pp. 73ff.

35 See the important discussion of this in Goertz *Die innere und aussere Ordnung* and more briefly his essay in Stayer ed. *The Anabaptists and Muentzer*.

36 The history of Anabaptism in its earliest phase can be found in G. Williams *Radical Reformation* and C.J. Dyck *An Introduction to Mennonite History* and W. Klassen ed. *Anabaptism in Outline*. On the links between Muenzer and the Anabaptists see Stayer and Packull eds *The Anabaptists and Thomas Muentzer* and the literature cited there.

37 Hill *Winstanley: The Law of Freedom* includes some of Winstanley's later writings. The edition of Winstanley's works is by G. Sabine (*The Works of Gerrard*

Winstanley). Unfortunately this edition does not include some of the important early pamphlets like *The Saints Paradise* and *The Breaking of the Day of God*. There are several studies of Winstanley available, the most accessible being Christopher Hill's *The World Turned Upside Down* which also includes discussions of other contempoarary radical groups. The religious ideas of Winstanley have been summarized by Hill in his *The Religion of Gerrard Winstanley, Past and Present* (Supplement 5) and by G.E. Aylmer 'The Religion of Gerrard Winstanley', in eds J.F. McGregor and B. Reay *Radical Religion in the English Revolution*.

38 Texts in Woodhouse *Puritanism and Liberty* and see the biography of Lilburn by P. Gregg *Free-Born John* and Hill *World* pp. 107ff.
39 A point well brought out in T. Wilson Hayes' book *Winstanley the Digger*.
40 On the social history of the period see K.E. Wrightson *English Society 1580–1680*.
41 *Breaking of the Day* (final pages) quoted in Hayes *Winstanley* p. 40.
42 See Hill *The Antichrist in Seventeenth Century England*.
43 *True Levellers Standard* (Hill *Law* pp. 88ff, Aylmer 'Religion of Winstanley' p. 98); *New Law* (Sabine *Works of Winstanley* pp. 190, 199); Hill *Religion* p. 20).
44 See Aylmer 'Religion of Winstanley' p. 117 n. 49.
45 *New Year's Gift* Hill *Law* pp. 165 and 170; Hayes *Winstanley* p. 165.
46 *New Law* (Sabine *Works* p. 158). Cf. *True Levellers Standard* Hill *Law* p. 85.
47 Hayes *Winstanley* p. 152.
48 *True Levellers Standard*, Hill *Law* p. 79f, and Hayes *Winstanley* p. 147.
49 *New Law*, see Sabine *Works* p. 158.
50 *Fire in the Bush* (Hayes *Winstanley* pp. 188ff).
51 *New Year's Gift* Hill *Law* p. 202f and Hayes *Winstanley* p. 170.
52 On this idea see Sanders *Paul and Palestinian Judaism* pp. 418ff.
53 *True Levellers Standard*, Hill *Law* p. 86f and Hayes *Winstanley* p. 147.
54 *Fire*, Hill *Law* p. 268.
55 Aylmer 'Religion of Winstanley', p. 99.
56 *New Law*, Sabine *Works* p. 159.
57 *Saints Paradise* p. 122. See also Sabine *Works* pp. 153, 170, 184, 410.
58 Hill *Religion* p. 34. Cf. the Digger song 'Glory here Diggers All'; see Hill *Law* p. 395.
59 Sabine *Works* pp. 316f, 337; see Hill *Religion* p. 35.
60 *Truth Lifting* (Sabine *Works* pp. 162ff).
61 *New Year's Gift* (Sabine *Works* pp. 385ff).
62 Hill *Religion* pp. 5 and 30, *Saints Paradise*, Hayes *Winstanley* pp. 49ff.
63 *New Law* (Sabine *Works* p. 162) and *Saints Paradise* (Sabine *Works* p. 96); see also Hayes *Winstanley* p. 116.
64 Hill *Religion* p. 30f. *Truth Lifting* (Sabine *Works* p. 121).
65 Aylmer 'Religion of Winstanley' p. 98.
66 *True Levellers Standard* (Hill *Law* p. 78f).
67 *New Law* (Sabine *Works* pp. 190, 199) and Hill *Religion* pp. 21ff.
68 *True Levellers Standard* Hill *Law* p. 88 and Hayes *Winstanley* p. 148.
69 Hayes *Winstanley* p. 157.
70 *Breaking of the Day* (Sabine *Works* p. 90).

71 *True Levellers Standard* (Hill *Law* p. 83: 'The blessing shall arise out of the dust . . . even the poor despised people, and they shall uphold salvation to this land'), Hill *Religion* p. 30.

72 *New Year's Gift* (Sabine *Works* p. 380). Cf. also *New Law* and *Breaking of the Day*.

73 *Breaking of the Day*, see Hayes *Winstanley* p. 31 and p. 92.

74 *Truth Lifting* (Sabine *Works* p. 99f) and further Hayes *Winstanley* p. 92.

75 *New Law* (Sabine *Works* p. 223) and see Hayes *Winstanley* p. 135.

76 *New Law* (Sabine *Works* p. 227) Hayes *Winstanley* p. 117, Hill *Religion* p. 31.

77 *Saints Paradise* (Sabine *Works* p. 94).

78 Sabine *Works* pp. 112ff, 112, 127 and Hill *Religion* p. 7.

79 *Truth Lifting* (Sabine *Works* p. 114f) and Hayes *Winstanley* p. 91.

80 *Saints Paradise* Hayes *Winstanley* p. 69.

81 Hill *Law* p. 177. See Hill *World*, A.L. Morton *The World of the Ranters* and Hill *Law* p. 177 and Hayes *Winstanley* p. 172.

82 *New Law* and Hayes *Winstanley* p. 124.

83 *Saints Paradise* quoted by Hayes *Winstanley* p. 51 and *Saints Paradise* (Sabine *Works* p. 96).

84 *Breaking of the Day* (see abstract in Sabine *Works* p. 90) and Hayes *Winstanley* p. 44 and on Winstanley's gradualism see Hill *Religion* p. 41.

85 *True Levellers Standard*, Hill *Law* p. 94 and Hayes *Winstanley* p. 150.

86 Hayes *Winstanley* p. 49.

87 *Ibid.* pp. 35 and 97. There is some evidence of Joachite periodization in the *True Levellers Standard* (see Hill *Law* p. 80f).

88 For evidence of some of the harassment see *New Year's Gift* (Hill *Law* p. 205f.) and on the disappointment Hill *The Experience of Defeat* pp. 37ff.

89 Hill *Religion* p. 44.

90 *Ibid.* p. 49.

91 Hill *Law* p. 389.

92 See Hill *The Experience of Defeat*.

93 Hill *Milton and the English Revolution* and *The World Turned Upside Down* pp. 395ff.

94 See the essays by B. Reay in McGregor and Reay *Radical Religion in the English Revolution*.

95 See E.P. Thompson *The Making of the English Working Class* pp. 411ff.

96 On Blake see D.V. Erdman *Blake : Prophet against Empire* and E. Larissy *William Blake* and on utopianism in English thought and A.L. Morton *English Utopia*. Cf. J.C. Davis *Utopia and the Ideal Society*. On the theme in early North American society see R. Bloch *Visionary Republic. Millenial Themes in American Thought 1756-1800*. In a rather different way Irving picked up some of the recurring themes of renewal linked with the prophetic spirit and a rebirth of a sense of Christian community. See e.g. G. Strachan *The Pentecostal Theology of Edward Irving*.

97 *New Year's Gift* (Hill *Law* p. 204).

5 The Theology of Liberation
Proclaiming God as Father in a World that is Inhumane

1 For the final documents see *Medellin Conclusions* and *Puebla Conclusions*. There is a general introductory survey of the churches in Latin America in Trevor Beeson and Jenny Pearce *A Vision of Hope. The Churches and Change in Latin America*.

2 On the varied character of the influence see T.C. Bruneau *The Political Transformation of the Brazilian Catholic Church* and his *The Church in Brazil. The Politics of Religion*.

3 On the Kiriri see Omar da Rocha Jr 'O Movimento Kiriri', *Cadernos do CEAS* no. 97 pp. 29ff; the same author's *A Politica dos Brancos* National Museum, Rio de Janeiro 1982; Maria de Lurdes *Os Kiriri de Mirandela: Um Grupo Indigena Integrado* Salvador (Bahía) 1972 (Serie Estudos Bahianos, 6); Jose Augusto L. Sampaio and Maria Goncalves de Carvalho *Os Povos Indigenas na Bahía* Salvador 1981. On the Brazilian Indians see J. Hemming *Red Gold* and *Amazon Frontier*.

4 Comments made in Cambridge on 25 January 1988.

5 For a report on this meeting I am indebted to my friend Derek Winter's report (Christian Aid September 1986) and to the Latinamerica Press report (Noticias Aliadas) vol. 18 no. 31, 28 August 1986.

6 Examples of treatment of the Exodus may be found in J. Severino Croatto *Exodus. A Hermeneutics of Freedom*; N. Gottwald *The Hebrew Bible*; and Jorge Pixley's commentary *Exodo: una lectura evangelica y popular* Mexico City 1983, and more briefly in English in his contribution to *La Iglesia Popular* (see n. 42). There is a concise description of the character of biblical study in Latin America in Carlos Mesters 'Como se faz teologia biblica hoje no Brazil?', in *Estudos Biblicos* vol. 1 Petropolis 1983 (*Estudos Biblicos* is an offshoot of the journal *Revista Eclesiastica Brasileira*).

7 Much material on the problem of land distribution in Brazil is published by the CPT (Commisão Pastoral da Terra: CP 749, 74000 Goaiânia). A good example of the relationship between this issue and the struggle for the land may be found in Marcelo de Barros Souza *A Biblia e a Luta pela Terra* (CPT) Petropolis 1983.

8 On Brazilian Catholicism see T.C. Bruneau *The Political transformation of the Brazilian Catholic Church* and Bruneau *The Church in Brazil. The Politics of Religion* and E. de Kadt *Catholic Radicals in Brazil*.

9 See *Os Nordestinos em São Paulo* (Edicões Paulinas 1982). The challenge of the north-east is well exemplified in *Nordeste: Desafio a Missão da Igreja no Brasil* CNBB São Paulo 1984 found in an abridged form in *Liberate the Land* Catholic Institute for International Relations London 1986.

10 *Brasil. Nunca Mais* São Paulo 1985.

11 Fr. G. Gorgulho *The Church of the Poor* Unpublished paper São Paulo n.d. Some indication of the problems in São Paulo at this period may also be gleaned from the São Paulo Justice and Peace Commission's report *São Paulo. Growth and Poverty*, published in England by the Catholic Institute for International Relations, London in 1977.

12 The literature on the theology of liberation is immense and it is impossible to

deal with it all. In addition to the primary sources, there is a readable and well-informed introduction to the whole phenomenon by T. Witvliet *A Place in the Sun*; also P. Berryman *Liberation Theology*. There is an important survey of the historical context for the theology of liberation written from a sympathetic perspective by Enrique Dussel *A History of the Church in Latin America. Colonialism to Liberation*. See also the general survey in Beeson and Pearce *A Vision of Hope*. For a sympathetic but critical exposition in English see A. Fierro *Militant Gospel* and further Berryman *Liberation Theology* pp. 179ff, and now C. and L. Boff, *Introducing Liberation Theology*.

13 This is one of the problems of the discussion of liberation theology in the first instruction by the Congregation for the Doctrine of the Faith. The two documents published by the Congregation are *Libertatis Nuntius* and *Instruction on Christian Freedom and Liberation* published in Rome 1986. There is a collection of reactions to the latter document in *Latinamerica Press* for May 1 1986. The first document has been subjected to critical scrutiny by J.L. Segundo in his *Theology and Church*. See also Gibellini, *The Liberation Theology Debate*.

14 In *Contribução da CED para Leitura da 'Instrução sobre alguns aspectos da Teologia da Libertação'* prepared for the 23rd Assembly of the Brazilian Bishop's Conference in Itaicí 10–19 April 1985.

15 E.g. H. Assmann *A Practical Theology of Liberation* cf. Clodovis Boff *Theology and Praxis*.

16 G. Gutierrez *The Power of the Poor in History* p. 60f.

17 Ibid. p. 57.

18 In Derek Winter ed. *Putting Theology to Work* Papers of the Latin America/UK Theological Consultation Fircroft, Birmingham BCC London 1980 p. 75f. There is an important discussion of the epistemology of the theology of liberation in C. Boff *Theology and Praxis*.

19 Libanio *Putting Theology to Work* p. 75f. The sequence 'seeing, judging and acting' has its origin in the Catholic Action movement. See Berryman *Liberation Theology* pp. 14ff and 65.

20 See Jon Sobrino in J. Filochowski et al. *Reflections on Puebla* p. 31, paraphrasing Jn. 8.7.

21 L. Boff *Jesus Christ Liberator* p. 265. There is a more extended approach of a similar kind in the important critique of theology by J.L. Segundo *The Liberation of Theology*. He has also attempted to discuss the relationship between Christian commitment and ideology in *Faith and Ideologies*.

22 E.g. M. de Barros Souza's *A Biblia*. Two extended treatments of Paul from a liberationist perspective which bring out the foundations of his thought in issues of social justice may be found in J.P. Miranda *Marx and the Bible* and J.L. Segundo *The Humanist Christology of Paul*, but cf. George Pixley's more trenchant critique of the social conservatism of Paul in *God's Kingdom*.

23 Quoted in J. Pitt *Good News for All* CAFOD London 1978.

24 'The use of the Bible in Christian Communities of the Common People' in ed. Norman Gottwald *The Bible and Liberation* and C. Boff *Teologia* pp. 132ff. Evidence of recent liberationist exegesis may be found in J.L. Segundo and from an evangelical perspective T. Hanks *God So Loved the Third World*.

25 *Estudos Biblicos* vol. 1 1984.

26 *Parabolas de Hoje* (Instituto de Acão Cultural) São Paulo 1982.

27 Ernesto Cardenal *Love in Practice: The Gospel in Solentiname* pp. 128ff; also *The Gospel in Solentiname*. Solentiname, an island in Lake Nicaragua, is where Cardenal spent many years before the Revolution.

28 Rev. 7.14.

29 See e.g. J. Sobrino *Christology at the Crossroads* and L. Boff *Jesus Christ Liberator*.

30 F. Belo *A Materialist Reading of the Gospel of Mark* and M. Clevenot *Materialist Approaches to the Bible* and further ed. N. Gottwald *The Bible and Liberation*. The work done by the Brazilian exegetes Ana Flora Anderson and Gilbert Gorgulho O.P. is indicative of the creative application of what they call a 'socio-structural' approach. Their work may be sampled in *Estudos Biblicos*.·

31 See the penetrative comments of N. Lash in the essays on biblical interpretation in *Theology on the Way to Emmaus*.

32 See E.R. Norman *Christianity and the World Order* and *Christianity in the Southern Hemisphere*.

33 On the Afro-Brazilian religions see R. Bastide *The Afro-Brazilian Religions* English translation of *As Religiões Africanas no Brasil* and Bastide *O Candomblé da Bahía*; Bastide *Estudos Afro-brasileiros*; O.G. Cacciatori *Dicionario de Cultos Afro-brasileiros*.

34 S. Hall 'Religious Ideologies and Social Movements in Jamaica' in Bocock and Thompson *Religion and Ideology* and Barrett *The Rastafarians*. See also Eugene Genovese *Roll Jordan Roll*. On popular religion see the collection of essays edited by Greinacher and Mette *Popular Religion, Concilium* vol. 186.

35 The title of a Christian Aid film on internal emigration in north-east Brazil.

36 On political theology in Europe see e.g. J.B. Metz *The Emergent Church* and *Faith in History and Society* and note the comments of Witvliet *A Place in the Sun* p. 24f.

37 On the CEBs (*comunidades eclesiais de base*) see S. Torres and J. Eagleson eds *The Challenge of Basic Christian Communities* Maryknoll 1981; S. Torres et al. *A Igreia que surge da Base* São Paulo 1982; A.R. Guimaraes *Comunidades de Base no Brasil* Petropolis 1978; Cook's *The Expectation of the Poor* and his short article 'The Protestant Predicament: From Base Ecclesial Community to Established Church – A Brazilian Case Study', *International Bulletin of Missionary Research* vol. 8 (1984). Cf. the reservations expressed by the conservatives in Bonaventura Kloppenburg *Igreja Popular* Rio de Janeiro 1983.

38 The basic texts relevant for understanding evangelization are to be found in the collection *Proclaiming Justice and Peace* eds. M. Walsh and B. Davies London 1984. Particularly relevant is the encyclical *Evangelii Nuntiandi* from which this quotation is taken.

39 On the impact of fundamentalist protestantism see e.g. H. Assmann *La Iglesia Electronica y su Impacto en America Latina* (1987), the studies of the Rio-based Institute for Religious Studies (ISER) and J. Coleman and G. Baum *New Religious Movements Concilium* vol. 161 (1983).

40 See above pp. 6ff.

41 *Jesus Christ Liberator* p. 44. *Ecclesiogenesis* pp. 9ff and A Fierro *The Militant Gospel* pp. 257ff. It should be noted that Boff's use of the language of utopianism does

not correspond exactly with the usage elsewhere in this book. It is both more eschatological and less specific in its prescriptions. For him utopia is more intimately linked with what we have described as the millenarian tradition rather than the specific detalied constructions of ideal societies. For this reason this section has described their concern as millenarian rather than utopian, in line with usage in the rest of the book.

42 See e.g. Enrique Dussel 'Populus Dei in Populo Pauperum' in eds Boff and Elizondo *La Iglesia Popular* Concilium 176 (1984) pp. 35ff.

43 *Church. Charism and Power* p. 133.

44 *Ecclesiongenesis* p. 13.

45 See Taylor and Goodwin *The Politics of Utopia*.

46 Mannheim *Ideology and Utopia* p. 175.

47 Boff *Ecclesiogenesis* p. 9f.

48 Reported in *Latinamerica Press* 1 May 1986 and see the comment of Joseph Ratzinger noted above p. 121.

49 On Nicaragua see P. Berryman *The Religious Roots of Rebellion* London 1983 and most recently the introductory study by A. Bradstock *Saints and Sandinistas*; A. Arguello *Fé Christiana y Revolucion Sandinista en Nicaragua* Managua 1980. A commentary on the situation in Nicaragua, including material relating to church–state affairs, can be found in in the bulletin of the Instituto Historico of the University of Central America in Managua. See also the balanced summaries in the regular 'Comment' on Nicaragua produced by the Catholic Institute for International Relations (latest edition 1987) and their study of the present human rights situation *Right to Survive. Human Rights in Nicaragua*, prepared by George Gelber (C.I.I.R. 1987).

50 An example of Uriel Molina's ideas may be found in his contribution to *La Iglesia Popular. Between Fear and Hope* eds L. Boff and V. Elizondo (*Concilium* 176 December 1984): 'How a People's Christian community is structured and how it functions' and in the material published by the Centro Antonio Valdivieso in Managua. See also *Church and Politics. Internal Upheaval and State Confrontation in Nicaragua* Central American Institute, vol. 5 no. 1 January 1986.

51 Berryman *Liberation Theology*.

52 Fernando Cardenal *A Letter to My Friends* 1984. There is a discussion of the situation of the priests in the Nicaraguan government in *Envio* volume 5 issue 50, August 1985 and on Fernando Cardenal in volume 4 issue 43, January 1985.

53 Casaldaliga's sentiments on the struggle for liberation and the situation in Central America are well illustrated in his *Prophets in Combat*.

54 *Challenge to the Church. The Kairos Document* Catholic Institute for International Relations 1985 (2nd edition by Paternoster Press 1986).

55 *Evangelical Witness in South Africa* Centre of Mission Studies Oxford 1986.

56 On the character of the theology of liberation in Africa see G.S. Wilmore and J.H. Cone *Black Theology: A Documentary History 1966–79* and T. Witvliet *The Way of the Black Messiah*. An example of a South African reading of Revelation can be seen in Allan Boesak's *Comfort and Protest*.

57 Matt. 16.3.

58 See e.g. ed. Jon Sobrino *Martyr for Liberation* and the collection of his works *Voice of the Voiceless*.

59 See Charles Elliott *Is there a Liberation Theology for the UK?*, Heslington Lecture, the University of York 1985. Of importance in this process is the catalytic effect of the work of John Vincent, Director of the Urban Theology unit in Sheffield who has pioneered a contextual theology in this country. His work is well exemplified by *Into the City* and *Radical Jesus* and the series of popular Bible studies on Mark *Mark at Work* which he wrote with John Davies, now Bishop of Shrewsbury.

60 Cardinal Lorscheider's contribution to *La Iglesia Popular*, 'The Redefined Role of a Bishop in a Poor, Religious People', is an example of the way in which the episcopacy, at least in Brazil, have been influenced by the theology of liberation in their pastoral practice.

Concluding Reflections

1 E.g. Ps. 46.5 and the story to back up the myth in Is. 37-9: the overwhelming of Sennacherib's army outside the walls of Jerusalem. On the character of this ideology see R.E. Clements *God and Temple* and on its continuing significance see M. Barker *The Older Testament*.

2 Jer. 7.

3 Mk. 11.17.

4 Acts 6-7.

5 Lk. 11.47f.

6 Lk. 11.52.

7 Jer. 31.33f.

8 Rupp *Patterns of Reformation* p. 176.

9 Sabine *Works* p. 198. The biblical quotations printed in this extract come from Winstanley.

10 Turner *Marxism and Christianity* p. 167.

11 Ibid. p. 182.

12 Ibid. p. 145f.

13 See M. Weber *Economics and Society* vol. 1 pp. 1151ff and more recently V. Turner *Drama, Fields and Metaphors*. There are suggestive comments on this theme in D. Martin's *The Breaking of the Image* pp. 155ff.

14 On this theme see the suggestive essays by J.H. Yoder in *The Priestly Kingdom*.

15 See the helpful contrasts drawn by R.H. Bainton 'The Left Wing of the Reformation' in his *Studies on the Reformation* (summary in Stayer and Packull *The Anabaptists and Thomas Muentzer* pp. 41ff).

16 Words used at a sermon to mark the end of Miguel d'Escoto's fast for peace in Managua in September 1985 by Leonardo Boff and also by Bishop Pedro Casaldaliga in a lecture in San Salvador later that month.

Select Bibliography

Abrams, M.H. 'Apocalypse: Theme and Variations', in eds. Patrides and Wittreich *The Apocalypse in English Renaissance Thought and Literature* Manchester 1984.

Ackroyd, P.R. *Exile and Restoration* London 1968.

Allison, D. *The End of the Ages Has Come* Edinburgh 1987.

Arguello, A. *Fé cristiana y Revolucion Sandinista en Nicaragua* Managua 1980.

Armytage, W.H.G. *Heavens Below: Utopian Experiments in England 1560–1960* London 1961.

Ashton, J. *The Interpretation of John* London 1986.

Aune, D.E. *The Cultic Aspect of Realised Eschatology in Early Christianity* Leiden 1972.

Aune, D.E. *Prophecy in Early Christianity and the Ancient Mediterranean World* Grand Rapids 1983.

Avila, C. *Ownership. Early Christian Teaching* London 1983.

Avineri, S. *The Social and Political Thought of Karl Marx* Cambridge 1968.

Aylmer, G.E. 'The Religion of Gerrard Winstanley', in eds. McGregor and Reay *Radical Religion in the English Revolution* Oxford 1984.

Ball, B.W. *The Great Expectation* Leiden 1975.

Bammel, E. and Moule, C.F.D. eds. *Jesus and the Politics of his Day* Cambridge 1984.

Barclay, J. *Obeying the Truth* Edinburgh 1988.

Bardy, G. 'Cérinthe', *Revue Biblique* vol. 20 (1921) pp. 344ff.

Barnard, L.W. *Justin Martyr* Cambridge 1967.

Barrett, C.K. *New Testament Background. Selected Documents* new edition London 1987.

Barrett, C.K. *The Gospel of John and Judaism* London 1975.

Barth, K. *Protestant Theology in the Nineteenth Century* London 1972.

Barton, J. *The Oracles of God* London 1986.

Bastide, R. *The African Religions of Brazil* Baltimore 1978.

Bauckham, R. 'The Delay of the Parousia', *Tyndale Bulletin* 31 (1980) pp. 3ff.

Bauckham Moltmann, R. *Messianic Theology in the Making* Basingstoke 1987.

Bauer, W. *Orthodoxy and Heresy in Early Christianity* London 1971.

van Beek, C. *Passio Sanctarum Perpetuae et Felicitatis* Bonn 1938.

Beeson, T. and Pearce, J. *A Vision of Hope* London 1984.

Beker, J.C. *Paul the Apostle. The Triumph of God in Life and Thought* Edinburgh 1980.

Belo, F. *A Materialist Reading of the Gospel of Mark* New York 1981.

Bentley, J. *Between Marx and Christ* London 1982.

Berger, K. *Die griechische Daniel-Diegese* Leiden 1976.

Berryman, P. *The Religious Roots of Rebellion* London 1983.

Berryman, P. *Liberation Theology. The Essential Facts about the Revolutionary Movement in Latin America and Beyond* London 1987.

Biale, D. *Gershom Scholem: Kabbalah and Counter-History* Cambridge Mass. 1982.

Blickle, P. *The Revolution of 1525. The German Peasants' War from a New Perspective* Baltimore 1981.

Bloch, E. *Thomas Muentzer als Theolog der Revolution* Frankfurt 1962.

Bloch, E. *The Principle of Hope* Oxford 1986.

Bloch, E. *Atheism in Christianity* London 1972.

Bloch, R. *Visionary Republic* Cambridge 1985.

Bocock, R. and Thompson, K. eds. *Religion and Ideology* Manchester 1985.

Boesak A. *Comfort and Protest* Edinburgh 1987.

Boff, C. *Teologia e Pratica* Petropolis, Brazil 1982 (English translation, Maryknoll, New York 1986).

Boff, C. and Boff, L. *Introducing Liberation Theology* London 1987.

Boff, L. *Jesus Christ Liberator* London 1980.

Boff, L. *Church. Charism and Power* London 1985.

Boff, L. *Ecclesiogenesis* New York 1986.

Boff, L. 'Martyrdom: An Attempt at Systematic Reflection', in eds. Metz, J.B. and Schillebeeckx, E. *Martyrdom Today* Concilium vol. 163 1983 pp. 12ff.

Boff, L. and Elizondo, V. *Popular Religion* Concilium vol. 163 December 1984.

Borgen, P. 'God's Agent in the Fourth Gospel', in ed. Ashton *The Interpretation of John.*

Bornkamm, H. *Luther in Mid-Career 1521–1530* London 1983.

Bousset, W. *Die Offenbarung Johannis* Goettingen 1906.

Bousset, W. *The Antichrist Legend* London 1896.

Bousset, W. *Kyrios Christos* Abingdon 1970.

Bowker, J.W. *Jesus and the Pharisees* Cambridge 1973.

Bradstock, A. *Saints and Sandinistas* London 1987.

Brady, D. *The Contribution of British Writers between 1560 and 1830 to the Interpretation of Revelation 13.16–18* Tuebingen 1983.

Brandon, S.G.F. *The Fall of Jerusalem and the Christian Church* London 1957.

Brandt, O. *Thomas Muentzer. Sein Leben und seine Schriften* Jena 1933.

Brown, P. *The Making of Late Antiquity* Cambridge Mass. 1978.

Brueggemann, W. *The Prophetic Imagination* Philadelphia 1978.

Bruneau, T.C. *The Political Transformation of the Brazilian Catholic Church* Cambridge 1974.

Bruneau, T.C. *The Church in Brazil. The Politics of Religion* University of Texas 1982.

Bultmann, R. *Theology of the New Testament* London 1952.

Burridge, K. *New Heaven New Earth* New York 1969.

Byrne, L. *Mary Ward. A Pilgrim Finds Her Way* Dublin 1984.

Byrne, L. *Women Before God* London 1988.

Caird, G.B. *Jesus and the Jewish Nation* Ethel M. Wood Lecture, London 1965.

Caird, G.B. *The Language and Imagery of the Bible* London 1980.

Calder, W.M. 'Philadelphia and Montanism', *Bulletin of the John Rylands Library* vol. 7 (1923).

von Campenhausen, H. *Ecclesiastical Authority and Spiritual Power in the Church of the First Three Centuries* London 1969.

von Campenhausen, H. *The Formation of the Christian Bible* London 1972.

Cardenal, E. *Love in Practice: The Gospel in Solentiname* London 1977.

Carnley, P. *The Structure of Resurrection Belief* Oxford 1987.

Carroll, R. *When Prophecy Failed* London 1979.

Casaldaliga, P. *Prophets in Combat* Catholic Institute for International Relations London 1987.

Chilton, B. *The Kingdom of God* London 1984.

Chadwick, H. *Priscillian of Avila. The Occult and the Charismatic in the Early Church* Oxford 1976.

Chadwick, H. *enkrateia* in *Reallexikon fuer Antike und Christentum* vol. 5 (1962) pp. 343ff.

Chitty, D. *The Desert a City* Oxford 1966.

Clevenot, M. *Materialist Approaches to the Bible* New York 1985.

Cohn, N. *The Pursuit of the Millennium* London 1957.

Cohn, N. 'Medieval Millenarism: its bearing on the comparative study of millenarian movements', in ed. Thrupp, S. *Millenial Dreams in Action: Comparative Studies in History and Society* Supplement 2 (1962) pp. 32ff.

Coleman, J. and Baum, G. *New Religious Movements Concilium* vol. 161 (1983).

Collins, A.Y. 'The Political Perspective of the Revelation to John', *Journal of Biblical Literature* 96 (1977) pp. 44ff.

Collins, J. *Daniel with an Introduction to the Apocalyptic Literature* Grand Rapids 1984.

Collins, J.J. *The Apocalyptic Imagination* New York 1985.

Collins, J.J. *Between Athens and Jerusalem* New York 1983.

Cook, G. 'The Protestant Predicament: From Base Ecclesial Community to Established Church – A Brazilian Case Study', *International Bulletin of Missionary Research* vol. 8. (1984).

Cook, G. *The Expectation of the Poor* Maryknoll, New York 1985.

Crouch, J.L. *The Origin of the Colossian Haustafeln* Goettingen 1972.

Cullmann, O. *The State in the New Testament* London 1957.

Cullmann, O. *Salvation in History* London 1967.

Dale Morris, W. *The Christian Origins of Social Revolt* London 1950.

Danby, H. *The Mishnah* Oxford 1933.

Daniélou, J. *The Theology of Jewish Christianity* London 1964.

Daniélou, J. *The Gospel Message and Hellenistic Culture* London 1973.

Daniélou, J. *The Origins of Latin Christianity* London 1977.

Davis, J.C. *Utopia and the Ideal Society* Cambridge 1983.

De Divitiis (Translation by Haslehurst, R.S.T. in *The Works of Fastidius* London 1927).

Dodds, E.R. *The Greeks and the Irrational* Berkeley 1951.

Dodds, E.R. *Pagan and Christian in an Age of Anxiety* Cambridge 1965.

Dussel, E. *A History of the Church in Latin America* Grand Rapids 1981.

Davies, W.D. *Paul and Rabbinic Judaism* London 1965.

Davies, W.D. *The Gospel and the Land* Berkeley 1974.

Davies, W.D. *Jewish and Pauline Studies* London 1984.

Deppermann, K. *Melchior Hoffmann. Social Unrest and Apocalyptic Visions in the Age of Reformation* Edinburgh 1987.

Dunn, J.D.G. *Unity and Diversity in the New Testament* London 1977.

Dunn, J.D.G. *Christology in the Making* London 1980.

Dunn, J.D.G. *The Kingdom of God and North East England* London 1986.

Dyck, C.J. ed. *An Introduction to Mennonite History* Scottdale, Pa. 1967.

Edwards, M. *Luther and the False Brethren* Stanford 1973.

Eliade, M. *Myths, Dreams and Mysteries* London 1968.

Eliade, M. *Cosmos and History: The Myth of the Eternal Return* New York 1954.

Elliger, W. *Thomas Muentzer. Leben und Werk* Goettingen 1975.

Elliot, C. *Is there a Liberation Theology for the UK?* Heslington Lecture, the University of York 1985.

Engels, F. *The Peasants War in Germany* in *Marx and Engels on Religion* Moscow 1957 pp. 86ff.

Erdman, D.V. *Blake: Prophet Against Empire* New York 1969.

Esler, P. *Community and Gospel in Luke–Acts* Cambridge 1987.

Farmer, W.R., Moule, C.F.D. and Niebuhr, R. eds. *Christian History and Interpretation* Cambridge 1967.

Festinger, L., Reichen, H.W. and Schachter, S. *When Prophecy Fails* Minneapolis 1956.

Feuerbach, L. *The Essence of Christianity* New York 1957.

Fierro, A. *The Militant Gospel* London 1977.

Firth, K. *The Apocalyptic Tradition in Reformation Britain* Oxford 1979.

Ford, D. *The Abomination of Desolation in Biblical Eschatology* Washington 1979.

Foucault, M. *A History of Sexuality* London 1979.

Francis, F.O. and Meeks, W. eds. *Conflict at Colossae* Missoula 1972.

Frend, W.H.C. *Martyrdom and Persecution in the Early Church* Oxford 1955.

Frend, W.H.C. *The Rise of Christianity* London 1985.

Freyne, S. *Galilee from Alexander the Great to Hadrian 323 BCE to 135CE* Notre Dame 1980.

Friesen, A. *Reformation und Utopia* Wiesbaden 1974.

Gager, J. *Kingdom and Community* Englewood Cliffs 1975.

Geertz, C. 'Religion as a Cultural System', in ed. M. Banton *Anthropolgical Approaches to the Study of Religion* London 1966.

Gelber, G. ed. *Right to Survive. Human Rights in Nicaragua* Catholic Institute for International Relations London 1987.

Genovese, E. *Roll Jordan Roll* New York 1976.

Gerhardsson, B. *Memory and Manuscript* Lund 1961.

Gibellini, R. *The Liberation Theology Debate* London 1987.

Goertz, H.J. and Friesen, A. eds. *Thomas Muentzer* Darmstadt 1978.

Goertz, H.J. ed. *Profiles of Radical Reformers* Scottdale 1982.

Goertz, H.J. *Innere und auessere Ordnung in der Theologie Thomas Muentzers* Leiden 1967.

Gollwitzer, H. *Reich Gottes und Sozialismus bei Karl Barth* Munich 1972.

Goodwin, B. and Taylor, K. *The Politics of Utopia* London 1982.

Gottwald, N. *The Tribes of Yahweh* London 1980.

Gottwald, N. ed. *The Bible and Liberation* New York 1983.

Gottwald, N. *The Hebrew Bible* Philadelphia 1985.

Gowan, D. *Eschatology in the Old Testament* Edinburgh 1986.

Grant, R.M. *Early Christianity and Society* London 1977.

Grant, R.M. *Second Century Christianity* London 1957.

Greer, R.A. *Broken Lights and Mended Ways* Pennsylvania 1986.

Greinacher, N. and Mette, N. *Popular Religion* Concilium 186 Edinburgh 1986.

Grillmeier, A. *Christ in Christian Tradition* London 1975.

Guimares, A. *Comunidades de Base no Brasil* Petropolis 1978.

Gutierrez, G. *The Theology of Liberation* London 1974.

Gutierrez, G. *The Power of the Poor in History* London 1983.

Hall, S. 'Religious Ideologies and Social Movements in Jamaica' in Bocock and Thompson eds. *Religion and Ideology*.

Hanks, T. *God So Loved the Third World* Maryknoll New York 1983.

Hanks, T. 'El testimonio evangelico a los pobres y oprimidos' *Vida y Pensamiento* vol. 4 (1984).

Hanson, P.D. *The Dawn of Apocalyptic* Philadelphia 1975.

Hartmann, L. *Prophecy Interpreted* Lund 1966.

Hayes, J. and Miller, M. *Israelite and Judean History* London 1977.

Hayes, W. *Winstanley the Digger* Cambridge Mass. 1979.

Heine, S. *Women and Early Christianity* London 1987.

Hemming, J. *Red Gold* London 1987.

Hengel, M. *Between Jesus and Paul* London 1983.

Hengel, M. *The Atonement* London 1981.

Hengel, M. *Property and Riches in the Early Church* London 1974.

Hengel, M. *Judaism and Hellenism* London 1974.

Hengel, M. *Die Zeloten* Leiden 1976.

Hennecke, E. and Schneemelcher, W. *NTApocrypha* London 1965.

Hill, C. *The World Turned Upside Down* London 1972.

Hill, C. *The Antichrist in Seventeenth Century England* Oxford 1971.

Hill, C. *Winstanley: 'The Law of Freedom' and other writings* Cambridge 1973.

Hill, C. *Milton and the English Revolution* London 1977.

Hill, C. *The Experience of Defeat* London 1985.

Hill, C. *The Religion of Gerrard Winstanley* in *Past and Present Supplements* no. 5.

Hill, M. *The Sociology of Religion* London 1973.

Hinkelammert, F.J. *The Ideological Weapons of Death. A Theological Critique of Capitalism* New York 1986.

Hobsbawm, E. 'The Principle of Hope', in *Revolutionaries* London 1977 pp. 136ff.

Hobsbawm, E. *Primitive Rebels* Manchester 1959.

Hobsbawm, E. *Bandits* London 1969.

Hoehner, H. *Herod Antipas* Cambridge 1972.

Holmberg, B. *Paul and Power* Philadelphia 1978.

Horbury, W. and Rowland, C. eds. *Essays for Ernst Bammel Journal for the study of the New Testament* vol. 19. Sheffield 1983.

Hudson, W. *The Marxist Philosophy of Ernst Bloch* London 1982.

Hurd, J.C. *The Origin of 1 Corinthians* London 1965.

Isenberg, S.R. 'Millenarism in Greco-Roman Palestine', *Religion* vol. 4 (1974) pp. 20ff.

Jameson, F. *The Political Unconscious* London 1981.

Jeremias, J. *New Testament Theology* London 1971.

de Kadt, E. *Catholic Radicals in Brazil* Oxford 1970.

The Kairos Document Challenge to the Church London 1985.

Kaesemann, E. *Commentary on Romans* London 1980.

Kaminsky, H. *The Hussite Revolution* Berkeley 1967.

Kaminsky, H. 'Chiliasm and the Hussite Revolution', *Church History* 26 (1957) pp. 43ff.

Kautsky, K. *The Foundations of Christianity* London 1925.

Kaye, H. *The British Marxist Historians* Cambridge 1984.

Kee, A. *Constantine versus Christ* London 1982.

Kelly, J.N.D. *Early Christian Doctrines* London 1968.

Kempe, M. *The Book of Margery Kempe* Harmondsworth 1985.

Kidd, B.J. *Documents Illustrating the Continental Reformation* Oxford 1967.

Klassen, W. ed. *Anabaptism in Outline* Scottdale, Pennsylvania 1981.

Klassen, W. *Anabapism. Neither Catholic nor Protestant* Waterloo, Ontario 1981.

Klijn, A.F.J. and Reinink, G.S. *Patristic Evidence for Jewish-Christian Sects* Leiden 1973.

Knowles, D. *From Pachomius to Ignatius* Oxford 1966.

Koch, K. *The Rediscovery of Apocalyptic* London 1972.

Kolakowski, L. *Main Currents of Marxism* Oxford 1978.

Kreider, A. *Journey towards Holiness* Basingstoke 1986.

Kuemmel, W.G. *Introduction to the New Testament* London 1975.

Kuhn, H.W. *Enderwartung und gegenwaertiges Heil* Goettingen 1966.

Kyrtatas, D.J. *The Social Structure of the Early Christian Communities* London 1987.

Labriolle, P. *La Crise montaniste* Paris 1913.

Labriolle, P. *Les Sources de l'histoire du Montanismus* Paris 1913.

Lake, K. ed. *The Apostolic Fathers* London 1912.

Lane Fox, R. *Pagans and Christians* London 1987.

Larissy, E. *William Blake* Oxford 1985.

Larain, J. *The Concept of Ideology* London 1979.

Leff, G. *Heresy in the Later Middle Ages* Manchester 1967.

Lincoln, A.T. *Paradise Now and Not Yet* Cambridge 1981.

Loewen, H. *Luther and the Radicals* Waterloo, Ontario 1974.

Louth, A. *Early Christian Writings* London 1987.

Luttikhuizen, G.P. *The Revelation of Elchesai* Tuebingen 1985.

Maccoby, H. *Paul the Mythmaker* London 1986.

Maccoby, H. *Revolution in Judaea* London 1973.

McGann, A. *Christian Realism* New York 1983.

McGinn, B. *Apocalyptic Spirituality* London 1979.

McGinn, B. *Visions of the End: Apocalyptic Traditions in the Middle Ages* New York 1979.

McGregor, J.F. and Reay, B. *Radical Religion in the English Revolution* Oxford 1984.

McKown, D.B. *The Classical Marxist Critiques of Religion* The Hague 1975.

McLellan, D. *Ideology* Milton Keynes 1986.

McLellan, D. *Marxism and Religion* London 1987.

Macmullen, R. *Christianising the Roman Empire* New Haven 1984.

Maier, J. *The Temple Scroll* Sheffield 1986.

Mannheim, K. *Ideology and Utopia* London 1960.

Markus, R.A. *Saeculum* Cambridge 1970.

Martin, D. *The Breaking of the Image* London 1980.

The Medellin Conclusions New York 1973.

Meeks, W.A. *The First Urban Christians* New Haven 1983.

Meeks, W.A. 'The Man from Heaven in Johannine Sectarianism', in ed. Ashton *The Interpretation of John*.

Meeks, W.A. *The Moral World of the Early Christians* London 1987.

Mesters, C. *Esperanca de um povo que luta. O apocalipse de São João. Uma chava de leitura* São Paulo n.d.

Mesters, C. 'Como se faz teologia biblica hoje no Brasil' *Estudos Biblicos* vol. 1 Petropolis 1983.

Miranda, J.P. *Marx and the Bible* New York 1974.

Mohler, J.A. *The Heresy of Monasticism* Staten Island 1971.

Mojtabai, A. *Blessed Assurance* London 1987.

Morris, P. 'Pelagian Literature', *Journal of Theological Studies* vol. 16 (1965) pp. 50ff.

Morton, A.L. *The World of the Ranters* London 1970.

Morton, A.L. *English Utopia* London 1978.

Munck, J. *Pual and the Salvation of Mankind* London 1959.

Murray, R. *Symbols of Church and Kingdom* Cambridge 1975.

Neusner, J. *From Politics to Piety* Englewood Cliffs 1973.

Nicholson, E.W. *Deuteronomy and Tradition* Oxford 1967.

Nickelsburg, G. *Resurrection. Immortality and Eternal Life* Cambridge Mass. 1972.

Nipperdey, T. *Reformation, Revolution, Utopie* Goettingen 1975.

Norman, E.R. *Christianity and the World Order* Oxford 1979.

Norman, E.R. *Christianity in the Southern Hemisphere* Oxford 1981.

Pannenberg, W. *Jesus God and Man* London 1968.

Patrides, C. and Wittreich, J. *The Apocalypse in English Renaissance Thought and Literature* Manchester 1984.

Pearson, B.A. *The Pneumatikos Psychikos Terminology in 1 Corinthians* Missoula 1973.

Pearson, B.A. 'Philo, Gnosis and the New Testament', in Wedderburn and Logan *The New Testament and Gnosis* Edinburgh 1983.

Peel, M.L. *The Epistle to Rheginos* London 1969.

Perkins, P. *Resurrection* London 1984.

Petegorsky, D.W. *Left Wing Democracy in the English Civil War* London 1940.

Pitt, J. *Good News for All* London 1978.

Pixley, G. *God's Kingdom* London 1981.

Pixley, G. *Exodo: una lectura evangeica y popular* Mexico City 1983.

Ploeger, O. *Theocracy and Eschatology* Oxford 1968. *The Puebla Conclusions* London 1983.

Rajak, T. *Josephus* London 1983.

Ramsay, W.M. *Letters to the Seven Churches* London 1904.

Reeves, M. *Joachim of Fiore and the Prophetic Future* London 1976.

Rhoads, D. *Israel in Revolution 6–74CE* Philadelphia 1976.

Rissi, M. *The Future of the World* London 1972.

Rivkin, E. *What Crucified Jesus?* Abingdon 1984.

Rivkin, E. *The Hidden Revolution* London 1975.

Robinson, J.M. ed. *The Nag Hammadi Library* Leiden 1978.

da Rocha, O. 'O movimento Kiriri', *Cadernos do CEAS* 97 pp. 29ff.

Romero, O. *Voice of the Voiceless* London 1985.

Rousseau, P. *Pachomius. The Making of a Community in Fourth Century Egypt* University of California 1985.

Rowland, C. *Christian Origins* London 1985.

Rowland, C. *The Open Heaven. A Study of Apocalyptic in Judaism and Early Christianity* London 1982.

Ruether, R. and McLaughlin, E. eds. *Woman of Spirit* New York 1979.

Safrai, S. and Stern, M. *Jewish People in the First Christian Century* Assen 1974–6.

Sabine, G. *The Works of Gerrard Winstanley* Cornell 1941.

de Ste Croix, G. *The Class Struggle in the Ancient Greek World* London 1981.

de Ste Croix, G. 'Early Christian Attitudes to Property and Slavery' *Studies in Church History* 12 (1973) pp. 1ff.

Sanders, E.P. ed. *Jewish and Christian Self-Definition* London 1981–3.

Sanders, E.P. *Paul and Palestinian Judaism* London 1977.

Sanders E.P. *Jesus and Judaism* London 1985.

Schepelern, W. *Der Montanismus und die phrygische Kult* Tuebingen 1929.

Scholem, G. *Sabbatai Sevi* London 1973.

Scholem, G. article 'Kabbalah', *Encyclopedia Judaica* vol. x col. 489ff.

Scholem, G. *Major Trends in Jewish Mysticism* London 1955.

Schottroff, W. and Stegemann, W. eds. *God of the Lowly* New York 1984.

Schuerer, E. (eds. Vermes, G. and Millar, F.) *History of the Jewish People in the Age of Jesus Christ* Edinburgh 1973–7.

Schuessler Fiorenza, E. *In Memory of Her* London 1983.

Schuessler Fiorenza, E. *The Book of Revelation. Justice and Judgement* Philadelphia 1985.

Scott, T. 'The "Volksreformation" of Thomas Muenzer in Allstedt and Muehlhausen', *Journal of Ecclesiastical History* vol. 22 (1983) pp. 194ff.

Schwarz, R. *Die apokalyptische Theologie Thomas Muentzers und der Taboriten* Tuebingen 1977.

Schweizer, E. *Church Order in the New Testament* London 1961.

Schweitzer, A. *The Quest of the Historical Jesus* London 1931.

Schweitzer, A. *The Mystery of the Kingdom of God* London 1925.

Schweitzer, A. *The Mysticism of Paul the Apostle* London 1931.

Scribner, Bob and Benecke, G. *The German Peasants War 1525. New Viewpoints.* London 1979.

Segundo, J.L. *The Liberation of Theology* New York 1976.

Segundo, J.L. *Theology and Church* London 1985.

Segundo, J.L. *The Historical Jesus of the Synoptic Gospels* London 1986.

Segundo, J.L. *The Humanist Christology of Paul* London 1987.

Skinner, Q. *The Foundations of Modern Political Thought* Cambridge 1978.

Sloan, R.B. *The Favorable Year of the Lord. A Study in the Jubilary Theology of the Gospel of Luke* Austin 1977.

Smith, M. *Clement of Alexandria and a Secret Gospel of Mark* Cambridge Mass. 1971.

Sobrino, J. *Christology at the Crossroads* London 1978.

Sobrino, J. ed. *Romero. Martyr for Liberation* London 1982.

Sobrino, J. *The True Church and the Poor* London 1984.

Stegemann, E. 'From Criticism to Enmity' in Scottroff and Stegemann *God of the Lowly* New York 1984.

Stendahl, K. ed. *The Scrolls and the New Testament* New York 1957.

Stone, M. ed. *Jewish Writings of the Second Temple Period* Assen 1984.

Souza, M. de Barros *A Biblia e a Luta pela Terra* Petropolis 1983.

Stayer, J. and Packull, W. eds. *The Anabaptists and Thomas Muentzer* Toronto 1980.

Strobel, A. *Das Heilige Land des Montanismus* Berlin 1980.

Sweet, J.P.M. *Revelation* London 1979.

Talmon, Y. 'The Pursuit of the Millennium: the Relation between Religions and Social Change', *Archives Européennes de Sociologie* vol. 3. (1962) pp. 125ff.

Taubes, J. 'The Price of Messianism', in *Essays in Honour of Yigael Yadin* in *Journal of Jewish Studies* vol. 33 (1982) pp. 595ff.

Theissen, G. *The First Followers of Jesus* London 1978.

Theissen, G. *The Social Setting of Pauline Christianity* London 1982.

Theissen, G. *The Miracle Stories of the Early Christian Tradition* Edinburgh 1983.

Thiselton, A.C. 'Realised Eschatology at Corinth', *New Testament Studies* vol. 24 pp. 510ff.

Thomas, K. *Religion and the Decline of Magic* Harmondsworth 1971.

Thrupp, S. ed. *Millenial Dreams in Action* Paris 1962.

Torres, S. and Eagleson, J. eds. *The Challenge of Basic Christian Communities* New York 1981.

Torres, S. ed. *A Igreja que surge da Base* São Paulo 1982.

Troeltsch, E. *The Social Teaching of the Christian Churches* London 1931.

Turner, D. *Marxism and Christianity* Oxford 1983.

Ullendorff, E. *Ethiopia and the Bible* London 1968.

Vermes, G. *The Dead Sea Scrolls. Qumran in Perspective* London 1975.

Vielhauer, P. 'Apocalyptic in Early Christianity' in eds. Hennecke and Schneemelcher *New Testament Apocrypha* vol. 2 pp. 608ff.

Vincent, J.J. *Radical Jesus* London 1986.

Vincent, J.J. *Into the City* London 1982.

Voegtle, A. *Das Neue Testament und die Zukunft der Kosmos* Duesseldorf 1971.

Vööbus, A. *A History of Asceticism in the Syrian Orient* Paris 1958.

Walsh, M. and Davies, B. eds. *Proclaiming Justice and Peace* London 1984.

Watson, F. *Paul, Judaism and the Gentiles* Cambridge 1986.

Weber, M. *The Protestant Ethic and the Spirit of Capitalism.* New York 1948.

Weber, M. *Ancient Judaism* London 1952.

Weber, M. *Economy and Society* New York 1968.

Wedderburn, A.J.M. and Logan, A. eds. *New Testament and Gnosis* Edinburgh 1983.

Weiss, J. *Jesus' Proclamation of the Kingdom of God* London 1971.

Wengst, K. *Pax Romana and the Peace of Jesus Christ* London 1987.

Werner, M. *The Formation of Christian Dogma* London 1957.

Williams, A. ed. *Prophecy and Millenarianism. Essays in Honour of Marjorie Reeves* London 1980.

Williams, G. *The Radical Reformation* Philadelphia 1962.

Wilmore, G.S. and Cone, J.H. *Black Theology: A Documentary History 1966-79* Maryknoll, New York 1986.

Wilson, B. *Patterns of Sectarianism* London 1967.

Wilson, B. *Magic and the Millennium* London 1973.

Wilson, R. *Prophecy and Society in Ancient Israel* Philadelphia 1980.

Wilson, R. *Sociological Approaches to the Old Testament* Philadelphia 1984.

Wink W. *Naming the Powers* New York 1984.

Winter, D. ed. *Putting Theology to Work* London 1980.

Witvliet, T. *A Place in the Sun. An Introduction to Liberation Theology in the Third World* London 1985.

Witvliet, T. *The Way of the Black Messiah* London 1987.

Woodhouse, A.S.P. ed. *Puritanism and Liberty* London 1938.

Worsley, P. *The Trumpet Shall Sound* New York 1968.

Worsley, P. *Three Worlds* London 1984.

Wrightson, K.E. *English Society 1580-1680* London 1982.

Yadin, Y. *Masada* London 1966.

Yadin, Y. *The Temple Scroll* Jerusalem 1984.

Yoder, J.H. *The Politics of Jesus* Grand Rapids 1972.

Yoder, J.H. *The Priestly Kingdom* Notre Dame 1984.

Young, F. *The Sacrifice and the Death of Christ* London 1975.

Index

satan, 12, 26, 84, 147, 153
Schweitzer, A., 5, 162
scripture, 3, 28-9, 35, 36-7, 59, 94-5, 97-8, 105, 109, 110-11, 120, 130-1, 134; canon of, 1, 82; interpretation of, 49-50, 53, 85-6; Jewish, 80; priority of, 152
Segundo, J. L., 137
Sobrino, J., 126, 133, 134, 137
social change, 1, 41, 83, 96, 104, 120, 143, 146, 159
Son of Man, 5, 7, 33, 69, 79, 108, 126
South Africa, 146-9
Spirit, 18, 29, 36-8, 40, 44, 46, 70-1, 81, 84-5, 91, 94-5, 97, 99, 110-11, 153; of asceticism, 63; of prophecy, 61-2, 82, 109
spirituality, 47, 149
symbol(ism), 67, 68, 75, 108, 136, 156

Temple, 18-20, 22, 32, 47-9, 81, 138, 150-1
text, 58, 68, 130-1, 134-5, 152, 157
theology, 11, 14-15, 20, 47, 66, 71, 84, 127, 147; as catholic, 9, 115; and ethics, 55-6; as feminist, 10; of Judaism, 72; of liberation, 9, 115-49, 152, 159, 160, 182; of Muenzer, 101; of Paul, 34, 42; as political, 33, 97, 137, as prophetic, 148; of Winstanley, 110
theologians, 51, 55, 116, 120; of liberation, 126, 128, 156

tradition, 1, 7, 9, 14, 46, 54, 67, 105, 116, 120, 125, 128-9, 136, 149, 152, 155, 160; of anabaptists, 102; anacalyptic, 4, 44, 50, 108; biblical, 47, 148; eschatalogical, 6; Joachimite, 112; Lutheran, 66; marxist, 103; mystical, 10; pacific, 101; pharisaic, 48; prophetic, 29, 82; theological, 117; utopian, 140
tribute, 24-5
Tutu, D., 146

USA, 67, 143, 145
utopia, 7-8, 112-14, 138-40, 159; of the mishnah, 48; monastic, 84, 87; of More, 11

Vatican Council II, 115-16, 137, 139

war, 4
Weiss, J., 6, 138
Wengst, K., 78-9
Winstanley, G., 2, 12, 88, 115, 152, 154, 159, 160, 179; and Meunzer, 102-114; and the New Law of Righteousness, 153
women, 28, 34, 38, 41, 62-5, 111, 130, 132, 174
Wycliff, J., 91

zealots, 23-4
Zwickau, 90-1

Index by Nick O'Sullivan

Printed in Great Britain
by Amazon